Managerial
Accounting

For the US CPA Exam

Volume
8

목차

PART I
Cost Accounting

Chapter 01 | Managerial Accounting

Chapter 02 | Job–order costing

Chapter **09** | Variable and Absorption Costing

Chapter **10** | Planning and Budgeting

Chapter **11** | Pricing

Chapter **15** | Performance Measure

Chapter **16** | Quality Control

서문 · Preface

Managerial accounting for the US CPA exam 의 특징입니다.

● WHO?

미국 공인회계사 시험을 응시하는 수험생을 대상으로 한 교재이다. 미국 공인회계사 시험 4과목 중 하나인 'Business Analysis and Reporting (BAR)' 과목에서 중요한 부분을 차지하고 있는 'Business Analysis' 영역을 대비하기 위한 교재이다.

● WHAT?

미국공인회계사 시험의 추세 및 난이도에 맞게 구성된 내용으로 각 장마다 미국 공인회계사 시험에 출제되는 'Task-Based Simulation' 유형의 문제를 대비하기 위한 문제를 수록하였다. 또한 미국 관리회계사 자격증인 CMA(certified management accountant)의 MCQ(multiple choice questions) 기출문제를 포함하였다.

● HOW?

미국공인회계사 오랜 강의 경력의 경험과 노하우를 압축한 교재이다. 'Business Analysis and Reporting (BAR)' 과목은 Discipline exam의 과목이므로 Core exam보다 난이도가 높다. 따라서 Managerial accounting에서 높은 점수를 획득하여야 하므로 이 교재와 강의로 스마트한 합격을 기원한다.

● CHAPTER

관리회계의 대분류 영역별로 본서의 순서는 구성되어있다. 1장~6장은 원가계산에 대한 내용이며, 7장 ~12장은 원가예측 및 의사결정에 대한 내용이고, 13장~16장은 원가통제 및 성과평가에 대한 내용이다.

● MANAGEMENT

직원들은 불과 5%에서 10%의 능력 밖에 발휘하지 않는다. 나머지 90%에서 95%의 미개발 능력을 매일 일터로 가져오게 하는 것, 그것이 바로 경영자가 하는 일이다.
〈퍼시 바네빅(Percy Barnevik)〉

A house of cards
"기초가 약하면 오래가지 못한다."
이 책은 관리회계 공부를 시작하는 학습자들에게 반석처럼 튼튼한 기초를 만들어 줄 것이다.

공인회계사/미국공인회계사/미국재무분석사(CFA)

김용석.

CBT Introduction

I. CBT 과목구성

　미국 공인회계사 시험은 2004년도에 PBT에서 CBT로 변경이 되었으며, 2017년에는 TBS(Task—Based Simulation)의 비중을 높인 새로운 방식으로 변경되었다. 2023년에 시험제도는 새롭게 변경이 되어 2024년 1월 1일 이후의 시험은 아래의 표와 같다.

Section	Section time	MCQ	TBS
AUD—Core	4 hours	50%(78)	50%(7)
FAR—Core	4 hours	50%(50)	50%(7)
REG—Core	4 hours	50%(72)	50%(8)
BAR—Discipline	4 hours	50%(50)	50%(7)
ISC—Discipline	4 hours	60%(82)	40%(6)
TCP—Discipline	4 hours	50%(68)	50%(7)

MCQ : Multiple Choices Questions
TBS: Task-Based Simulation

The CPA licensure model requires all candidates to pass three Core exam sections and one Discipline exam section of a candidate's choosing.

The Core exam sections assess the knowledge and skills that all newly licensed CPAs (nlCPAs) need in their role to protect the public interest. The three Core exam sections, each four hours long, are: Auditing and Attestation(AUD), Financial Accounting and Reporting (FAR) and Taxation and Regulation(REG).

The Discipline exam sections assess the knowledge and skills in the respective Discipline domain applicable to nlCPAs in their role to protect the public interest.The three Discipline exam sections, each four hours long, are: Business Analysis and Reporting (BAR), Information Systems and Controls (ISC) and Tax Compliance and Planning (TCP).

The Business Analysis and Reporting section of the Uniform CPA Examination assesses the knowledge and skills nlCPAs must demonstrate with respect to:

- Financial statement and financial information analysis with a focus on an nlCPA's role in comparing historical results to budgets and forecasts, deriving the impact of transactions, events (actual and proposed) and market conditions on financial and nonfinancial performance measures and comparing investment alternatives.

- Select technical accounting and reporting requirements under the Financial Accounting Standards Board (FASB) Accounting Standards Codification and the U.S. Securities and Exchange Commission (SEC) that are applicable to for-profit business entities and employee benefit plans.

- Financial accounting and reporting requirements under the Governmental Accounting Standards Board (GASB) that are applicable to state and local government entities.

The following table summarizes the content areas and the allocation of content tested in the BAR section of the Exam:

	Content area	Allocation
Area I	Business Analysis	40~50%
Area II	Technical Accounting and Reporting	35~45%
Area III	State and Local Governments	10~20%

(1) Area I : Business Analysis

- Financial statement analysis, including comparison of current period financial statements to prior period or budget and interpretation of financial statement fluctuations and ratios.

- Non-financial and non-GAAP measures of performance, including use of the balanced scorecard approach and interpretation of non-financial and non-GAAP measures to assess an entity's performance and risk profile.

- Managerial and cost accounting concepts and the use of variance analysis techniques.

- Budgeting, forecasting and projection techniques.

- Factors that influence an entity's capital structure, such as leverage, cost of capital, liquidity and loan covenants.

- Financial valuation decision models used to compare investment alternatives.

- The Committee of Sponsoring Organizations of the Treadway Commission (COSO) Enterprise Risk Management framework, including how it applies to environmental, social and governance (ESG) related risks.

- The effect of changes in economic conditions and market influences on an entity's business.

(2) Area II : Technical Accounting and Reporting

- Indefinite-lived intangible assets, including goodwill.

- Internally developed software.

- Revenue recognition, specifically focusing on the analysis and interpretation of agreements, contracts and other supporting documentation to determine whether revenue was appropriately recognized.

- Stock compensation.

- Research and development costs.

- Business combinations.

- Consolidated financial statements, specifically focusing on topics including variable interest entities, noncontrolling interests, functional currency and foreign currency translation adjustments.

- Derivatives and hedge accounting.

- Leases, specifically focusing on recalling and applying lessor accounting requirements and analyzing the provisions of a lease agreement to determine

- whether a lessee appropriately accounted for the lease.

- Public company reporting topics, specifically focusing on Regulation S-X, Regulation S-K and segment reporting.

- Financial statements of employee benefit plans.

(3) Area III : State and Local Governments

- Basic concepts and principles of the government-wide, governmental funds, proprietary funds and fiduciary funds financial statements.

- Preparing government-wide, governmental funds, proprietary funds and fiduciary funds financial statements and other components of the financial section of the annual comprehensive financial report.

- Deriving the government-wide financial statements and reconciliation requirements.

- Accounting for specific types of transactions such as net position, fund balances, capital assets, long-term liabilities, interfund activity, nonexchange revenue, expenditures and expenses and budgetary accounting within the governmental entity financial statements.

PART I

Cost Accounting

Chapter

01

Managerial Accounting

Managerial Accounting

01 Basic concepts

1 Accounting

회계는 정보이용자가 합리적 의사결정을 하는데 유용한 경제적 정보를 측정, 기록 및 요약하여 정보이용자에게 전달하는 과정이다. 정보이용자는 주주, 채권자, 정부 등 기업 외부의 정보이용자와 경영자, 중간관리자 등 기업 내부의 정보이용자로 구분된다. 회계는 정보이용자에 따라 재무회계(financial accounting)와 관리회계(managerial accounting)으로 구분된다.

2 Financial accounting

Financial accounting focuses on reporting financial information to external parties based on Generally Accepted Accounting Principles (GAAP).

재무회계는 외부 정보이용자가 합리적 의사결정을 하는데 유용한 경제적 정보를 제공하는 것을 목적으로 하는 회계를 말하며 재무제표를 작성하여 제공한다. 재무제표는 일반적으로 인정된 회계원칙(GAAP)에 의하여 작성되며 강조되는 정보의 특성은 신뢰성(reliability)이다.

3 Managerial accounting

Management accounting is the process of measuring, analyzing, and reporting financial and non-financial information that helps managers make decisions to fulfill the goals of an organization.

관리회계는 내부 정보이용자가 합리적 의사결정을 하는데 유용한 경제적 정보를 제공하는 것을 목적으로 하는 회계를 말하며 일반적으로 인정된 회계원칙(GAAP)의 영향을 받지 않으며 제공되는 정보의 형태와 내용 등의 제약이 없으며 강조되는 정보의 특성은 목적적합성(relevance)이다.

4 Differences between managerial and financial accounting

	Financial accounting	Managerial accounting
Primary Users	External users*	Internal users**
Types of Reports	Financial statement	Internal reports
Frequency of Reports	Quarterly and annually	As frequently as needed
Focus	Past-oriented	Future-oriented
GAAP	Yes	No
Information quality	Reliability	Relevance

* External users : stockholders, creditors & regulators.

** Internal users : CEO, officers & managers.

5 Elements of managerial accounting

관리회계에서 제공하는 정보는 원가계산, 원가계획 및 원가통제로 구성된다.

(1) Cost accounting

관리회계나 재무회계의 목적으로 재고자산의 원가를 계산한다.

(2) Planning (decision making)

기업이 목표를 설정하고 예산(budget)을 편성한 후 목표를 어떻게 달성할 것인가에 대한 정

보를 제공하며 경영자가 경영활동을 수행하는 과정에서 대안을 선택해야 하는 의사결정에 필
요한 정보를 제공한다.

(3) Control

성과평가를 통하여 기업이 목표로 하는 원가 또는 이익을 달성하는 과정에 필요한 정보를
제공한다.

02 Cost concepts

1 Cost terminology

(1) Cost object (원가대상)

1) A cost object is anything for which a manager needs a separate measurement of cost.

원가대상은 개별적으로 원가를 측정할 필요가 있는 목적물로서 경영자의 사용목적에 따라 제품, 서비스, 고객이 원가대상이 된다.

2) Examples of cost objects

- Product : A Tesla vehicle, A Honda motorcycle
- Service : An airline flight from Seoul to LA
- Project : An airplane assembled by Boeing for KAL
- Customer : A customer of business-class seats of KAL

(2) Cost assignment (원가할당)

1) Cost tracing (원가추적)

the assignment of direct costs to a cost object

2) Cost allocation (원가배분)

the assignment of indirect costs to a cost object

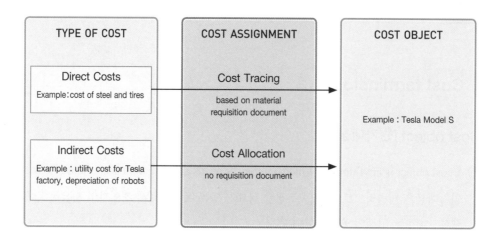

(3) Direct cost (직접원가)

- A direct cost is any cost that is related to a particular cost object and can be traced to that cost object in an economically feasible way.
- 특정 원가 대상에 직접 추적할 수 있는 원가
- Tesla Model S : costs of steel and tires
- Starbucks : costs of coffee bean

(4) Indirect cost (간접원가)

- Indirect costs are related to a particular cost object but cannot be traced to it in an economically feasible way.
- 특정 원가 대상에 직접 추적할 수 없는 원가
- 합리적 배분기준을 선정하여 원가대상에 배분
- Tesla Model S : utility costs for Tesla factory, depreciation of robots
- Starbucks : depreciation of a coffee machine, utility costs for a store
- The same cost can be direct for one cost object and indirect for another cost object.

2 Product costs versus period costs

	Product costs	Period costs
Synonym	Manufacturing costs = Inventoriable costs	Non-manufacturing costs = Non-inventoriable costs
Definition	Can be associated with the production of specific goods.	Can not be associated with the production of specific goods.
Expense recognition	When inventory is sold. (Matching principles)	When period costs are incurred.
Components	Direct materials Direct labors Manufacturing overhead	Selling expense Administrative expense R&D expense
Freight costs	Freight-in	Freight-out

(1) Product cost

제품원가는 제조과정에서 발생한 원가로서 제품원가계산에 반영하여야 하므로 제조원가(Manufacturing costs) 또는 재고가능원가(Inventoriable costs)라고도 한다. 제품원가는 발생 시 재고자산에 할당한 후 제품이 판매될 때 매출원가로 비용 처리된다. 제품원가에는 직접재료원가(DM, direct materials), 직접노무원가(DL, direct labors), 제조간접원가(MOH, manufacturing overhead)로 구성된다.

(2) Period cost

기간원가는 제조활동과 관계없이 발생한 원가로서 제품원가계산에 반영하지 않으므로 비제조원가(Non-manufacturing costs) 또는 재고불능원가(Non-inventoriable costs)라고도 한다. 기간원가는 발생 시 즉시 비용으로 처리되며 판매비(Selling expense), 일반관리비 (General and administration expense), 연구개발비(R&D)로 구성된다.

3 Direct materials(DM)

제품을 생산하기 위해서는 여러 종류의 원재료를 투입하여야 하는데, 특정 제품에 직접 추적할 수 있는 재료원가를 직접재료원가(direct material)라고 하며, 직접 추적이 불가능하거나 추적이 가능하더라도 비용이 많이 발생되어 추적이 비경제적인 재료원가를 간접재료원가(indirect material)라고 하며 이는 제조간접원가에 포함된다.

(1) Direct material

1) Cost of materials directly and conveniently traceable to a product.

2) Example

- Car : steel, plastics and tires
- Computer: plastics, hard drives and processing chips

(2) Indirect materials

1) Raw materials that cannot be easily traceable to a product.

2) Indirect materials are classified as manufacturing overhead.

3) Example: lubricants, glue

4 Direct labor(DL)

제품을 생산하기 위해서는 노동력이 투입이 되는데, 특정 제품에 직접 추적할 수 있는 노무원가를 직접노무원가(direct labor)라고 하며, 직접 추적이 불가능하거나 추적이 가능하더라도 비용이 많이 발생되어 추적이 비경제적인 노무원가를 간접노무원가(indirect labor)라고 하며 이는 제조간접원가에 포함된다.

(1) Direct labor

1) Direct labor is cost of labor directly and conveniently traceable to a product.

2) Example: machine operators, CPA in accounting firms

(2) Indirect labor

1) Labor costs that cannot be easily traceable to a product.

2) Indirect labor is classified as manufacturing overhead.

3) Example: factory supervisor or foreman, machine mechanics

5 Manufacturing overhead (MOH)

제조원가 중 직접재료원가와 직접노무원가 이외의 모든 제조원가를 제조간접원가(manufacturing overhead)라고 한다.

(1) Costs that are indirectly associated with the production.

(2) Manufacturing costs that cannot be classified as direct material or direct labor.

(3) Example

1) Indirect materials

2) Indirect labor

3) Depreciation on factory building and machine.

4) Insurances, taxes and maintenance on factory.

5) Electricity for a manufacturing plant

6 Prime cost and Conversion costs

제조원가 중 직접재료원가와 직접노무원가를 기초원가(prime cost)라고 하며, 직접노무원가와 제조간접원가를 가공원가(conversion cost) 또는 전환원가라고 한다.

(1) Prime cost: all direct manufacturing costs

(2) Conversion cost: all manufacturing costs other than direct material costs

Prime cost	Conversion cost
Direct material	Direct labor
Direct labor	Manufacturing overhead

03 / Cost Flow

1 Inventory

상기업(유통업)은 상품을 구입한 후 가공하지 않고 그대로 판매하기 때문에 재고자산을 상품(Merchandise)으로 기록한다. 제조기업은 생산요소를 외부에서 구입하여 제조과정을 통하여 재화를 생산하여 판매하므로 재고자산을 다음과 같이 기록한다.

(1) Raw materials: purchased but not yet issued
(2) Working in process(WIP): issued but not yet completed
(3) Finished goods(FG): completed but unsold

2 T-account analysis

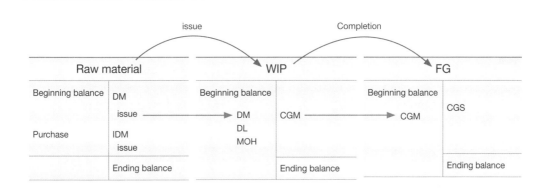

[그림 1-1]

3 Accounting

Purchase of raw materials	Raw materials xxx Account payable xxx
Issuance of raw materials	WIP xxx Raw materials xxx
Direct labor incurred	WIP xxx Accrued payable xxx
Manufacturing overhead incurred	WIP xxx Various accounts xxx
Completion of goods	Finished goods xxx WIP xxx

Sale of goods	Account receivables xxx
	     Sales revenue xxx
	Cost of goods sold(CGS) xxx
	     Finished goods xxx

4 Income statements

Merchandise company		Manufacturing company	
Beginning merchandise	xxx	Beginning finished goods	xxx
Cost of goods purchased	xxx	Cost of goods manufactured(CGM)	xxx
Cost of goods available for sale	xxx	Cost of goods available for sale	xxx
Ending merchandise	(xxx)	Ending finished goods	(xxx)
Cost of goods sold	xxx	Cost of goods sold	xxx

5 Cost of goods manufactured schedule

Beginning WIP		xxx
Direct materials	xx	
Direct labor	xx	
Manufacturing overhead	xx	
Total current manufacturing costs		xxx
Total cost of WIP		xxx
Ending WIP		(xxx)
Cost of goods manufactured		xxx

6 Example-Merchandising sector

The following data are for Amazon Outlet. The account balances (in thousands) are for 20X1.

Marketing and advertising costs	$ 48,000
Merchandise inventory, January 1, 20X1	104,000
Shipping of merchandise to customers	4,000
Building depreciation	8,000
Purchases	520,000
General and administrative costs	64,000
Merchandise inventory, December 31, 20X1	90,000
Merchandise freight-in	20,000
Purchase returns and allowances	22,000
Purchase discounts	18,000
Revenues	640,000

Required

1. Compute the cost of goods purchased.
2. Compute the cost of goods sold.
3. Prepare the income statement for 20X1.

Answers

1. Cost of goods purchased = $520,000 - 22,000 - 18,000 + 20,000 = \$500,000$
2. Cost of goods sold = 기초재고 + 당기매입 - 기말재고
   $= 104,000 + 500,000 - 90,000 = \$514,000$
3. Income Statement

   Selling expense = $48,000 + 4,000 = 52,000$

   Administration expense = $8,000 + 64,000 = 72,000$

Sales revenue	$640,000
Cost of goods sold	(514,000)
Gross profit	126,000
Selling expense	(52,000)
Administration expense	(72,000)
Operating income	2,000

7 Example-Manufacturing sector

Apple Inc. has the following costs for the year ending December 31, 20X1			
Raw materials 1/1/X1	$30,000	Factory insurance	$14,000
Raw materials 12/31/X1	20,000	Factory property taxes	6,000
Raw material purchased	200,000	Sales revenue	1,500,000
Indirect materials issued	5,000	Freight-outs	100,000
WIP 1/1/X1	80,000	Sales commissions	150,000
WIP 12/31/X1	50,000	Factory utilities	40,000
Finished goods 1/1/X1	100,000	Factory depreciation	24,000
Finished goods 12/31/X1	110,000	Headquarter depreciation	20,000
Direct labor	350,000	Officer's salary	50,000
Factory manager's salary	35,000	Interest expense	100,000

Required

Prepare a cost of goods manufactured schedule and an income statements for 20X1

Answers

(1) T−account analysis:

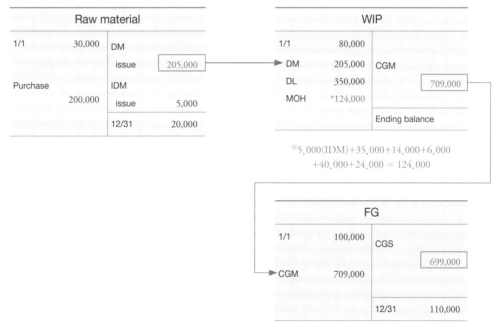

[그림 1-2]

(2) Cost of goods manufactured schedule

Beginning WIP		$80,000
Direct materials	$205,000	
Direct labor	350,000	
Manufacturing overhead	124,000	
Total current manufacturing costs		$679,000
Total cost of WIP		$759,000
Ending WIP		($50,000)
Cost of goods manufactured		$709,000

(3) Income statement

Sales revenue	$1,500,000
Cost of goods sold	(699,000)
Gross profit	801,000
Selling expense	(250,000)
Administration expense	(70,000)
Operating income	481,000
Other expense	(100,000)
Income from continuing operations	381,000

8 Example-Manufacturing sector

Tesla Inc. specializes in manufacturing automobiles. Tesla's monthly manufacturing cost and other expense data are as follows:

1) Rent on factory equipment	$5,000
2) Insurance on factory building	3,000
3) Raw materials (frames and tires)	20,000
4) Utility costs for factory	800
5) Supplies for general office	200
6) Wages for assembly line workers	35,000
7) Depreciation on office equipment	500
8) Miscellaneous materials (lubricants)	1,000
9) Maintenance costs on factory building	300
10) Factory manager's salary	6,000
11) Advertising for automobiles	10,000
12) Sales commissions	5,000
13) Depreciation on factory building	700

Required

(1) Indicate each of the cost items in the following lists
  a. Direct material
  b. Direct labor
  c. Manufacturing overhead
  d. Period costs
(2) Calculate the current total manufacturing costs

Answers

(1) 1−C, 2−C, 3−A, 4−C, 5−D, 6−B, 7−D,
  8−C, 9−C, 10−C, 11−D, 12−D, 13−C
(2) Direct material: $20,000
  Direct labor: 35,000
  Manufacturing overhead: 16,800
  Total manufacturing costs: $71,800

9 Summary

(1) Direct material issued

= Beginning Raw material + Purchase (including fright−in)

  − indirect material issued − Ending Raw material

(2) Current total manufacturing costs

= DM + DL + MOH

(3) CGM (Cost of goods manufactured)

= Beginning WIP + Current total manufacturing costs − Ending WIP

(4) CGS (Cost of goods sold)

= Beginning FG + CGM − Ending FG

(5) Prime cost = DM + DL

(6) Conversion cost = DL + MOH

04 MCQ (Multiple Choice Questions)

01. Which of the following costs would be included in manufacturing overhead of a computer manufacturer?

a. The cost of CD drivers   b. The salaries of computer assemblers

c. The cost of the memory chips   d. Depreciation of factory equipment.

02. Which of the following is not an element of manufacturing overhead?

a. Sales manager's salary   b. Plant manager's salary

c. Factory repairman's salary   d. Product inspector's salary

03. Which one of the following items would not be considered a manufacturing cost? (CMA)

a. Cream for an ice cream maker.

b. Sales commissions for a car manufacturer.

c. Plant property taxes for an ice cream maker.

d. Tires for an automobile manufacturer.

04. The schedule of cost of goods manufactured of Gruber Fittings, Inc. shows the following balances for its fiscal year-end.

Direct manufacturing labor	$ 280,000
Manufacturing overhead	375,000
Ending work-in-process inventory	230,000
Raw materials used in production	450,000
Cost of goods manufactured	1,125,000

The value of the WIP inventory at the beginning of the fiscal year was (CMA)

a. $625,000   b. $250,000   c. $210,000   d. $20,000

05. Indirect labor cost is a

a. period cost

b. prime cost

c. conversion cost

d. non-manufacturing cost

Questions 6 through 9 are based on the following information.

Nike Company's beginning and ending inventories for May are

	May 1	May 31
Direct materials	$52,000	$57,000
Work-in-process	135,000	121,000
Finished goods	65,000	78,000

Production data for the month of May follow:

Direct labor	$185,000
Actual factory overhead	98,000
Direct materials purchased	134,000
Freight-in	5,000
Freight-out	7,000
Purchase returns	3,000

---

06. What is the company's prime cost for May?

a. $131,000   b. $316,000   c. $414,000   d. $428,000

07. What is the company's total manufacturing cost for May?

a. $131,000   b. $316,000   c. $414,000   d. $428,000

08. What is the cost of goods transferred to finished goods inventory for May?

a. $316,000   b. $414,000   c. $428,000   d. $415,000

09. What is the company's cost of goods sold for May?

a. $316,000   b. $414,000   c. $428,000   d. $415,000

10. Mello Joy produces 200,000 units of a good that has the following costs.

Direct material costs	$2,000,000
Direct manufacturing labor costs	1,000,000
Indirect manufacturing labor costs	600,000

Mello Joy's per unit prime costs and conversion costs, respectively, are (CMA)

a. $8 and $15   b. $8 and $18   c. $10 and $8   d. $15 and $8

11. The following is selected information from the records of ZARA:
    - Purchases of raw materials : $6,000
    - Raw materials, beginning : 500
    - Raw materials, ending : 800
    - Work-in-process, beginning : 0
    - Work-in-process, ending : 0
    - Cost of goods sold : 12,000
    - Finished goods, beginning : 1,200
    - Finished goods, ending : 1,400
    What is the total amount of conversion costs?

a. $5,700   b. $6,500   c. $6,800   d. $12,200

· 정답 및 해설

1. a ⇨ DM, b ⇨ DL, c ⇨ DM   정답 : d

2. 판매사원의 급여는 product cost가 아닌 period cost이다.   정답 : a

3. IDM은 제조원가 이면서 가공비이지만 기초 원가는 아니다.   정답 : b

4. TMC = DM (450,000) + DL (280,000) + OH (375,000) = 1,105,000
   BWIP = CGM (1,125,000) + EWIP (230,000) − TMC (1,105,000) = 250,000
   정답 : b

5. a ⇨ DM, b ⇨ period cost, c ⇨ OH, d ⇨ DM   정답 : c

6. DM = 기초재고 (52,000) + 당기매입 (134,000 + 5,000 − 3,000)
         − 기말재고 (57,000) = 131,000
   Prime cost = DM (131,000) + DL (185,000) = 316,000   정답 : a

7. TMC = DM (131,000) + DL (185,000) + OH (98,000) = 414,000
   정답 : c

8. CGM = BWIP (135,000) + TMC (414,000) − EWIP (121,000) = 428,000
   정답 : c

9. CGS = BFG (65,000) + CGM (428,000) − EFG (78,000) = 415,000
   정답 : d

10. Prime cost = DM (2,000,000) + DL (1,000,000) = 3,000,000
    Conversion cost = DL (1,000,000) + OH (600,000) = 1,600,000
    Unit cost of prime cost = 3,000,000 ÷ 200,000 units = $15
    Unit cost of conversion cost = 1,600,000 ÷ 200,000 units = $8
    정답 : d

11. DM issue = 500 + 6,000 − 800 = 5,700
    1,200 + CGM = 12,000 + 1,400 ⇨ CGM = 12,200
    12,200 = 5,700 + Conversion cost ⇨ Conversion cost = 6,500
    정답 : b

05 / TBS (Task-Based Simulation)

Problem-1

The following items (in millions) pertain to Intel Corporation:
Intel's manufacturing costing system uses a three-part classification of direct materials, direct manufacturing labor, and manufacturing overhead costs.

⟨For Specific Date⟩

Work-in-process inventory, Jan. 1, 20X1	$15
Direct materials inventory, Dec. 31, 20X1	9
Finished goods inventory, Dec. 31, 20X1	19
Accounts payable, Dec. 31, 20X1	28
Accounts receivable, Jan. 1, 20X1	57
Work-in-process inventory, Dec. 31, 20X1	7
Finished goods inventory, Jan 1, 20X1	43
Accounts receivable, Dec. 31, 20X1	30
Accounts payable, Jan. 1, 20X1	40
Direct materials inventory, Jan. 1, 20X1	39

⟨For Year 20X1⟩

Plant utilities	$ 6
Indirect manufacturing labor	25
Depreciation—plant and equipment	8
Revenues	354
Miscellaneous manufacturing overhead	17
Marketing, distribution, and customer-service costs	91
Property taxes on plant	3
Direct materials purchased	82
Direct manufacturing labor	41
Plant supplies used	5

· Instructions ·

Prepare an income statement and a supporting schedule of cost of goods manufactured.

Problem-2

P&G Company's selected data for October 20X1 are presented here (in millions):

Direct materials inventory 10/1/20X1	$ 105
Direct materials purchased	365
Direct materials used	385
Total manufacturing overhead costs	450
Variable manufacturing overhead costs	265
Total manufacturing costs incurred during October 20X1	1,610
Work-in-process inventory 10/1/20X1	230
Cost of goods manufactured	1,660
Finished goods inventory 10/1/20X1	130
Cost of goods sold	1,770

• Instructions •

Calculate the following costs:

1. Direct materials inventory 10/31/20X1
2. Fixed manufacturing overhead costs for October 20X1
3. Direct manufacturing labor costs for October 20X1
4. Work-in-process inventory 10/31/20X1
5. Cost of finished goods available for sale in October 20X1
6. Finished goods inventory 10/31/20X1

Problem-3

Each of the following cost items pertains to one of these companies:

- Costco (a merchandising-sector company)
- LG (a manufacturing-sector company)
- Google (a service-sector company)

1) Cost of lettuce and tomatoes on sale in Costco' store
2) Electricity used to provide lighting for assembly-line workers at a LG refrigerator-assembly plant
3) Depreciation on Google' computer equipment used to update its Web site
4) Electricity used to provide lighting for Costco' store aisles
5) Depreciation on LG' computer equipment used for quality testing of refrigerator components during the assembly process
6) Salaries of Costco' marketing personnel planning local-newspaper advertising campaigns
7) Perrier mineral water purchased by Google for consumption by its software engineers
8) Salaries of Google' marketing personnel selling advertising
9) Depreciation on vehicles used to transport LG refrigerators to retail stores

• Instructions •

Distinguish between inventoriable costs and period costs.

06 Case study

❖ 현대차 국내 사업망

본사	영동대로 GBC 양재동 사옥 원효로 사옥
공장	울산공장 아산공장 전주공장
연구소	남양 기술연구소 환경기술연구소
연수원	용인 마북 캠퍼스 파주 캠퍼스 울산 기술교육원 등
출고센터	시흥, 신갈, 울산, 남양 등
영업망	영업지점 영업대리점
고객서비스	서비스센터(직영)

Chapter

02

Job-order costing

Job-order costing

01 Job-order costing

	Job-order costing	Process costing
Product	Unique	Homogeneous
Topic	Application of MOH	Equivalent Units of production
Advantage	Accurate costing	Less expensive
Disadvantage	More expensive	Inaccurate costing
Example	Law or accounting firm Aircraft assembly House construction Movie production Mainframe computer (IBM) Advertising	Deposit processing Oil refining Beverage production Automobiles Personal computer (Apple) Chemicals

1 Job-costing system (개별원가계산)

- The cost object is a unit or multiple units of a distinct product or service called a job.

- Each job generally uses different amounts of resources.

- Because the products and services are distinct, job-costing systems are used to accumulate costs separately for each product or service.

2 Process-costing system (종합원가계산)

- The cost object is masses of identical or similar units of a product or service.

- In each period, process costing systems divide the total costs by the total number of units produced to obtain a per-unit cost.

- This per-unit cost is the average unit cost that applies to each of the identical or similar units produced in that period.

02 / Job-order cost flow

1 Approach to job-order costing

(Step 1) Identify the job

(Step 2) Trace the direct costs for the job: DM & DL

(Step 3) Allocate the indirect costs to the job (MOH Application)

DM, DL은 직접적으로 추적가능하기 때문에 발생한 원가를 원가추적으로 할당하지만, MOH는 특정작업과 관련하여 직접 추적이 불가능하기 때문에 적정한 기준으로 원가배분을 하여야 하는데, 이러한 원가배분 과정을 배부(application)라고 한다.

2 Assigning manufacturing costs

Direct material	Material requisition slips	
Direct labor	Labor time tickets	Job cost sheet
Manufacturing Overhead	Overhead rate	

Completed job cost sheet

Job No   101   Quantity   1,000

Item   Aircrafts   Date   Requested February

For   KIMCPA   Date   Completed

Date	Direct Materials	Direct Labor	Manufacturing Overhead
1/6	$ 1,000		
1/10		$9,000	$7,200
1/12	7,000		
1/26	4,000		
1/31		6,000	4,800
	$12,000	$15,000	$12,000

Cost of completed job

Direct materials $ 12,000

Direct labor   15,000

Manufacturing overhead   12,000

Total cost $ 39,000

Unit cost($39,000÷1,000) $ 39.00

[그림 2-1]

3 Accumulating manufacturing costs

Purchase of raw materials	Raw materials xxx Account payable xxx
Issuance of Direct materials	WIP xxx Raw materials xxx
Direct labor incurred	WIP xxx Accrued payable xxx
Manufacturing overhead incurred	**Manufacturing overhead control** xxx Various accounts xxx

Manufacturing overhead Application	WIP xxx
	     Manufacturing overhead allocated xxx
	     (contra account to MOH−Control)

There are two indirect-cost accounts in the general ledger.

- Manufacturing Overhead Control

  the record of the actual costs in all the individual overhead categories

- Manufacturing Overhead Allocated

  the record of the manufacturing overhead allocated to individual jobs

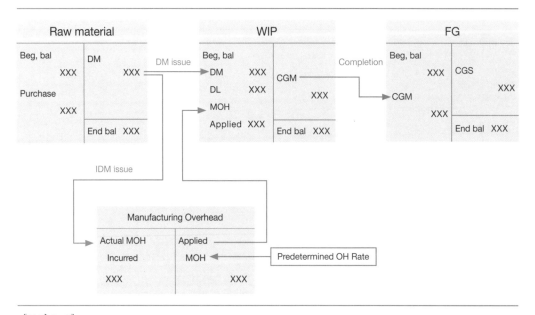

[그림 2−2]

03　Application of manufacturing overhead

1　Application

Assigning overhead costs to specified jobs on cost allocation base.

Direct material	Traced actual costs
Direct labor	
Manufacturing Overhead	Applied costs

2　Cost-allocation base

(1) DL costs

(2) DL hours

(3) Machine hours

3　Actual costing (실제개별원가계산)

$$\text{Actual indirect cost rate} = \frac{\text{Actual indirect}}{\text{Actual annual quantity of the cost-allocation base}}$$

- DM, DL : 실제발생액을 개별 작업에 직접 추적하여 집계

- MOH : 실제배부율을 이용하여 배부

- MOH 배부액 : 개별 작업의 실제배부기준수량 × MOH 실제배부율

- 장점 : 원가계산의 결과를 그대로 재무제표에 반영할 수 있음

- 단점 : 제품원가계산이 지연되어 원가정보의 적시성이 떨어짐

4 Normal costing (정상개별원가계산)

$$
\text{Budgeted indirect cost rate} = \frac{\text{Budgeted annual indirect costs}}{\text{Budgeted annual quantity of the cost-allocation base}}
$$

- DM, DL : 실제발생액을 개별 작업에 직접 추적하여 집계
- MOH : 예정배부율(predetermined MOH rate)을 이용하여 배부
- MOH 배부액 : 개별 작업의 실제배부기준수량 × MOH 예정배부율
- 장점 : 제품원가계산이 빨라져 원가정보의 적시성이 증가
- 단점 : MOH 배부차이에 대한 회계처리를 수행하여야 함

조업도(capacity)는 기업의 생산능력의 이용정도를 말하며, 기준조업도는 예정배부율을 계산하기 위하여 미리 설정한 조업도를 말한다. 많이 사용되는 기준조업도는 다음과 같다.

(1) Theoretical capacity

The maximum capacity assuming no holidays or downtime.

이론적 조업도는 정상적인 수선과 유지 등을 허용하지 않고 생산활동이 100% 전부 가동된다고 할 때 달성될 수 있는 조업도이다.

(2) Practical capacity

The maximum level at which output is produced efficiently.

⇨ Adjusted for holidays or downtime.

실제적 조업도는 정상적인 수선과 유지 등을 허용하면서 달성될 수 있는 연간 최대수준의 조업도이다.

(3) Normal capacity

Capacity based on the long-term average periods that include seasonal factors.

정상 조업도는 과거 몇 년 동안의 평균수요량에 기초한 기준조업도이며 기준조업도 중에서는 가장 많이 사용된다.

(4) Master-budget capacity

Capacity based on the anticipated capacity for the next budget period.

연간 예상 조업도는 다음 회계연도의 예상수요량에 기초한 생산능력을 말하며 이 조업도는
종합예산편성의 기초로 많이 이용된다.

Example-1

Boeing uses a job-costing system with one manufacturing overhead cost pool. Boeing allocates manufacturing overhead costs using direct manufacturing labor costs. Boeing provides the following information:

[Budget for 20X1]
Direct material costs	$2,000,000
Direct manufacturing labor costs	1,500,000
Manufacturing overhead costs	2,700,000

[Actual Results for 20X1]
Direct material costs	$1,900,000
Direct manufacturing labor costs	1,450,000
Manufacturing overhead costs	2,755,000

During March, the job-cost record for Job #747 contained the following information:
Direct materials used	$40,000
Direct manufacturing labor costs	$30,000

Compute the cost of Job #747 using (1) actual costing and (2) normal costing. At the end of 20X1, compute the under- or over-allocated manufacturing overhead under normal costing.

정답

(1) Actual costing

   1) Actual MOH rate = 2,755,000 ÷ 1,450,000 = $1.90 per DL

   2) Applied MOH = 30,000 × 1.90 = $57,000

   3) Cost of job #747 = 40,000 + 30,000 + 57,000 = $127,000

(2) Normal costing

   1) Actual MOH rate = 2,700,000 ÷ 1,500,000 = $1.80 per DL

   2) Applied MOH = 30,000 × 1.80 = $54,000

   3) Cost of job #747 = 40,000 + 30,000 + 54,000 = $124,000

(3) Under − or over − allocated manufacturing overhead

    1) Applied MOH = 1,450,000 × 1.80 = $2,610,000

    2) Under applied = 2,755,000 − 2,610,000 = $145,000

Journal entry	
Application	Dr) WIP 2,610,000 Cr) Manufacturing OH allocated 2,610,000
Actual costs	Dr) Manufacturing OH control $2,755,000 Cr) Various Accounts 2,755,000

5 Under-applied or over-applied manufacturing overhead

		Under-applied	Over-applied
Definition		Actual MOH > Applied MOH	Actual MOH < Applied MOH
Manufacturing overhead account		Debit balance	Credit balance
Causes	Activity	Actual < Expected	Actual > Expected
	Costs	Actual > Expected	Actual < Expected
Year-end		과소 또는 과대배부 제조간접비를 배분하는 방법 (1) Adjusted allocation-rate approach (2) Proration approach (3) Write off to cost of goods sold approach.	

Normal costing system에서는 제조간접원가 실제발생액과 배부액과의 차이가 발생하며 이러한 배부차이는 과소배부(under-applied)와 과대배부(over-applied)로 구분된다. 기말에 외부보고목적을 위해서는 재고자산과 매출원가의 제조간접원가 예정배부액을 실제발생액으로 전환하여야 하며, 배부차이를 조정할 때에는 재고자산과 매출원가에 과소배부(under-applied)는 증가하고, 과대배부(over-applied)는 감소한다. 이러한 배부차이 조정방법은 다음과 같은 3가지 방법이 있다.

(1) Adjusted allocation-rate approach

실제배부율을 적용한 배부금액과 예정배부율을 적용한 배부금액과의 차이를 재고자산과 매출원가를 증가 또는 감소시키는 방법으로 배부차이가 매우 중요한 경우 사용한다.

(2) Proration approach

배부차이를 재공품, 제품 및 매출원가의 금액에 비례하여 조정하는 방법으로 배부차이가 중요한 경우에 사용한다. 비례법은 총원가기준법(Method-1)과 원가요소법(Method-2)으로 구분되며, 이 방법에서는 원재료에 배부차이를 배분하지는 않는다.

1) 총원가기준법(Method-1)

기말재공품(EWIP), 기말제품(EFG), 매출원가의 총액에 비례하여 조정

2) 원가요소법(Method-2)

기말재공품(EWIP), 기말제품(EFG), 매출원가에 포함된 MOH에 비례하여 조정

(3) Write off to cost of goods sold approach.

배부차이를 전액 매출원가에서 조정하는 방법으로 배부차이가 중요하지 않은 경우에 사용한다.

Example-2

- Total estimated OH costs for the year is $500
- Total estimated DL hours for the year is 100 hours
- OH Rate = $500 ÷ 100 hours = $5.00 per hour
- Job #101: 60 hours
- Job #102: 30 hours
- Actual OH incurred is $490
- Year-end account balances before adjustment

	Total costs	MOH
CGS	500	200
FG	375	200
WIP	125	100
RM	300	0

Application	• Application for #101: $5 × 60 hours = $300
	• Application for #102: $5 × 30 hours = $150
	• Journal entry)
	   Dr) WIP 450
	       Cr) Manufacturing OH allocated 450

Actual costs	Dr) Manufacturing OH control $490 Cr) Various Accounts 490

Year-end	(1) Write off to CGS approach
	    Dr) CGS $40
	       MOH allocated 450
	       Cr) MOH control 490
	
	(2) Proration approach-method 1
	    Dr) CGS 20
	       Finished goods 15
	       Work-in-process 5
	       MOH allocated 450
	       Cr) MOH control 490

Year-end	* Total ending balances = 500 + 375 + 125 = 1,000 CGS proration = 40 × 500/1000 =20 FG proration = 40 × 375/1000 =15 WIP proration = 40 × 500/1000 =20

(3) Proration approach-method 2

    Dr) CGS   16
        Finished goods   16
        Work-in-process   8
        MOH allocated   450
            Cr) MOH control   490

* Total MOH ending balances = 200 + 200 + 100 = 500

CGS proration = 40 × 200/500 =16

FG proration = 40 × 200/500 =16

WIP proration = 40 × 100/500 =8

Year-end account balance after adjustment

	(1)	(2)	(3)
CGS	540	520	516
FG	375	390	391
WIP	125	130	133
RM	300	300	300

04 Allocation of support department cost

1 Support departments

(1) A production department (=an operating department)

- directly adds value to a product or service.
- examples : machining, assembly

(2) A support department (= a service department)

- provides the services that assist other internal departments (operating departments and other support departments) in the company.
- examples : information systems, production control, materials management, plant maintenance, plant utility production

보조부문(support department)은 직접 제품생산 활동을 수행하는 것이 아니라 제조부문 (production department)의 제품생산에 필요한 용역을 제공함으로써 간접적으로 제품생산에 기여하므로 보조부문의 제조간접원가는 제품과의 관련성을 찾기 어려우므로 보조부문의 제 조간접원가는 제조부문에 배분한 후 다시 제품에 배부하여야 한다.

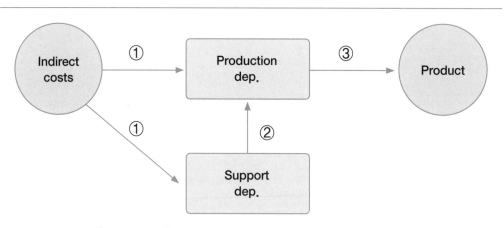

① Accumulation ② Allocation ③ Application

[그림 2-3]

보조부문이 존재할 경우 제품원가계산 절차는 다음과 같으며 이는 개별원가계산과 종합원 가계산에 공통적으로 적용된다.

① Accumulation : 제조간접원가를 보조부문과 제조부문으로 집계한다.

② Allocation : 보조부문원가를 제조부문에 배분한다.

③ Application : 제조간접원가를 제품에 배부한다.

2 Allocating costs of multiple support departments to production departments

보조부문이 다른 보조부문에 용역을 제공하지 않고 제조부문에만 제공한다면 Allocation은 복잡 하지 않다. 하지만 보조부문이 다른 보조부문에 용역을 제공한다면 보조부문 상호간에 용역제공관 계를 어느 정도 인식하는가에 따라 배분방법은 3가지로 나눌 수 있다.

(1) Direct method (직접배분법)

1) Allocates each support-department's costs to operating departments only. The direct method does not allocate support department costs to other support departments.

   보조부문원가를 다른 보조부문에는 배분하지 않고 제조부문에만 배분하는 방법

2) Advantage : it is easy to use

3) Disadvantage : it ignores information about reciprocal services provided among support departments and can therefore lead to inaccurate estimates of the cost of operating departments.

(2) Step-down method (단계배분법)

1) Allocates support-department costs to other support departments and to operating departments in a sequential manner that partially recognizes the mutual services provided among all support departments.

   보조부문 상호간에 용역제공을 부분적으로 인식하여 배분하는 방법으로 배분순서를 정한 후 순서에 따라 보조부문원가를 다른 보조부문과 제조부문에 배분

2) A step-down sequence begins with the support department that renders the highest percentage of its total services to other support departments.

배분순서를 정하는 경우 다른 보조부문에 용역제공비율이 큰 보조부문부터 배분

3) Once a support department's costs have been allocated, no subsequent support-department costs are allocated back to it.

배분이 끝난 보조부문에는 배분하지 않음

4) The step-down method does not recognize the total services that support departments provide to each other.

보조부문 상호간에 용역제공을 완전히 인식하지 않음

(3) Reciprocal method (상호배분법)

1) Allocates support-department costs to operating departments by fully recognizing the mutual services provided among all support departments.

보조부문 상호간에 용역제공을 완전히 인식하여 배분하는 방법

2) Advantage : the most precise method because it considers the mutual services provided among all support departments.

3 Comprehensive example

Siemens Engineering manufactures engines used in electric power generating plants. Siemens has two support departments and two operating departments in its manufacturing facility.

Operating department	Support department
Machining (P1)	Plant maintenance(S1)
Assembly (P2)	Information system (S2)

The two support departments provide reciprocal support to each other as well as support to the two operating department.

	Support		Production	
	S1	S2	P1	P2
Costs before allocation	$80,000	90,000	200,000	300,000
Support work by S1	0	20%	30%	50%
Support work by S2	10%	0	20%	70%

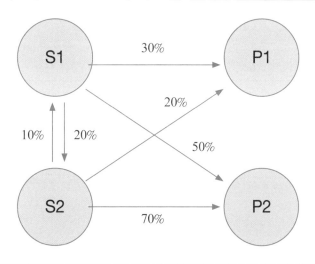

(1) Direct Method

		Service		Production	
		S1	S2	P1	P2
	Cost	$80,000	90,000	200,000	300,000
S1	Ratio	0	0	3/8	5/8
	Amount	(80,000)	0	30,000	50,000
S2	Ratio	0	0	2/9	7/9
	Amount	0	(90,000)	20,000	70,000
	Total	0	0	250,000	420,000

(2) Step-down method

		Service		Production	
		S1	S2	P1	P2
	Cost	$80,000	90,000	200,000	300,000
S1	Ratio	0	20%	30%	50%
	Amount	(80,000)	16,000	24,000	40,000
S2	Ratio	0	0	2/9	7/9
	Amount	0	(106,000)	23,556	82,444
	Total	0	0	247,556	422,444

- S1의 다른 서비스부문의 비중이 S2보다 더 크기 때문에 S1을 우선 배분

(3) Reciprocal method

상호 배분법은 우선 다음과 같은 연립방정식을 만들어 S1과 S2를 다시 결정한다.

S1 = 80,000 + 0.1 × S2

S2 = 90,000 + 0.2 × S1

Therefore S1 = \$90,816, S2 = \$108,163

		Service		Production	
		S1	S2	P1	P2
	Cost	\$80,000	90,000	200,000	300,000
S1	Ratio	0	20%	30%	50%
	Amount	(90,816)	18,163	27,245	45,408
S2	Ratio	10%	0	20%	70%
	Amount	10,816	(108,163)	21,633	75,714
	Total	0	0	248,878	421,122

05 / MCQ (Multiple Choice Questions)

01. Which one of the following alternative correctly classifies the business application to the appropriate cost system?

Job Costing System	Process Costing System
a. Wallpaper manufacturer	Oil refinery
b. Aircraft assembly	Public accounting firm
c. Paint manufacturer	Retail banking
d. Print shop	Beverage drink manufacturer

02. Which of the following is not one of the source documents for assigning costs to job cost sheets?

a. Time tickets   b. The predetermined overhead rate

c. Material requisition slips   d. The actual overhead costs

03. In recording the issuance of raw material in a job order cost system, it would be incorrect to?

a. debit work-in-process inventory

b. debit finished good inventory

c. debit manufacturing overhead account

d. credit raw material inventory.

04. In determining next year's overhead application rates, a company desires to focus on manufacturing capacity rather than output demand for its products. To derive a realistic application rate, the denominator activity level should be based on (CMA)

 a. practical capacity.

 b. maximum capacity.

 c. normal capacity.

 d. master-budget(expected annual) capacity.

05. A review of the year-end accounting records of the Walt Disney Company discloses the following information.

Raw materials	$ 80,000
Work−in−process	128,000
Finished goods	272,000
Cost of goods sold	1,120,000

The company's under-applied overhead equals $133,000. On the basis of this information, the company's cost of goods sold is most appropriately reported as (CMA)

 a. $987,000   b. $1,213,100

 c. $1,218,000   d. $1,253,000

06. Wilcox Industrial has two support departments, the Information Systems Department and the Personnel Department, and two manufacturing departments, the Machining Department and the Assembly Department. The support departments service each other as well as the two production departments. Company studies have shown that the Personnel Department provides support to a greater number of departments than the Information Systems Department. If Wilcox uses the step-down method of departmental allocation, which one of the following cost allocations would not occur? Some of the costs of the (CMA)

a. Personnel Department would be allocated to the Information Systems Department.

b. Information Systems Department would be allocated to the Personnel Department.

c. Personnel Department would be allocated to the Assembly Department.

d. Personnel Department would be allocated to the Assembly Department and the Machining Department.

07. Patterson Corporation expects to incur $70,000 of factory overhead and $60,000 of general and administrative costs next year. Direct labor costs at $5 per hour are expected to total $50,000. If factory overhead is to be applied per direct labor hour, how much overhead will be applied to a job incurring 20 hours of direct labor? (CMA)

a. $28　　　　　　　　　　　b. $120

c. $140　　　　　　　　　　d. $260

08. In a job order cost system, the issue of indirect materials increases

a. raw material inventory control　　b. work in process control.

c. factory overhead control.　　　　d. factory overhead allocated.

09. PwC uses job-costing system. Costs are allocated to jobs using a budgeted machine-hour rate. At the end of the month, over-applied overhead might be explained by which of the following situations?

Actual machine-hours	Actual overhead costs
a. Greater than budgeted	Greater than budgeted
b. Greater than budgeted	Less than budgeted
c. Less than budgeted	Greater than budgeted
d. Less than budgeted	Less than budgeted

10. PwC uses job-costing system. Costs are allocated to jobs using a budgeted machine-hour rate. At the end of the month, under-applied overhead might be explained by which of the following situations?

Actual machine-hours	Actual overhead costs
a. Greater than budgeted	Greater than budgeted
b. Greater than budgeted	Less than budgeted
c. Less than budgeted	Greater than budgeted
d. Less than budgeted	Less than budgeted

Questions 11 through 14 are based on the following information.

Hyundai Heavy Industries's beginning and ending inventories for May are

	May 1	May 31
Direct materials	$52,000	$57,000
Work-in-process	135,000	121,000
Finished goods	65,000	78,000

Production data for the month of May follows:

Direct labor	$185,000
Actual factory overhead	98,000
Direct materials purchased	134,000
Freight-in	5,000
Freight-out	7,000
Purchase returns	3,000

Hyundai uses one factory overhead control account and charges factory overhead to production at 60% of direct labor cost. The company does not formally recognize over/under-applied overhead until year-end. The company allocates over-and under-applied overhead to appropriate inventories and cost of goods sold based on year-end balances.

11. What is the company's cost of goods sold for May?

    a. $427,000   b. $428,000
    c. $441,000   d. $415,000

12. Hyundai's net charge to factory overhead control for the month of May is

    a. $13,000 debit, overapplied   b. $13,000 debit, underapplied
    c. $13,000 credit, overapplied   d. $13,000 credit, underapplied

13. If the company formally recognizes over/under-applied overhead at May 31, what is the cost of goods sold for May?

    a. $419,126   b. $428,000
    c. $441,000   d. $415,000

14. If the company formally recognizes over/under-applied overhead at May 31 and any amount of under- or over-allocation is written off to cost of goods sold, what is the cost of goods sold for May?

    a. $419,126   b. $428,000
    c. $441,000   d. $415,000

• 정답 및 해설

1. a. Wall paper ⇨ process costing
   b. Public accounting firm ⇨ job-order costing
   c. Paint ⇨ process costing　　　　　　　　　　　　　　　**정답 : d**

2. 제조 간접비는 실제금액이 원가명세서에 배분하지 않고 예정 배부율로 배부된 금액
   이 원가명세서에 배분된다.　　　　　　　　　　　　　　　**정답 : d**

3. Dr) WIP　　　　　　xxx
   　　Dr) MOH　　　　　　　　　xxx
   　　Cr) Raw material　　　　　　xxx

   　　　　　　　　　　　　　　　　　　　　　　　　　　　　정답 : b

4. 수요보다는 공급에 초점을 둔 조업도는 maximum capacity와 practical capacity이다.

   　　　　　　　　　　　　　　　　　　　　　　　　　　　　정답 : a

5. WIP + FG + CGS = $1,520,000 CGS 배분금액
   = 133,000 × 1,120,000 ÷ 1,520,000 = 98,000배분 후 CGS
   = 1,120,000 + 98,000 = 1,218,000　　　　　　　　　　　**정답 : c**

6. Personnel Department가 더 중요한 보조부문이므로 PD는 MD, AD, ID에 배분하지
   만 ID는 MD와 AD에만 배분한다.　　　　　　　　　　　　**정답 : b**

7. Estimated hours = $50,000 ÷ $5 = 10,000 hours
   Predetermined OH rate = $70,000 ÷ 10,000 H = $7/H
   Applied OH = 20 H × $7 = $140

   　　　　　　　　　　　　　　　　　　　　　　　　　　　　정답 : c

8. Dr) MOH-control　　　　　　　　xx
   　　Cr) Raw material　　　　　　　xxx　　　　　　　　　　**정답 : c**

9. Actual hours 〉 Budgeted hours ⇨ Over-applied overhead
   Actual hours 〈 Budgeted hours ⇨ Under-applied overhead
   Actual OH 〉 Budgeted OH ⇨ Under-applied overhead

Actual OH $\langle$ Budgeted OH $\Rightarrow$ Over-applied overhead

정답 : b

10. 9번 답안을 참조한다. 정답 : c

11. (1) DM = BRM (52,000) + Purchase (134,000 + 5,000 − 3,000) − ERM (57,000)
    = 131,000
    (2) TMC = DM (131,000) + DL (185,000) + OH (111,000) = 427,000
    (3) CGM = BWIP (135,000) + TMC (427,000) − EWIP (121,000) = 441,000
    (4) CGS = BFG (65,000) + CGM (441,000) − EFG (78,000) = 428,000

정답 : b

12. Actual (98,000) $\langle$ Applied (111,000) 이므로 over-applied 정답 : c

13. WIP + FG + CGS = $627,000
    CGS 배분금액 = 13,000 × 428,000 ÷ 627,000 = 8,874
    배분 후 CGS = 428,000 − 8,874 = 419,126

정답 : a

14. 배분 후 CGS = 428,000 − 13,000 = 415,000

정답 : d

06 / TBS (Task-Based Simulation)

Problem-1

In each of the following situations, determine whether job costing or process costing would be more appropriate.

(1) A CPA firm

(2) An oil refinery

(3) A custom furniture manufacturer

(4) A tire manufacturer

(5) A textbook publisher

(6) A pharmaceutical company

(7) An advertising agency

(8) An architecture firm

(9) A paint manufacturer

(10) A nursing home

(11) A landscaping company

(12) A cola-drink-concentrate producer

(13) A movie studio

(14) A law firm

(15) A commercial aircraft manufacturer

(16) A management consulting firm

(17) A plumbing contractor

(18) A catering service

(19) A paper mill

(20) An auto repair shop

Problem-2

Hyundai Construction assembles residential houses. It uses a job-costing system with two direct-cost categories (direct materials and direct labor) and one indirect-cost pool (assembly support). Direct labor-hours is the allocation base for assembly support costs. Hyundai budgets 20X1 assembly-support costs to be $8,000,000 and 20X1 direct labor hours to be 160,000.

At the end of 20X1, Anderson is comparing the costs of several jobs that were started and completed in 20X1.

⟨Model-AA⟩

Construction period : Feb–June 20X1

Direct material costs : $106,650 127,970

Direct labor costs : $36,276

Direct labor-hours : 920

⟨Model-AB⟩

Construction period : May–Oct 20X1

Direct material costs : $127,970

Direct labor costs : $ 41,750

Direct labor-hours : 1,040

Direct materials and direct labor are paid for on a contract basis. The costs of each are known when direct materials are used or when direct labor-hours are worked. The 20X1 actual assembly-support costs were $7,614,000, and the actual direct labor-hours were 162,000.

· Instructions ·

1. Compute the (a) budgeted indirect–cost rate and (b) actual indirect–cost rate.

2. What are the job costs of the Model–AA and the Model–AB using (a) normal costing and (b) actual costing?

Problem-3

AIFA assembles prestige manufactured homes. Its job costing system has two direct-cost categories and one indirect-cost pool (manufacturing overhead allocated at a budgeted $31 per machine-hour in 20X1).

The following data (in millions) show operation costs for 20X1:

Materials Control, beginning balance, January 1, 20X1	$ 18
Work-in-Process Control, beginning balance, January 1, 20X1	9
Finished Goods Control, beginning balance, January 1, 20X1	10
Materials and supplies purchased on credit	154
Direct materials used	152
Indirect materials (supplies) issued to various production departments	19
Direct manufacturing labor	96
Indirect manufacturing labor incurred by various production departments	34
Depreciation on plant and manufacturing equipment	28
Miscellaneous manufacturing overhead incurred	13
Manufacturing overhead allocated, 3,000,000 actual machine-hours	?
Cost of goods manufactured	298
Revenues	410
Cost of goods sold	294

• Instructions •

1. Prepare journal entries.
2. What is the ending balance of Work−in−Process Control?
3. Show the journal entry for disposing of under− or over−allocated manufacturing overhead directly as a year−end write off to Cost of Goods Sold.
4. How did AIFA perform in 20X1

Problem-4

Kim & Associates is a law firm specializing in labor relations and employee-related work. It employs 30 professionals (5 partners and 25 associates) who work directly with its clients. The average budgeted total compensation per professional for 20X1 is $97,500. Each professional is budgeted to have 1,500 billable hours to clients in 20X1. All professionals work for clients to their maximum 1,500 billable hours available. All professional labor costs are included in a single direct-cost category and are traced to jobs on a per-hour basis. All costs of Kim & Associates other than professional labor costs are included in a single indirect-cost pool (legal support) and are allocated to jobs using professional labor-hours as the allocation base. The budgeted level of indirect costs in 20X1 is $2,475,000.

• Instructions •

1. Compute the 20X1 budgeted direct-cost rate per hour of professional labor.
2. Compute the 20X1 budgeted indirect-cost rate per hour of professional labor.
3. Kim & Associates is considering bidding on two jobs:
    (1) Litigation work for Richardson, which requires 120 budgeted hours of professional labor
    (2) Labor contract work for Punch, which requires 160 budgeted hours of professional labor
       Prepare a cost estimate for each job.

Job costing, accounting for manufacturing overhead, budgeted rates. The AIFA Company uses a job-costing system at its Seoul plant. The plant has a machining department and a finishing department. AIFA uses normal costing with two direct-cost categories (direct materials and direct manufacturing labor) and two manufacturing overhead cost pools (the machining department with machine hours
as the allocation base and the finishing department with direct manufacturing labor costs as the allocation base). The 20X1 budget for the plant is as follows:

[Machining Department]

Manufacturing overhead costs	$9,065,000
Direct manufacturing labor costs	$ 970,000
Direct manufacturing labor-hours	36,000
Machine-hours	185,000

[Finishing Department]

Manufacturing overhead costs	$8,181,000
Direct manufacturing labor costs	$4,050,000
Direct manufacturing labor-hours	155,000
Machine-hours	37,000

· Instructions ·

1. During the month of January, the job-cost record for Job 431 shows the following:

	Machining Department	Finishing Department
Direct materials used	$13,000	$ 5,000
Direct manufacturing labor costs	$ 900	$1,250
Direct manufacturing labor-hours	20	70
Machine-hours	140	20

Assuming that Job 431 consisted of 300 units of product, what is the cost per unit?

2. Amounts at the end of 20X1 are as follows:

	Machining Department	Finishing Department
Direct materials used	$10,000,000	$7,982,000
Direct manufacturing labor costs	$ 1,030,000	$4,100,000
Machine-hours	200,000	34,000
Manufacturing overhead costs	$9,900,000	$8,200,000

Compute the under- or over-allocated manufacturing overhead for each department and for the Seoul plant as a whole.

Problem-6

KIMCPA uses job-costing system. Costs are allocated to jobs using a budgeted machine-hour rate.

Situations	A	B	C	D
Budgeted manufacturing overhead	$70,000	$70,000	$70,000	$70,000
Budgeted machine-hours	2,000	2,000	2,000	2,000
Actual manufacturing overhead	$70,000	$65,000	70,000	$75,000
Actual machine-hours	1,900	2,000	2,100	2,000

· Instructions ·

For each situation,

1. Calculate the budgeted manufacturing overhead rate.
2. Calculate the manufacturing overhead allocated.
3. Calculate the amount of under- or over-allocated manufacturing overhead

Problem-7

㈜한라는 20X1년 초에 설립되었으며 정상원가계산(normal costing)을 적용하고 있다. 제조간접비는 직접노무시간을 기준으로 예정 배부한다. 회사는 제조간접비 배부차이를 기말재고자산 및 매출원가에 포함된 제조간접비 예정배부액에 비례하여 안분한다.

당기에 기말재공품, 기말제품 및 매출원가에는 1 : 3 : 4의 비율로 제조간접비가 각각 예정배부되었고, 기말재공품에 차감하여 조정된 배부차이는 ₩2,500이었다. 당기의 실제 제조간접비는 ₩180,000이고, 실제 직접노무시간은 총 1,250시간이었다. (K-CPA)

· Instructions ·

제조간접비 예정배부율은 직접노무시간당 얼마인가?

Problem-8

KIMCPA provides management consulting services to government and corporate clients. KIMCPA has two support departments—administrative services (AS) and information systems (IS)—and two operating departments—government consulting (GOVT) and corporate consulting (CORP). For the first quarter of 20X1, KIMCPA's cost records indicate the following:

	SUPPORT		OPERATING	
	AS	IS	GOVT	CORP
Budgeted overhead costs before inter-department cost allocations	$600,000	$2,400,000	$8,756,000	$12,452,000
Support work supplied by AS (budgeted head count)	-	25%	40%	35%
Support work supplied by IS (budgeted computer time)	10%	-	30%	60%

• Instructions •

Allocate the two support departments' costs to the two operating departments using the following methods:

1. Direct method
2. Step-down method (allocate AS first)
3. Step-down method (allocate IS first)
4. Reciprocal method

07 Case study

1 미국 워싱턴주 보잉 에버렛 공장

세계 최대 비행지 제조공장
상시근무인원 : 35000명
대형비행기 생산능력 : 1일 1대
비행기 1대당 부품수 : 600만개
면적 : 415m² (여의도 1.5배)

2 현대중공업 울산조선소

한국에서 가장 큰 조선소
면적 : 600만㎡ (여의도 면적 2배)
대형도크 : 9개

3 Ship Construction Process

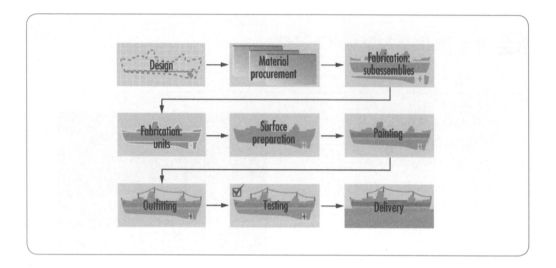

Chapter

03

Process Costing

Chapter 03 — Process Costing

01 Introduction

- In a process-costing system, the unit cost of a product or service is obtained by assigning total costs to many identical or similar units of output.

  종합원가계산 (process−costing)은 동종제품을 하나 또는 여러 개의 제조공정을 이용하여 연속적으로 대량생산하는 기업의 원가계산방법이다.

- Unit costs are calculated by dividing total costs incurred by the number of units of output from the production process

  종합원가계산에서는 생산되는 제품이 동질적이므로 발생한 제조원가를 제조공정별로 구분하여 집계한 후 이를 공정별로 생산된 수량을 기준으로 단위당 원가를 계산한다.

	Job-order costing	Process costing
WIP accounts	One	Multiple
Documents	Job cost sheets	Production cost reports
Unit cost	$\dfrac{\text{Costs per each job}}{\text{Units produced for the job}}$	$\dfrac{\text{Total manufacturing costs}}{\text{Units produced}}$

Job-order cost flow

Process cost flow

[그림 3-1]

Issuance of Direct materials	WIP-A xxx
	WIP-B xxx
	Raw materials xxx
Direct labor incurred	WIP-A xxx
	WIP-B xxx
	Accrued payable xxx
Manufacturing overhead incurred	Manufacturing overhead control xxx
	Various accounts xxx
Manufacturing overhead Application	WIP-A xxx
	WIP-B xxx
	Manufacturing overhead allocated xxx
Transfer to next department	WIP-B xxx
	WIP-A xxx
Transfer to FG	FG xxx
	WIP-B xxx

Example-1

The Coca-Cola Company uses a process cost system. The following information pertains to operation for the month of January 20X1:

	Units
Beginning work in process inventory, January 1	0
Started in production during January	10,000
Completed production during January	10,000
Ending work in process inventory, January 31	0

In January 20X1, all 10,000 physical units started were completed. Cost pertaining to the month of January are as follows:

Direct material costs : $200,000

Conversion costs : $360,000

Total costs added during January : $560,000

cost per unit = total costs ÷ total units produced

$560,000 ÷ 10,000 units = $56 per unit

종합원가계산에서는 직접재료원가(direct material)와 가공원가(conversion costs)로 구분하여 계산한다. 왜냐하면 직접재료원가는 공정의 일정 시점에서 전량 투입되는 반면에 가공원가는 공정전반에 걸쳐 균등하게 발생하기 때문이다.

02 Process costing

1 Five steps of process costing

종합원가는 다음과 같이 5단계의 계산절차를 적용한다.

> (Step 1) Identify the flow of physical units of output.
> 물량흐름 파악
>
> (Step 2) Compute output in terms of equivalent units.
> 완성품환산량 계산
>
> (Step 3) Summarize the total costs to allocate.
> 배분할 원가 요약
>
> (Step 4) Compute the cost per equivalent units.
> 완성품환산량 단위당 원가 계산
>
> (Step 5) Allocate the total costs to units completed and to units in EWIP
> 완성품원가 및 기말재공품원가 계산

2 Process costing with some ending WIP inventory

(1) Process costing with some EWIP inventory

기말재공품(EWIP)이 있는 경우에는 단순한 물리적 수량이 아닌 완성품환산량(EUP, equivalent units of production)을 기준으로 완성품(CGM)과 기말재공품(EWIP)에 배분하여 원가를 계산하여야 한다. Job-order costing에서 원가배분에서 가장 중요한 요소가 제조간접원가(MOH)의 원가배분이라면, process costing에서 가장 중요한 요소는 EUP를 이용한 원가배분이다.

(2) Equivalent units of production (EUP)

Equivalent units are a derived measure of output calculated by converting the quantity of input into the amount of completed output units that could be produced with that quantity of input.

완성품환산량은 완성품으로 환산하였을 경우의 수량을 의미한다.

(3) Equivalent units for DM and conversion costs

1) 제조과정에서 여러 가지 재료가 투입되는 경우 각 재료의 투입시점에 따라 완성품환산량을 구분하여 계산한다.

2) 가공원가의 발생형태에 대해서 언급이 없는 경우에는 공정의 진행에 따라 균등하게 발생하는 것으로 간주하여 완성품환산량을 계산한다.

(4) Work-in-process

완성품 환산량을 적용한 원가배분은 재공품(WIP)에만 적용되며, 원재료와 제품에는 적용되지 않는다. 원재료와 제품은 기말재고자산과 투입 또는 판매된 재고자산의 수량개념이 동일하기 때문에 완성품 환산량의 개념이 필요가 없다.

Example-2

The Coca-Cola Company uses a process cost system. The following information pertains to operation for the month of January 20X1:

	Units
Beginning work in process inventory, January 1	0
Started in production during January	10,000
Completed production during January	8,000
Ending work in process inventory, January 31	2,000

In January 20X1, all 10,000 physical units started were completed. Cost pertaining to the month of January are as follows:

Direct material costs : $200,000

Conversion costs : $360,000

Total costs added during January : $560,000

The ending work-in-process inventory was 50% complete. All materials are added at the beginning of the process.

Step 1, 2, 3

	Physical units	EUP	
		DM	Conversion costs
CGM	8,000	8,000	8,000
EWIP	2,000	2,000	1,000
Equivalent units	10,000	10,000	9,000
Total costs	$560,000	$200,000	$360,000

완성품(CGM)의 경우에는 완성도가 100%이기 때문에 physical units = EUP가 성립된다. 기말재공품(EWIP)의 경우 직접재료원기(DM)는 공정의 기초 시점에서 전량 투입되었기 때문에 비록 완성도가 50%라 하더라도 EUP는 100%기준인 2,000개로 계산이 된다. 가공원가의 경우에는 공정전반에 걸쳐 균등하게 발생하기 때문에 2,000개를 50% 완성하는 노력은 1,000개를 100% 완성하는 노력과 동일하므로 EUP = 1,000개로 계산한다.

Step 4

the cost per equivalent units for DM = $200,000 ÷ 10,000 = $20

the cost per equivalent units for conversion costs = $360,000 ÷ 9,000 = $40

Step 5

CGM = 8,000 × @20 + 8,000 × @40 = $480,000

EWIP = 2,000 × @20 + 1,000 × @40 = $80,000

the cost per CGM = $480,000 ÷ 8,000 = $60

the cost per EWIP = $80,000 ÷ 2,000 = $40

Example-3

The Coca-Cola Company uses a process cost system. The following information pertains to operation for the month of January 20X1:

	Units
Beginning work in process inventory, January 1	0
Started in production during January	10,000
Completed production during January	8,000
Ending work in process inventory, January 31	2,000

In January 20X1, all 10,000 physical units started were completed. Cost pertaining to the month of January are as follows:

Direct material costs : $200,000

Conversion costs : $360,000

Total costs added during January : $560,000

The ending work-in-process inventory was 50% complete. All materials are added when a process is 60% complete.

Step 1, 2, 3

	Physical units	EUP	
		DM	Conversion costs
CGM	8,000	8,000	8,000
EWIP	2,000	0	1,000
Equivalent units	10,000	8,000	9,000
Total costs	$560,000	$200,000	$360,000

직접재료원가(DM)를 공정의 기초 시점이 아닌 60% 공정시점에서 전량 투입된다고 가정한다면 50% 공정의 기말재공품(EWIP)에는 아직 직접재료원가(DM)가 투입되지 않았기 때문에 EWIP의 직접재료원가의 EUP는 0개로 계산한다.

Step 4

the cost per equivalent units for DM = \$200,000 ÷ 8,000 = \$25

the cost per equivalent units for conversion costs = \$360,000 ÷ 9,000 = \$40

Step 5

CGM = 8,000 × @25 + 8,000 × @40 = \$520,000

EWIP = 0 × @25 + 1,000 × @40 = \$40,000

  the cost per CGM = \$520,000 ÷ 8,000 = \$65

  the cost per EWIP = \$40,000 ÷ 2,000 = \$20

만일 A라는 원재료는 기초시점에 투입하고 B라는 원재료는 60%시점에서 투입한다면 EUP의 계산은 DM-A와 DM-B로 구분하여 다음과 같이 계산이 된다.

Assume that material A is added at the beginning of the process and material B is added when a process is 60% complete.

	Physical units	EUP		
		DM-A	DM-B	Conversion cost
CGM	8,000	8,000	8,000	8,000
EWIP	2,000	2,000	0	1,000
Equivalent units	10,000	10,000	8,000	9,000

3 Process costing with some beginning WIP inventory

(1) Weighted-average method

- 전기에 발생한 기초재공품(BWIP)원가와 당기투입원가를 구분하지 않고 이를 합하여 완성품(CGM)과 기말재공품(EWIP)에 배분
- 실제물량흐름과는 다른 방법
- Total equivalent units = 총작업량

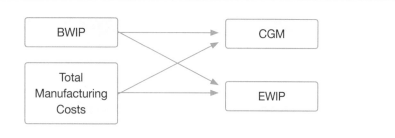

[그림 3-2]

(2) FIFO(First-in First-out) method

- 기초재공품(BWIP)은 당기에 모두 완성하고, 당기 착수량의 일부는 완성되고 일부는 기말 재공품(EWIP)으로 나누어진다고 가정
- 전기에 발생한 기초재공품(BWIP)원가 : 모두 완성품(CGM)원가에 포함
- 당기투입원가 : 당기작업량기준으로 완성품(CGM)과 기말재공품(EWIP)에 배분
- 실제물량흐름에 보다 충실한 방법
- Total equivalent units = 당기작업량

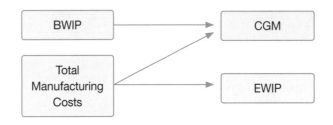

[그림 3-3]

(3) LIFO(Last-in First-out) method

- 기초재공품(BWIP)은 기말재공품(EWIP)으로 되어 있으며, 당기 착수량의 일부는 완성되고 일부는 기말재공품(EWIP)로 나누어진다고 가정
- 전기에 발생한 기초재공품(BWIP)원가 : 모두 기말재공품(EWIP)원가에 포함
- 당기투입원가 : 당기작업량기준으로 완성품(CGM)과 기말재공품(EWIP)에 배분
- 실제물량흐름과는 반대의 방법
- Total equivalent units = 당기작업량
- 재무회계 목적으로 절세효과를 누리기 위하여 선택하는 방법으로 관리회계목적으로는 거의 사용하지 않음

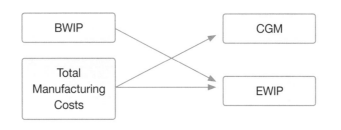

[그림 3-4]

(4) Summary

1) Step 2

평균법의 EUP = 총작업량, FIFO의 EUP = 당기작업량

기초재공품 재고가 있는 경우 EUP의 크기는 다음과 같다.

Weighted-average > FIFO

기초 재공품 재고가 없는 경우라면 EUP의 크기는 다음과 같다.

Weighted-average = FIFO

2) Step 3~4

완성품환산량 단위당 원가를 계산하는 과정에서 기초재공원 원가와 당기투입원가의 포함 여부를 요약하면 다음과 같다.

	Weighted-average	FIFO
기초재공품원가	Yes	No
당기투입원가	Yes	Yes

Example-4

The Coca-Cola Company uses a process cost system. The following information pertains to operation for the month of May 20X1:

	Units
Beginning work in process inventory, May 1	2,000
Started in production during May	8,000
Completed production during May	7,000
Ending work in process inventory, May 31	3,000

The beginning inventory was 30% complete and the ending inventory was 50% complete. All materials are added at the beginning of the process. Cost pertaining to the month of May are as follows:

- The beginning inventory costs are:

      Materials: $400,000, Conversion costs: $254,000

- Costs incurred during May are:

      Materials used: $1,760,000, Conversion costs: $3,792,000

(1) Weighed-average method

평균법은 물량흐름을 알 수 없기 때문에 총 제조원가 $6,206,000을 CGM과 EWIP로 배분하여야 한다.

Step 1, 2

	Physical units	EUP	
		DM	Conversion costs
CGM	7,000	7,000	7,000
EWIP	3,000(50%)	3,000	1,500
Total	10,000	10,000	8,500

Step 3, 4

	Total costs	DM	Conversion costs
BWIP	$654,000	$400,000	$254,000
Current costs	$5,552,000	$1,760,000	$3,792,000
Total	$6,206,000	$2,160,000	$4,046,000
EUP		10,000	8,500
Cost per EUP	@ $692	@ $216	@ $476

Step 5

CGM = 7,000 × @216 + 7,000 × @476 = $4,844,000

EWIP = 3,000 × @216 + 1,500 × @476 = $1,362,000

(2) FIFO method

FIFO 방법은 BWIP의 제조원가 $654,000은 먼저 제조가 완성된디고 가정하므로 CGM으로 분류하며 당기제조원가인 $5,552,000을 CGM과 EWIP로 배분하여야 한다.

Step 1, 2

	Physical units	EUP	
		DM	Conversion costs
BWIP	2,000(30%)	2,000	600
CGM	7,000	7,000	7,000
Current CGM	7,000	5,000	6,400
EWIP	3,000(50%)	3,000	1,500
Total	10,000	8,000	7,900

Step 3, 4

	Total costs	DM	Conversion costs
Current costs	$5,552,000	$1,760,000	$3,792,000
EUP		8,000	7,900
Cost per EUP	@$700	@$220	@$480

Step 5

BWIP = $400,000 + 254,000 = $654,000

Current CGM = 5,000 × @220 + 6,400 × @480 = $4,172,000

CGM = $4,172,000 + $654,000 = $4,826,000

EWIP = 3,000 × @220 + 1,500 × @480 = $1,380,000

(3) LIFO method

LIFO 방법은 BWIP의 제조원가 $654,000은 나중에 완성된다고 가정하므로 EWIP로 분류하며 당기제조원가인 $5,552,000을 CGM과 EWIP로 배분하여야 한다.

Step 1, 2

	Physical units	EUP	
		DM	Conversion costs
BWIP	2,000(30%)	2,000	600
EWIP	3,000(50%)	3,000	1,500
CGM	7,000	7,000	7,000
Current EWIP	3,000(50%)	1,000	900
Total	10,000	8,000	7,900

Step 3, 4

	Total costs	DM	Conversion costs
Current costs	$5,552,000	$1,760,000	$3,792,000
EUP		8,000	7,900
Cost per EUP	@$700	@$220	@$480

Step 5

BWIP = $400,000 + 254,000 = $654,000

Current EWIP = 1,000 × @220 + 900 × @480 = $652,000

CGM = 7,000 × @220 + 7,000 × @480 = $4,900,000

EWIP = $652,000 + $654,000 = $1,306,000

Example-5

The Coca-Cola Company uses a process cost system. The following information pertains to operation for the month of May 20X1:

	Units
Beginning work in process inventory, May 1	2,000
Started in production during May	8,000
Completed production during May	7,000
Ending work in process inventory, May 31	3,000

The beginning inventory was 50% complete for materials and 30% complete for conversion costs.

The ending inventory was 80% complete for materials and 50% complete for conversion costs.

Costs pertaining to the month of May are as follows:

- The beginning inventory costs are:

Materials: $398,000, Conversion costs: $254,000

- Costs incurred during May are:

Materials used: $1,764,000, Conversion costs: $3,792,000

(1) Weighed-average method

Step 1, 2

	Physical units	EUP	
		DM	Conversion costs
CGM	7,000	7,000	7,000
EWIP	3,000(80%, 50%)	2,400	1,500
Total	10,000	9,400	8,500

- EWIP의 경우 실제 공정률은 50% 이지만 직접재료원가는 80%가 이미 투입이 되었다고 의미로, 직접재료원가도 공정에 걸쳐 부분적으로 투입한다는 가정이다.

Step 3, 4

	Total costs	DM	Conversion costs
BWIP	$652,000	$398,000	$254,000
Current costs	$5,556,000	$1,764,000	$3,792,000
Total	$6,208,000	$2,162,000	$4,046,000
EUP		9,400	8,500
Cost per EUP	@$706	@$230	@$476

Step 5

CGM = 7,000 × @230 + 7,000 × @476 = $4,942,000
EWIP = 2,400 × @230 + 1,500 × @476 = $1,266,000

(2) FIFO method

FIFO 방법은 BWIP의 제조원가 $654,000은 먼저 제조가 완성된다고 가정하므로 CGM으로 분류하며 당기제조원가인 $5,552,000을 CGM과 EWIP로 배분하여야 한다.

Step 1, 2

	Physical units	EUP	
		DM	Conversion costs
BWIP	2,000(50%, 30%)	1,000	600
CGM	7,000	7,000	7,000
Current CGM	7,000	6,000	6,400
EWIP	3,000(80%, 50%)	2,400	1,500
Total	10,000	8,400	7,900

Step 3, 4

	Total costs	DM	Conversion costs
Current costs	$5,556,000	$1,764,000	$3,792,000
EUP		8,400	7,900
Cost per EUP	@$690	@$210	@$480

Step 5

BWIP = $398,000 + 254,000 = $652,000

Current CGM = 6,000 × @210 + 6,400 × @480 = $4,332,000

CGM = $4,332,000 + $652,000 = $4,984,000

EWIP = 2,400 × @210 + 1,500 × @480 = $1,224,000

4 Transferred-in costs in process costing

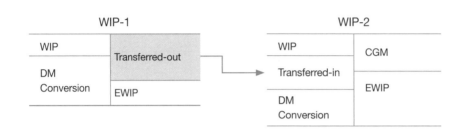

[그림 3-5]

2개 이상의 연속적인 제조공정을 통하여 제품을 생산하는 경우

● 제1공정의 완성품수량 = 제2공정의 당기착수량

● 제1공정의 완성품원가(Transferred-out costs)

= 제2공정의 전공정대체원가(Transferred-in costs)

● 제1공정의 완성품은 제2공정의 초기에 투입되므로

⇨ CGM, EWIP, BWIP, Spoilage 전공정 대체원가 완성도 = 100%

⇨ Transferred-in costs = 제2공정 기초시점에 투입하는 직접재료원가

제2공정의 경우 EUP의 계산과정에서 다음과 같은 양식으로 파악하여야 한다.

	Physical units	EUP		
		Transferred-in	DM	Conversion costs
CGM				
EWIP				
Total				

Example-6

Moncler is a manufacturer of winter clothes. It has a knitting department and a finishing department. During June, the following data were recorded for the finishing department.

	Units(tons)
Beginning work in process inventory, June 1	60
Started in production during June	100
Completed production during June	120
Ending work in process inventory, June 30	40

Direct materials are added at the end of the process. Conversion costs are added evenly during the process. The beginning inventory was 50% complete and the ending inventory was 75% complete for conversion costs.

Costs pertaining to the month of June are as follows:
- The beginning inventory costs are:
     T-in costs : $60,000, Materials: $0, Conversion costs: $24,000
- Costs incurred during June are:
     T-in costs : $132,000, Materials: $27,000, Conversion costs: $62,400

(1) Weighed-average method

Step 1, 2, 3, 4

	Units	%	T-in	DM	Conversion
CGM	120	100	120	120	120
EWIP	40	75	40	0	30
Total	160		160	120	150
Total cost	$305,400		$192,000	27,000	86,400
Unit cost	$2,001		$1,200	225	576

Step 5

$$CGM = 120 \times (1200 + 225 + 576) = \underline{\$240,120}$$
$$EWIP = 40 \times 1200 + 0 \times 225 + 30 \times 576 = \underline{\$65,280}$$

(2) FIFO method

Step 1, 2, 3, 4

	Units	%	T-in	DM	Conversion
BWIP	60	50%	60	0	30
CGM	120	100	120	120	120
Current CGM	120	100	60	120	90
EWIP	40	75	40	0	30
Total	160		100	120	120
Total cost	$221,400		$132,000	27,000	62,400
Unit cost			$1,320	225	520

Step 5

$$BWIP = \$60,000 + 0 + 24,000 = \$84,000$$
$$Current\ CGM = 60 \times 1320 + 120 \times 225 + 90 \times 520 = \$153,000$$
$$CGM = \$153,000 + \$84,000 = \underline{\$237,000}$$
$$EWIP = 40 \times 1320 + 0 \times 225 + 30 \times 520 = \underline{\$68,400}$$

03 / Spoilage

1 Spoilage, rework and scrap

(1) Spoilage(공손)

- Defective units that are discarded or sold for disposal value

  공정 중에 결함이 발생한 불량품으로 폐기 또는 처분외의 용도가 없는 것으로 정상공손 (normal spoilage)과 비정상공손(abnormal spoilage)으로 구분하여 처리한다.

(2) Reworked units(재작업품)

- Defective units that are reworked and sold for as normal product

  불량품이지만 재작업을 하여 판매가 가능한 것으로 제품원가(product cost)로 처리한다.

(3) Scrap(작업폐물)

- Residual material that results from manufacturing a product

  제품을 제작할 때 생기는 부수적인 물질로서 원가를 계산하지 않고, 판매시점에 수익으로 인식한다.

2 Types of spoilages

Normal Spoilage	1) A spoilage inherent in a particular production process that arises even under efficient operating conditions. 2) Product cost 3) Uncontrollable in the short run
Abnormal Spoilage	1) A spoilage through some unnecessary act, event, or condition. ⇨ It would not arise under efficient operating conditions. 2) Period cost (written off as a loss) ⇨ It should not be included in EWIP, EFG and CGS 3) Controllable in the short run

3 Spoilages in job-order costing

(1) When normal spoilage is attributable to general factory condition

1) Allocated to all jobs

2) Reflected in the predetermined overhead rate

(2) When normal spoilage is attributable to specific job condition

1) Charged to the specific job

2) Not reflected in the predetermined overhead rate

(3) Abnormal spoilage

1) Charged to "loss account"

2) Not reflected in the predetermined overhead rate

4 Spoilages in process costing

(1) Physical units of spoilage

공손(spoilage)이 발생하는 경우 1단계의 물량흐름 분석은 다음과 같다.

WIP(Physical units)			
		CGM	xxx
BWIP	xxx	Normal spoilages	xxx
Current issue	xxx	Abnormal spoilages	xxx
		EWIP	xxx

정상공손(normal spoilage)과 비정상공손(Abnormal spoilage)수량 파악은 다음과 같다.

> 1) Total spoilage = BWIP + Current issue − (CGM + EWIP)
> 2) Normal spoilage = units passing inspection × normal spoilage rate
>   = 검사를 통과한 정상품 × 정상품 공손 허용률
> 3) Abnormal spoilage = Total spoilage − Normal spoilage

➡ 정상공손수량파악은 검사시점 통과기준과 검사시점 도달기준이 있지만 US CPA시험에서는 일반적으로 검사시점 통과기준으로 계산한다.

정상품(units passing inspection)에 대한 판단은 검사시점에서 하며 수량은 다음과 같다.

- 기말재공품(EWIP)이 검사시점을 통과한 경우 : CGM + EWIP
- 기말재공품(EWIP)이 검사시점을 통과하지 않은 경우 : CGM

> **Example-7**

The Coca-Cola Company uses a process cost system. The following information pertains to operation for the month of May X1:

	Units
Beginning work in process inventory, May 1	2,000(30%)
Started in production during May	9,000
Completed production during May	7,000
Ending work in process inventory, May 31	3,000(50%)

Assume that normal spoilage is 8% of goods units passing inspection in a process. Calculate the normal spoilage and abnormal spoilage in units assuming the inspection point is at

(1) 40% stage of completion

(2) 80% stage of completion

Total spoilage = $(2,000 + 9,000) - (7,000 + 3,000) = 1,000$ units

(1) 완성도 40%에서 품질검사를 하는 경우

기말재공품(EWIP)이 검사시점을 통과하였기 때문에

units passing inspection = $7,000 + 3,000 = 10,000$ units

normal spoilage = $8\% \times 10,000$ units = 800 units

abnormal spoilage = $1,000$ units $-$ 800 units = 200units

(2) 완성도 80%에서 품질검사를 하는 경우

기말재공품(EWIP)이 검사시점을 통과하지 않았기 때문에

units passing inspection = $7,000$ units

normal spoilage = $8\% \times 7,000$ units = 560 units

abnormal spoilage = $1,000$ units $-$ 560 units = 440 units

5 Allocating costs of normal spoilage

It is to presume that normal spoilage occurs at the inspection point in the production cycle and to allocate its cost over all units that have passed that point during the accounting period.

- 공손은 검사시점에서 일시에 발생한다고 가정 ➡ 공손의 완성도 = 검사시점

- 정상공손의 원가는 검사시점을 통과한 정상품에 배분한다.

- FIFO는 기초재공품의 공손을 추정하여야 하는 어려움이 있기 때문에 US CPA 시험목적으로는 평균법으로 문제를 출제한다.

Normal spoilage	기말재공품(EWIP)이 검사를 받지 않은 경우 • 검사시점 〉 EWIP 완성도 • 정상공손은 전액 완성품(CGM)에 배분한다.
	기말재공품(EWIP)이 검사를 받은 경우 • 검사시점 〈 EWIP 완성도 • 정상공손은 완성품(CGM)과 기말재공품(EWIP)에 배분한다. ⇨ 배분기준은 완성품 환산량(EUP)가 아닌 물량기준으로 한다.
Abnormal spoilage	정상적인 제조활동과 관계가 없는 공손이므로 전액 기간비용으로 처리하여 영업외비용으로 보고한다.

Example-8

PARKER manufactures small pens. Direct materials are added at the beginning of the production and conversion costs are incurred evenly throughout the production cycle. Normal spoilage generally constitute 10% of the good units passing the inspection point. Data for 20X1 are as follows:

Beginning WIP (1/1/20X1)	400 units (20% complete)
Started during 20X1	1,600 units
Completed during 20X1	1,000 units
Ending WIP (12/31/20X1)	600 units (80% complete)

Costs for 20X1:

Beginning WIP:	
Direct materials	$28,000
Conversion costs	40,000
Direct material added	232,000
Conversion costs added	114,160

Calculate CGM by weighted-average method assuming the inspection point is at
      (1) 100% stage of completion   (2) 40% stage of completion

(1) 100% stage of completion

Step 3

total spoilage = 400 + 1600 − (1000 + 600) = 400

normal spoilage = 1,000 × 10% = 100

abnormal spoilage = 400 − 100 = 300

Step 2, 3, 4

	Units	%	DM	Conversion
CGM	1,000	100	1,000	1,000
normal spoilage	100	100	100	100
abnormal spoilage	300	100	300	300
EWIP	600	80	600	480
Total	2,000		2,000	1,880
Total cost	$414,160		$260,000	$154,160
Unit cost	$212		$130	$82

Step 5

CGM = 1,000 × $130 + 1,000 × $82 = $212,000

normal spoilage = 100 × $130 + 100 × $82 = $21,200

abnormal spoilage = 300 × $130 + 300 × $82 = $63,600

EWIP = 600 × $130 + 480 × $82 = $117,360

Allocating costs of normal spoilages

EWIP이 검사를 받지 않았기 때문에 정상공손은 전액 완성품(CGM)에 배분

 CGM = $212,000 + $21,200 = $233,200

 unit cost of CGM = $233,200 ÷ 1,000 = $233.2

Journal entry

Dr) Finished goods   233,200

   Loss   63,600

      Cr) WIP   296,800

(2) 40% stage of completion

Step 1

total spoilage = 400 + 1600 − (1000 + 600) = 400

normal spoilage = 1,600 × 10% = 160

abnormal spoilage = 400 − 160 = 240

Step 2, 3, 4

	Units	%	DM	Conversion
CGM	1,000	100	1,000	1,000
normal spoilage	160	40	160	64
abnormal spoilage	240	40	240	96
EWIP	600	80	600	480
Total	2,000		2,000	1,640
Total cost	$414,160		$260,000	$154,160
Unit cost			$130	$94

Step 5

CGM = 1,000 × \$130 + 1,000 × \$94 = \$224,000

normal spoilage = 160 × \$130 + 64 × \$94 = \$26,816

abnormal spoilage = 240 × \$130 + 96 × \$94 = \$40,224

EWIP = 600 × \$130 + 480 × \$94 = \$123,120

Allocating costs of normal spoilages

EWIP이 검사를 받았기 때문에 정상공손은 CGM과 EWIP에 배분

CGM = \$224,000 + \$26,816 × 1000/1600 = \$240,760

EWIP = \$123,120 + \$26,816 × 600/1600 = \$133,176

unit cost of CGM = \$240,760 ÷ 1,000 = \$240.76

Journal entry

Dr) Finished goods   240,760

    Loss   40,224

      Cr) WIP   280,984

04 / Hybrid costing

1 의의

최근의 대량생산 기업들은 소품종에서 다품종으로 전환하고 있다. 예를 들면 나이키나 자동차 기업의 경우에는 품목은 다양하면서도 수량을 대량으로 생산하고 있기 때문에 이러한 업종에는 기존의 process costing으로는 접근이 곤란하다. 따라서 이러한 업종에 대해서는 Job order costing 과 process costing을 접목한 hybrid costing(혼합원가계산)을 적용하여 원가를 계산하여야 한다.

2 Nature

(1) A hybrid-costing system blends characteristics from both job-costing and process-costing systems. This method is used when similar products are produced in different models or styles.

(2) Example

　1) Automobile manufacturer: GM, Ford

　2) Clothing manufacturer: Levi Strauss, ZARA

　3) Shoes manufacturer: Nike, Adidas

(3) Mass customization: Combination of customization with mass production.

3 Operation costing

- Operation costing is a hybrid-costing system that blends characteristics from both job-costing (for direct materials) and process-costing systems (for conversion costs).

- It is a better approach to product costing when production systems share some features of custom-order manufacturing and other features of mass-production manufacturing.

Example-9

ZARA Company, a clothing manufacturer, produces two lines of blazers for department stores: those made of wool and those made of polyester. Wool blazers use better-quality materials and undergo more operations than polyester blazers do. The operations information on work order #1 for 50 wool blazers and work order #2 for 100 polyester blazers is as follows:

	#1	#2
Direct materials	Wool	Polyester
	Bone buttons	Plastic buttons
Operations		
1. Cutting cloth	Yes	Yes
2. Sewing body	Yes	Yes
3. Hand sewing of collars	Yes	No
4. Machining sewing of collars	No	Yes

The cost data for these work orders, started and completed in 20X1, are as follows:

	#1	#2
Number of blazers	50	100
Direct materials	$6,000	$3,000
Operation 1	580	1,160
Operation 2	1,900	3,800
Operation 3	700	0
Operation 4	0	875
Total	$9,180	$8,835

Unit cost of wool blazer = $9,180 ÷ 50 units = $183.6

Unit cost of polyester blazer = $8,835 ÷ 100 units = $88.35

05 / MCQ (Multiple Choice Questions)

01. Kepler Optics makes lenses for telescopes. Because Kepler will only sell lenses of the highest quality, the normal spoilage during a reporting period is 1,000 units. At the beginning of the current reporting period, Kepler had 2,200 units in inventory, and during the period, production was started on 4,000 units. Units in inventory at the end of the current reporting period were 1,500, and the units transferred out were 3,000. During this period, the abnormal spoilage for Kepler's lense production was (CMA)

    a. 700 units

    b. 1,000 units

    c. 1,700 units

    d. 3,200 units

02. Waller Co. uses a weighted-average process-costing system. Material B is added at two different points in the production of shirms, 40% is added when the units are 20% completed, and the remaining 60% of Material B is added when the units are 80% completed. At the end of the quarter, there are 22,000 shirms in process, all of which are 50% completed. With respect to Material B, the ending shirms in process represent how many equivalent units? (CMA)

    a. 4,400 units.

    b. 8,800 units.

    c. 11,000 units.

    d. 22,000 units.

03. Colt Company uses a weighted-average process cost system to account for the cost of producing a chemical compound. As part of production, Material B is added when the goods are 80% complete. Beginning work-in-process inventory for the current month was 20,000 units, 90% complete. During the month, 70,000 units were started in process, and 65,000 of these units were completed. There were no lost or spoiled units. If the ending inventory was 60% complete, the total equivalent units for Material B for the month was (CMA)

    a. 65,000 units.

    b. 70,000 units.

    c. 85,000 units.

    d. 90,000 units.

04. Jones Corporation uses a first-in, first-out (FIFO) process costing system. Jones has the following unit information for the month of August.

	Units
Beginning work-in-process inventory, 100% complete for materials, 75% complete for conversion cost	10,000
Units complete and transferred out	90,000
Ending work-in-process inventory, 100% complete for materials, 60% complete for conversion costs	8,000

The number of equivalent units of production for conversion costs for the month of August is (CMA)

a. 87,300.   b. 88,000.

c. 92,300.   d. 92,700.

05. A company that uses a process costing system inspects its goods at the 60% stage of completion. If the firm's ending work-in-process inventory is 80% complete, how would the firm account for its normal and abnormal spoilage? (CMA)

a. Both normal and abnormal spoilage costs would be added to the cost of the good units completed during the period.

b. Both normal and abnormal spoilage costs would be written off as an expense of the period.

c. Normal spoilage costs would be added to the cost of the good units completed during the period; in contrast, abnormal spoilage costs would be written off as a loss.

d. Normal spoilage costs would be allocated between the cost of good units completed during the period and the ending work-in-process inventory. In contrast, abnormal spoilage costs would be written off as a loss.

06. When compared with normal spoilage, abnormal spoilage

a. arises more frequently from factors that are inherent in the manufacturing process.

b. is given the same accounting treatment as normal spoilage

c. is generally thought to be more controllable by production management than normal spoilage

d. is not typically influenced by the tightness of production standards.

07. In computing the cost per equivalent unit, the weighted-average method of process costing considers?

	the costs of the current period	the costs of beginning WIP
a.	Yes	Yes
b.	Yes	No
c.	No	Yes
d.	No	No

08. In computing the cost per equivalent unit, the first-in, first-out (FIFO) method of process costing considers?

	the costs of the current period	the costs of beginning WIP
a.	Yes	Yes
b.	Yes	No
c.	No	Yes
d.	No	No

09. During July, 3M Company completed 50,000 units costing $600,000, exclusive of spoilage allocation. Of these completed units, 25,000 were sold during the month. An additional 10,000 units, costing $80,000, were 50% complete at July 31. All units are inspected between the completion of manufacturing and transfer to finished goods inventory. Normal spoilage for the month was $60,000, and abnormal spoilage of $50,000 was also incurred during the month. 3M Company's cost of goods sold for July was:

a. $325,000   b. $330,000

c. $360,000   d. $380,000

10. During July, 3M Company completed 50,000 units costing $600,000, exclusive of spoilage allocation. Of these completed units, 25,000 were sold during the month. An additional 10,000 units, costing $80,000, were 50% complete at July 31. All units are inspected at the 30% stage of completion. Normal spoilage for the month was $60,000, and abnormal spoilage of $50,000 was also incurred during the month. 3M Company's cost of goods sold for July was:

a. $325,000   b. $330,000

c. $360,000   d. $380,000

11. Three commonly employed systems for product costing are job-order costing, operation costing, and process costing. Match the type of production environment with the costing method used.

Job-Order Costing	Operation Costing	Process Costing
a. Auto repair	Clothing manufacturing	Oil refining
b. Loan processing	Drug manufacturing	Custom printing
c. Custom printing	Paint manufacturing	Paper manufacturing
d. Engineering design	Auto assembly	Motion picture production

12. Johnson & Johnson employs a weighted average method in its process costing system. Johnson & Johnson's work in process inventory on June 30 consists of 4,000 units. These units are 100% complete with respect to materials and 60% complete with respect to conversion costs. The equivalent unit costs are $5.00 for materials and $7.00 for conversion costs. What is the total cost of the June 30 work-in-process inventory?

a. $20,000

b. $28,800

c. $36,800

d. $48,000

• 정답 및 해설

1. Abnormal spoilage = $2,200 + 4,000 - (3,000 + 1,000 + 1,500) = 700$ 정답 : a

2. EUP of EWIP for material B = $22,000 \times 40\% = 8,800$
   EUP of EWIP for conversion costs = $22,000 \times 50\% = 11,000$ 정답 : b

3. Material B는 80%에 투입이 되므로 EWIP가 60%이므로 아직 투입이 되지 않았음.
   EUP for material B = $65,000 + 25,000 \times 0 = 65,000$
   EUP for conversion costs = $65,000 + 25,000 \times 60\% = 80,000$ 정답 : a

4. EUP of BWIP for conversion costs = $10,00 \times 75\% = 7,500$
   EUP for conversion costs = $90,000 + 8,000 \times 60\% - 7,500 = 87,300$ 정답 : a

5. EWIP(80%)는 검사(60%)를 받았기 때문에 정상공손을 CGM과 EWIP에 배분
   비정상공손은 전액 손실로 기간비용 처리   정답 : d

6. 정상공손은 통제 불가능하고 비정상공손은 통제가능하다.   정답 : c

7. 평균법은 기초재고 원가와 당기원가를 모두 합산하여 배분한다.   정답 : a

8. FIFO는 당기원가만을 배분한다.   정답 : b

9. EWIP(50%)는 검사(100%)를 받지 않았기 때문에 정상공손은 전액 CGM에 배분
   CGM = $\$600,000 + \$60,000 = \$660,000$
   CGS = $\$660,000 \times 25,000\text{units}/50,000\text{units} = \$330,000$ 정답 : b

10. EWIP(50%)는 검사(30%)를 받았기 때문에 정상공손은 CGM과 EWIP에 배분
    CGM = $\$600,000 + \$60,000 \times 50,000\text{units}/60,000\text{units} = \$650,000$
    CGS = $\$650,000 \times 25,000\text{units}/50,000\text{units} = \$325,000$ 정답 : a

11. Custom printing $\Rightarrow$ Job-order costing
    Loan processing $\Rightarrow$ process costing
    Paint manufacturing $\Rightarrow$ process costing
    Motion picture $\Rightarrow$ Job-order costing   정답 : a

12. EWIP = $(4,000\text{units} \times \$5) + (4,000\text{units} \times 60\% \times \$7) = \$36,800$ 정답 : c

06 TBS (Task-Based Simulation)

Problem-1

AMD Company specializes in the manufacture of microchips for aircraft. Direct materials are added at the start of the production process. Conversion costs are added evenly during the process. Some units of this product are spoiled as a result of defects not detectable before inspection of finished goods. Normally, the spoiled units are 15% of the good units transferred out.

	Physical units	DM	Conversion
WIP, 1/1 *	400	$64,000	$10,200
Started in this year	1700		
Good units completed during this year	1400		
WIP, 12/31 **	300		
Costs added during this year		$377,000	$153,000

* Degree of completion : DM 100% and Conversion 30%

** Degree of completion : DM 100% and Conversion 40%

Required

What costs are allocated to FG, WIP, abnormal spoilage, using the weighted−average method of processing costing?

Problem-2

Mattel Company specializes in the manufacture of toys in a two-stage molding and finishing operation. The company uses the weighted-average method of process costing. During June, the following data were recorded for the finishing department.

Units of BWIP	10,000 units (25%):	
DM	$0	
Conversion costs	$42,000	
Transferred-in costs	$82,900	
Units started	70,000 units	
Units completed	50,000 units	
Units of EWIP	20,000 units (95%)	
Spoiled units	10,000 units	
Costs added during June.		
DM	$655,200	
Conversion costs	$1,251,600	
Transferred-in costs	$647,500	

Direct materials are added when production is 90% complete.

Conversion costs are added evenly during the process.

The inspection point is at the 80% stage of production.

Normal spoilage is 10% of all good units that pass inspection.

Required

For June, calculate CGM and EWIP.

Problem-3

Mattel Company specializes in the manufacture of toys in a two-stage molding and finishing operation. The company uses the weighted-average method of process costing. During June, the following data were recorded for the finishing department.

Units of BWIP	10,000 units (25%):
DM	$0
Conversion costs	$42,000
Transferred-in costs	$82,900
Units started	70,000 units
Units completed	50,000 units
Units of EWIP	20,000 units (50%)
Spoiled units	10,000 units
Costs added during June.	
DM	$655,200
Conversion costs	$1,251,600
Transferred-in costs	$647,500

Direct materials are added when production is 90% complete.

Conversion costs are added evenly during the process.

The inspection point is at the 80% stage of production.

Normal spoilage is 10% of all good units that pass inspection.

Required

For June, calculate CGM and EWIP.

Problem-4

Guiness Company makes a variety of specialty beers at its main brewery. Production of beer occurs in three main stages: mashing, boiling, and fermenting. Consider the fermenting department, where direct materials (bottles and other packaging) are added at the end of the process. Conversion costs are added evenly during the process. Guiness Company provides the following information related to its top-selling Gypsum for the fermenting department for the month of July:

	Physical Units	Transferred -In Costs	Direct Materials	Conversion Costs
Beginning work in process	2,500	$116,000	$ 0	$ 37,500
Transferred in during July from boiling department	10,000			
Completed during July	10,500			
Ending work in process, July 31	2,000			
Total costs added during July		$384,000	$110,775	$152,250

The units in beginning work in process are 25% complete for conversion costs, while the units in ending inventory are 50% complete for conversion costs.

· Instruction ·

1. Using the weighted-average method, assign costs to units completed (and transferred out) and to units in ending work in process.

2. Assume that the FIFO method is used for the fermenting department. Under FIFO, the transferred-in costs for work-in-process beginning inventory in July are $115,680 (instead of $116,000 under the weighted-average method), and the transferred-in costs during July from the boiling department are $376,000 (instead of $384,000 under the weighted-average method). All other data are unchanged. Assign costs to units completed and transferred out and to units in ending work in process using the FIFO method.

Problem-5

IKEA Company is a furniture manufacturer with two departments: molding and finishing. The company uses the weighted-average method of process costing. In August, the following data were recorded for the finishing department:

Units of beginning work in process inventory	25,000
Percentage completion of beginning work in process units	25%
Cost of direct materials in beginning work in process	$ 0
Units started	175,000
Units completed	125,000
Units in ending inventory	50,000
Percentage completion of ending work in process units	95%
Spoiled units	25,000

Total costs added during current period:	
Direct materials	$1,638,000
Direct manufacturing labor	$1,589,000
Manufacturing overhead	$1,540,000

Work in process, beginning:	
Transferred-in costs	$ 207,250
Conversion costs	$ 105,000
Cost of units transferred in during current period	$1,618,750

Conversion costs are added evenly during the process. Direct material costs are added when production is 90% complete. The inspection point is at the 80% stage of production. Normal spoilage is 10% of all good units that pass inspection. Spoiled units are disposed of at zero net disposal value.

• Instruction •

For August, assign these costs to units completed and transferred out (including normal spoilage), to abnormal spoilage, and to units in ending work in process.

Problem-6

(주)한국은 종합원가계산제도를 채택하고 있으며, 원재료는 공정의 초기에 전량 투입되며, 가공원가는 공정 전반에 걸쳐서 진척도에 따라 균등하게 발생한다. 재료원가의 경우 평균법에 의한 완성품환산량은 78,000단위이고, 선입선출법에 의한 완성품환산량은 66,000단위이다. 또한 가공원가의 경우 평균법에 의한 완성품환산량은 54,400단위이고, 선입선출법에 의한 완성품환산량은 52,000단위이다. 기초재공품의 완성도는 몇 %인가?
(K-CPA)

Problem-7

(주)신라는 한 가지 종류의 플라스틱 장난감을 제조한다. 이번 기의 자료는 다음과 같다.

	단위	재료원가	가공원가
기초 재공품	1,000	₩9,000	₩12,000
당기 착수	30,000	₩240,000	₩305,000
기말 재공품	500	–	–

모든 재료는 공정의 초기단계에 100% 투입된다. 기초 재공품은 가공원가가 40% 투입되었으며, 기말 재공품에는 80%가 투입되었다. 이 회사는 공정별원가계산방법(process costing)을 사용하고 있으며, 원가흐름에 대한 가정으로 선입선출법(FIFO)을 사용하고 있다. 이번 기에 발생한 전출원가(transfer-out cost)는 얼마인가? 단, 공손은 발생하지 않았다.
(K-CPA)

Problem-8

유정은 하나의 공정에서 단일 종류의 제품을 생산하며, 종합원가계산(process costing)을 적용하여 제품원가를 계산한다. 원재료는 공정의 초기단계에 100% 투입된다. 당기의 생산 및 원가자료는 다음과 같다.

재공품 평가방법은 선입선출법이고 당기 중에 공손이나 감손은 발생하지 않았다고 가정한다. 기말재공품원가는 얼마인가? (K-CPA)

구분	물량단위	가공비 완성도	직접재료비	가공비
기초재공품	600	1/3	₩ 5,000	₩ 60,950
	400	1/2		
당기착수(투입)	9,000	–	135,000	281,700
기말재공품	200	40%	?	?
	300	70%		

07 Case study

※ Coca-Cola Manufacturing Process

1. Water Treatment	9. Washer (세척)
2. Filtering	10. Filing
3. Sweetener (감미료)	11. Crowner & Date Corder
4. Concentrate (원액)	(마개부착 및 날짜 코딩)
5. Syrup Blending	12. Inspection
6. Proportioner (비례조절)	13. Case Packing
7. Carbonater (탄산화)	14. Palletizer
8. Pre-inspection (사전세척검사)	15. Delivery

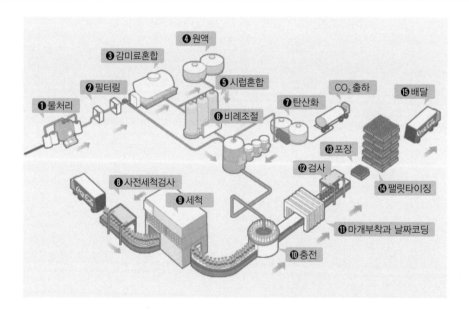

Chapter 04

Activity Based Costing

01 Introduction

　제조과정의 자동화로 제조간접원가의 비중이 증가함에 따라 보다 정확한 간접원가의 배분의 필요성이 대두되었으며, 전통적 배분기준을 수정한 활동기준원가(Activity-based costing : ABC)가 등장하게 되었다.

　전통적인 원가계산은 제조간접원가의 각 항목별 특성을 무시하고 노동시간과 같은 조업도를 기준으로 배분하였으며, 이는 다양한 발생원인과의 인과관계를 보여주지 못하기 때문에 부정확한 원가계산이 된다. 특히 원가배분이 잘못되면 한 제품의 원가가 잘못 계산되면 다른 제품의 원가도 잘못 계산되는 peanut-butter costing 현상이 발생한다.

　전통적인 원가계산에서는 원가중심점(Cost center)으로서 제조공정(process)나 부문(department)을 고려하였지만, ABC에서는 활동(activities)이 새로운 원가중심점이 된다. 전통적인 원가계산에서는 노동시간이나 기계시간과 같은 단일 기준이라면, ABC에서는 다양한 원가동인(cost driver)을 배분기준으로 원가를 제품에 배분한다.

전통적인 원가계산과 ABC를 비교 요약하면 다음과 같다.

	Traditional cost system	ABC system
Cost center	Process or department	Activities
Allocation base (cost driver)	Single	Multiple

　ABC는 제조업 또는 서비스업 모두 적용이 가능하며 개별원가 계산이나 종합원가 계산 모두 적용이 가능하다.

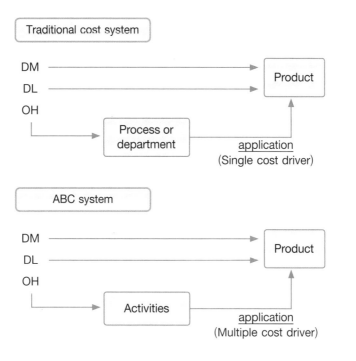

[그림 4-1]

02 / Activity-Based Costing

1 Steps

Step 1: Identify the major activities
제조 작업에서 수행하는 활동을 구분한다.

Step 2: Accumulate manufacturing overhead costs by activities.
각 활동별로 발생하는 원가를 집계한다.

Step 3: Identify cost drivers
각 활동과 관련된 원가동인을 파악하고 단위당 원가 배부율을 계산한다.

Step 4: Assign manufacturing overhead costs to products.
활동별 원가 배부율을 제품의 원가동인 수량에 곱하여 각 제품에 배분한다.

2 Terminology

(1) Activity

An event, task, or unit of work with a specified purpose

ex designing products, setting up machines, operating machines

(2) Resource

An element that is used to perform an activity

(3) Cost driver

A factor which has a direct cause and effect relationship to a particular cost.

(4) Cost pools

Accounts in which homogeneous costs with a common cause are accumulated.

(5) Cost objects

The intermediate and final disposition of cost pools.

(6) Cost allocation

The process of assigning costs to cost objects.

3 A cost hierarchy

ABC에서는 원가를 4가지 원가 계층으로 분류한다.

(1) Unit-level costs (단위수준원가)

- 한 단위의 제품을 생산할 때마다 발생하는 원가.
- 생산량(volume)에 비례하여 발생
- Example: DM, DL, machine operations costs
- Cost drivers: DL hours, machine hours, units of output.
- 전통적인 원가계산에서 사용하는 원가배부기준

(2) Batch-level costs (묶음수준원가)

- 생산량보다는 묶음(batch)단위로 수행하는 활동에서 발생하는 원가.
- 묶음 수에 비례하여 발생
- Example: setup costs, costs of purchase order, material handling costs
- Cost drivers: number of setups, number of purchase orders, number of inspections

(3) Product-sustaining costs (제품유지원가)

- 특정 제품의 생산을 지원하기 위하여 수행하는 활동에서 발생하는 원가
- 제품의 종류 수에 비례하여 발생
- Example: design costs, costs of making engineering changes, product R&D costs, marketing costs to launch new products
- Cost drivers: design time, number of engineering change, R&D time

(4) Facility-sustaining costs (설비유지원가)

- 공장의 설비전체를 지원하기 위하여 수행하는 활동에서 발생하는 원가
- 개별제품의 생산과 직접적인 관련성을 찾기 어려움
- Example: management of plant, rent, building security.
- 전통적인 원가계산과 마찬가지로 임의적인 배부기준에 의하여 제품에 배부

Example-1

	Product X	Product Y
Setup cost	$80,000	
Physical units	7,500 units	2,500 units
Batch size	2,500 units	500 units

1. Calculate the unit cost of product X under the traditional costing system.

2. Calculate the unit cost of product X under an activity-based costing system.

(1) Traditional approach

전통적인 원가계산에서는 제조 간접원가의 배부기준을 생산수량으로 한다.

	Product X	Product Y
Setup cost	$80,000	
Allocation base	7,500 units	2,500 units
Set-up cost per unit	$80,000 ÷ 10,000 units = $8	
Set-up cost per unit	$8	$8
Allocate costs	$60,000	$20,000

(2) ABC

setup cost는 batch-level 이므로 number of setup을 배분기준으로 한다.

	Product X	Product Y
Setup cost	$80,000	
Number of setups	3	5
Set-up cost per set-up	$80,000 ÷ 8 = $10,000/setup	
Set-up cost per unit	30,000 ÷ 7,500 units = $4	50,000 ÷ 2,500 units = $20
Allocate costs	$30,000	$50,000

⇨ The use of activity-based costing normally results in substantially greater unit costs for low-volume products than is reported by traditional product costing.

Example-2

Texas Instrument produces mathematical and financial calculators and operates at capacity. Data related to the two products are presented here:

	Mathematical	Financial
Annual production in units	50,000	100,000
Direct material costs	$150,000	$300,000
Direct manufacturing labor costs	$50,000	$100,000
Machine–hours	25,000	50,000
Number of production runs	50	50
Inspection hours	1,000	500

Total manufacturing overhead costs are as follows:

- Machining costs : $375,000
- Setup costs : $120,000
- Inspection costs : $105,000

1. Compute the manufacturing cost per unit for each product under the traditional costing system that allocated overhead on the basis of machine hours.

2. Compute the manufacturing cost per unit for each product under the activity-based costing system.

(1) Traditional costing system (machine hours)

Total manufacturing overhead = 375,000 + 120,000 + 105,000 = $600,000

Allocating MOH to Mathematical = $600,000 × 25,000/75,000 = $200,000
Allocating MOH to Financial = $600,000 × 50,000/75,000 = $400,000

Unit cost of Mathematical = ($150,000 + $50,000 + $200,000)/50,000 = $8
Unit cost of Financial = ($300,000 + $100,000 + $400,000)/100,000 = $8

(2) Activity-based costing system

Machining costs : Unit-level costs ⇨ Machine-hours 기준으로 배분
Setup costs : Batch-level costs ⇨ Number of production runs 기준으로 배분
Inspection costs : Batch-level costs ⇨ Inspection hours 기준으로 배분

Allocating MOH to Mathematical
 = $375,000 × 25,000/75,000 + $120,000 × 50/100 + $105,000 × 1000/1500
 = $255,000
Allocating MOH to Financial
 = $375,000 × 50,000/75,000 + $120,000 × 50/100 + $105,000 × 500/1500
 = $345,000

Unit cost of Mathematical = ($150,000 + $50,000 + $255,000)/50,000 = $9.10
Unit cost of Financial = ($300,000 + $100,000 + $345,000)/100,000 = $7.45

4 Advantages and disadvantages of ABC

(1) Advantages

1) More accurate costing system

제조간접원가를 원가동인에 의하여 배분하므로 정확한 원가계산이 됨

2) Better cost control and more efficient operation

각 활동별로 원가가 집계되므로 활동별로 원가관리가 되어 효율적인 원가통제가 가능

3) Better management decision

정확한 원가계산으로 가격결정, 손익분기점분석 등 의사결정에 유용한 정보 제공

(2) Disadvantages

1) Costs more to accumulate and analyze information

2) Time consuming

3) Need specialized knowledge

(3) Activity based costing is not useful

1) Small companies

2) Overheads are relatively small

3) Companies producing only one product or few products

4) Companies producing products that homogeneously consume resources

5) Batch-level and product-sustaining costs are immaterial

03 Activity-Based Management

1 Activity-Based Management (ABM)

- Activity-based management (ABM) is a method of management decision making that uses activity-based costing information.

- Activity-based costing establishes relationships between overhead costs and activities to allocate overhead costs.

- Activity-based management focuses on managing activities to reduce costs

ABC가 원가의 배부기준을 다양화한 정확한 원가계산에 초점이 있다면 ABM은 이러한 원가계산(Costing)뿐만 아니라 원가통제를(Control) 동시에 추구하는 관리 시스템이다.

ABM은 activity를 중심으로 원가를 통제함으로써 고객이 원하는 제품의 품질과 가격에 대응할 수 있도록 한다.

2 Improvement process

ABM의 원가절감 절차는 다음과 같이 3가지로 구성된다.

Activity analysis ⇨ Cost driver analysis ⇨ Performance analysis

(1) Activity analysis

Identify activities ⇨ reduce or eliminate Non−Value−Added activities

1) Value−added activities

Activities that cannot be eliminated without the customer perceiving a decline in product quality or performance.(고객에게 가치를 부여하는 활동)

2) Non-value-added activities

- Activities that can be eliminated without the customer perceiving a decline in product quality or performance. (고객에게 가치를 부여하지 못하는 활동)
- Example : rework costs, move time, waiting time, inspection time, storage costs

(2) Cost driver analysis

원가동인 분석의 목적은 활동원가의 근원적인 원인을 파악하고자 하는 것이다. 예를 들면 material handling cost의 원가동인은 재료운반 횟수이며 이를 기준으로 원가를 계산한다. 재료 운반비의 근원적인 원인은 공장설비의 배치와 관련이 되어 있다면 공장 설비를 재배치함으로써 재료운반횟수를 변화하여 재료운반비를 절감할 수 있다.

Root cause	Activity driver	Activity costs
Factory arrangement	Number of moves	Material handling costs

(3) Performance evaluation

활동성과의 측정은 재무적 또는 비재무적인 방법으로 이루어진다.

04 MCQ (Multiple Choice Questions)

01. In ABC, product design costs are a cost hierarchy in which of the four levels?

a. unit-level

b. batch-level

c. product-sustaining

d. facility-sustaining

02. The Chocolate Baker specializes in chocolate baked goods. The firm has long assessed the profitability of a product line by comparing revenues to the cost of goods sold. However, Barry White, the firm's new accountant, wants to use an activity-based costing system that takes into consideration the cost of the delivery person. Listed below are activity and cost information relating to two of Chocolate Baker's major products.

	Muffins	Cheesecake
Revenue	$53,000	$46,000
Cost of goods sold	26,000	21,000
Delivery Activity		
Number of deliveries	150	85
Average length of delivery	10 Minutes	15 Minutes
Cost per hour for delivery	$20.00	$20.00

Using ABC, which one of the following statements is correct? (CMA)

a. The muffins are $2,000 more profitable.

b. The cheesecakes are $75 more profitable.

c. The muffins are $1,925 more profitable.

d. The muffins have a higher profitability as a percentage of sales and, therefore, are more advantageous.

03. All of the following are likely to be used as a cost allocation base in activity-based costing except the (CMA)

    a. number of different materials used to manufacture the product.

    b. units of materials used to manufacture the product.

    c. number of vendors supplying the materials used to manufacture the product.

    d. cost of materials used to manufacture the product.

Questions 4 and 6 are based on the following information.

KIMCPA Company estimates the amount of overhead that should be allocated to the product A and product B from the information given as follows:

	Product A	Product B
Units produced	20	40
Material moves	6	9
Direct labor hour per unit	600	200
Materials handling costs	$50,000	

---

04. Under a traditional system that allocates overhead on the basis of direct labor hours, what is the materials handling costs per unit for product A?

    a. $833   b. $1,000   c. $1,333   d. $1,500

05. Under a traditional system that allocates overhead on the basis of units produced, what is the materials handling costs per unit for product A?

    a. $833   b. $1,000   c. $1,333   d. $1,500

06. Under activity-based costing (ABC), what is the materials handling costs per unit for product A?

    a. $833   b. $1,000   c. $1,333   d. $1,500

07. Each of the following statements is true except:

    a. Traditional costing seeks to assign all manufacturing costs to products

    b. ABC costing seeks to assign all manufacturing costs to products

    c. Traditional costing is more refined than an ABC system

    d. ABC systems reveal activities that can be eliminated.

Questions 8 and 9 are based on the following information.

L'Oreal Cosmetics has used a traditional cost accounting system to apply quality control costs uniformly to all products at a rate of 14% of direct labor cost. Monthly direct labor cost for Lancome makeup is $27,000. In an attempt to distribute quality control costs more equitably, L'Oreal Cosmetics is considering activity-based costing. The monthly data shown in the chart below have been gathered for Lancome makeup.

Activity	Cost driver	Cost rates	Lancome
Material inspection	Type of material	$11.50 per type	12 types
In-process inspection	Number of units	$0.14 per unit	17,500 units
Product certification	Per order	$77 per order	25 order

---

08. What is the monthly quality control cost assigned to Lancome makeup using traditional costing?

    a. $3,780   b. $4,000   c. $4,513   d. $4,700

09. What is the monthly quality control cost assigned to Lancome makeup using activity-based costing?

    a. $3,780   b. $4,000   c. $4,513   d. $4,700

1. 제품 디자인 원가는 제품의 성격에 따라 다르기 때문에 product—level이다.

정답 : c

2. Delivery cost for Muffin = 150 × 10M ÷ 60M × \$20 = \$500
   Delivery cost for Cheesecake = 85 × 15M ÷ 60M × \$20 = \$425
   Operating income of Muffin = \$53,000 − 26,000 − 500 = \$26,500
   Operating income of Cheesecake = \$46,000 − 21,000 − 425 = \$24,575

정답 : c

3. Cost of material에는 수량, 단가 및 횟수의 다양한 원가동인이 존재하므로 원가동인
   이 아닌 원가동인의 종속변수이다.

정답 : d

4. Total DLH = 20 × 600H + 40 × 200H = 20,000H
   Total cost for A = \$50,000 × 12,000H ÷ 20,000H = \$30,000
   Unit cost for A = \$30,000 ÷ 20 = \$1,500 per unit

정답 : d

5. Unit cost for A = \$50,000 ÷ 60 units = \$833 per unit

정답 : a

6. Total cost for A = \$50,000 × 6 moves ÷ 15 moves = \$20,000
   Unit cost for A = \$20,000 ÷ 20 = \$1,000 per unit

정답 : b

7. ABC는 전통적인 방법보다 정확한 배분기준으로 배분하기 때문에 보다 정교하다.

정답 : c

8. \$27,000 × 0.14 = \$3,780

정답 : a

9. (\$11.50 × 12 types) + (\$0.14 × 17,500 units) + (\$77 × 25 orders) = \$4,513

정답 : c

05 TBS (Task-Based Simulation)

Problem-1

Bonaok manufactures wireless blue-tooth karaoke microphone. The machines differ significantly in their complexity and their manufacturing batch sizes. The following costs were incurred in 20X1:

a. Indirect manufacturing labor costs such as supervision that supports direct manufacturing labor,$825,000

b. Procurement costs of placing purchase orders, receiving materials, and paying suppliers related to the number of purchase orders placed, $525,000

c. Cost of indirect materials, $160,000

d. Costs incurred to set up machines each time a different product needs to be manufactured, $365,000

e. Designing processes, drawing process charts, and making engineering process changes for products, $287,500

f. Machine-related overhead costs such as depreciation, maintenance, and production engineering, $950,000 (These resources relate to the activity of running the machines.)

g. Plant management, plant rent, and plant insurance, $512,000

· Instruction ·

Classify each of the preceding costs as output unit—level, batch—level, product—sustaining, or facility—sustaining.

Problem-2

Vineyard Test Laboratories does heat testing (HT) and stress testing (ST) on materials and operates at capacity. Under its current costing system, Vineyard aggregates all operating costs of $1,190,000 into a single overhead cost pool. Vineyard calculates a rate per test-hour of $17 ($1,190,000÷ 70,000 total test-hours). HT uses 40,000 test-hours, and ST uses 30,000 test-hours.

Vineyard' controller, believes that there is enough variation in test procedures and cost structures to establish separate costing and billing rates for HT and ST. The market for test services is becoming competitive. Without this information, any miscosting and mispricing of its services could cause Vineyard to lose business. Celeste divides Vineyard' costs into four activity-cost categories.

a. Direct-labor costs, $146,000. These costs can be directly traced to HT, $100,000, and ST, $46,000.

b. Equipment-related costs (rent, maintenance, energy, and so on), $350,000. These costs are allocated to HT and ST on the basis of test-hours.

c. Setup costs, $430,000. These costs are allocated to HT and ST on the basis of the number of setup-hours required. HT requires 13,600 setup-hours, and ST requires 3,600 setup-hours.

d. Costs of designing tests, $264,000. These costs are allocated to HT and ST on the basis of the time required for designing the tests. HT requires 3,000 hours, and ST requires 1,400 hours.

• Instruction •

1. Classify each activity cost as output unit – level, batch–level, product–sustaining, or facility–sustaining.
2. Calculate the cost per test–hour for HT and ST.

Problem-3

IKEA produces two types of doors, interior and exterior. The company's simple costing system has two direct cost categories (materials and labor) and one indirect cost pool. The simple costing system allocates indirect costs on the basis of machine-hours. Recently, the owners of the company have been concerned about a decline in the market share for their interior doors, usually their biggest seller. Information related to IKEA production for the most recent year follows:

	Interior	Exterior
Units sold	3,200	1,800
Selling price	$ 250	$ 400
Direct material cost per unit	$ 60	$ 90
Direct manufacturing labor cost per hour	$ 32	$ 32
Direct manufacturing labor–hours per unit	1.50	2.25
Production runs	40	85
Material moves	72	168
Machine setups	45	155
Machine–hours	5,500	4,500
Number of inspections	250	150

The owners have heard of other companies in the industry that are now using an activity-based costing system and are curious how an ABC system would affect their product costing decisions. After analyzing the indirect cost pool for IKEA, the owners identify six activities as generating indirect costs: production scheduling, material handling, machine setup, assembly, inspection, and marketing. IKEA collected the following data related to the indirect cost activities:

Activity	Cost Activity	Cost Driver
Production scheduling	$190,000	Production runs
Material handling	$ 90,000	Material moves
Machine setup	$ 50,000	Machine setups
Assembly	$120,000	Machine-hours
Inspection	$ 16,000	Number of inspections

Marketing costs were determined to be 3% of the sales revenue for each type of door.

• Instruction •

1. Calculate the cost of an interior door and an exterior door under the existing simple costing system.
2. Calculate the cost of an interior door and an exterior door under an activity-based costing system.

Problem-4

A company with three products classifies its costs as belonging to five functions.

Functions	Cost driver
1. R&D	A. Number of customer phone calls
2. Production	B. Number of shipments.
3. Marketing	C. Number of sales persons
4. Distribution	D. Number of research scientists
5. Customer services	E. Production volume.

• Instruction •

Match each function with its representative cost driver.

Problem-5

㈜한호기계는 활동기준원가계산(activity-based costing)을 적용하고 있다. 회사는 제품생산을 위해 세 가지 활동을 수행하고 있다. 당기에 발생된 활동별 실제원가는 기계가동활동 ₩84,000, 엔지니어링활동 ₩60,000, 품질검사활동 ₩41,000이었다. 당기에 두 종류의 제품 A와 B를 생산하였으며, 생산관련 실제자료는 다음과 같았다. 제품 A에 배부되는 총 활동원가는 얼마인가? 단, 괄호 안은 각 활동의 원가동인을 의미한다. (K-CPA)

항 목	제품 A	제품 B
생산량	500단위	1,200단위
기계가동(기계시간)	2,000시간	3,000시간
엔지니어링(작업시간)	500시간	700시간
품질검사(품질검사 횟수)	10회	15회

Problem-6

㈜대한은 휴대전화기를 생산한다. 현재 회사는 제조간접원가를 단일 배부율을 사용하여 공장 전체에 배부하고 있다. 회사의 경영진은 제조간접원가를 좀 더 정교하게 배부할 필요가 있다고 판단하고, 회계담당부서로 하여금 주요 생산활동과 그 활동에 대한 원가동인을 파악하라고 지시하였다. 다음은 활동, 원가동인 그리고 배부율에 대한 자료이다.

현재의 전통적인 원가계산방법은 직접노무시간에 기초하여 1시간당 ₩150,000의 배부율을 사용한다. 휴대전화 제작을 위하여 한 번의 작업(batch)으로 50대의 휴대전화가 제조되었다. 전통적인 원가계산방법과 활동기준원가계산방법을 사용할 경우 휴대전화 한 대당 배부될 제조간접원가는 각각 얼마인가? 한 번의 작업(batch)에는 1,000개의 부품, 직접노무시간 8시간, 그리고 검사시간 15분이 필요하다. (K-CPA)

활동	원가동인	배부율
재료취급	부품의 수	부품당 ₩1,000
조립	직접노무시간	시간당 ₩40,000
검사	검사부문에서의 검사시간	분 당 ₩10,000

06　Case study

Hospitals using time-driven activity-based costing (TDABC)

M.D. Anderson Cancer Center in Houston is using time-driven activity-based costing (TDABC) to help bring accurate cost and value measurement practices into the health care delivery system.

TDABC assigns all of the organization' resource costs to cost objects using a framework that requires two sets of estimates. TDABC first calculates the cost of supplying resource capacity, such as a doctor' time. The total cost of resources—including personnel, supervision, insurance, space occupancy, technology, and supplies—is divided by the available capacity—the time available for doctors to do their work—to obtain the capacity cost rate. Next, TDABC uses the capacity cost rate to drive resource costs to cost objects, such as the number of patients seen, by estimating the demand for resource capacity (time) that the cost object requires.

Medical centers implementing TDABC have succeeded in reducing costs. For the M.D. Anderson Cancer Center, the TDABC-modified process resulted in a 16% reduction in process time, a 12% decrease in costs for technical staff, and a 36% reduction in total cost per patient. Prior to implementing TDABC, managers did not have the necessary information to make decisions to reduce costs.

Chapter

05

Joint Products

Chapter 05

Joint Products

01 Introduction

　동일한 원재료가 동일한 공정에 투입되어 동시에 두 종류 이상의 서로 다른 제품들이 생산될 때 이 제품을 결합제품(joint products)이라고 한다. 예를 들면 정유산업의 경우 원유를 투입하여 가솔린, 등유, 경유, 중유, 윤활유, LPG 등의 제품으로 가공된다.

다음 산업들이 결합제품의 대표적인 예이다.

Industry	Raw materials	Joint products
Agriculture processing	Pineapples	Rings, juice, crushed pineapple
Food processing	Pig	Bacon, ham, spare ribs, pork roast
Extractive industries	Coal	Coke, gas, benzol, tar
Chemical industries	Crude oil	Gasoline, Diesel, LPG, Asphalt.

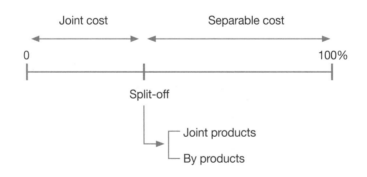

[그림 5-1]

(1) Joint products (연산품)

결합제품 중 상대적으로 판매가치가 비교저 큰 제품을 말한다.

(2) Byproducts (부산물)

연산품의 제조과정에서 부수적으로 생산되는 제품으로서 결합제품 중 상대적으로 판매가치가 작은 큰 제품을 말한다. 정유업의 아스팔트와 비누제조의 글리세린이 대표적인 예이다.

(3) Split-off point (분리점)

결합제품을 개별적으로 식별할 수 있는 제조공정 중의 한 시점

(4) Joint costs (결합원가)

결합제품을 생산하기 위하여 분리점까지 발생한 모든 제조원가를 말하며 각 제품별로 추적이 불가능한 원가이다.

(5) Separable costs (분리원가)

분리점에서 개별제품으로 분리한 후 최종제품으로 만드는 과정에서 추가로 발생하는 원가를 말한다.

02 / Allocation method

1 Joint products

결합원가(joint costs)는 여러 제품의 생산에 공통적으로 발생하는 원가이므로 결합제품에 배분하여야 하며 배분방법은 다음과 같다.

- Physical measures method (물량기준법)
- Relative sales value at split-off point method (분리점에서의 판매가치법)
- Net realizable value (NRV) method (순실현가치법)
- Constant gross margin percentage method (균등이익률법)

(1) Physical measures method

1) 물리적 특성인 수량, 부피, 중량 등을 기준으로 배분하는 방법

2) 제품의 가격을 알 수 없는 경우에도 사용 가능

3) 제품의 경제적 가치를 반영하지 못함

(2) Relative sales value at split-off point method

1) 분리점에서의 판매가치를 기준으로 배분하는 방법

2) 이론적으로 가장 우수한 방법

3) 분리점에서의 판매가치는 판매량이 아닌 생산량을 기준으로 계산

4) 분리점에서의 판매가격을 알 수 없는 경우에는 사용할 수 없음

(3) Net realizable value (NRV) method

1) 분리점에서의 순실현가치(NRV)를 기준으로 배분하는 방법

2) '분리점에서의 판매가치 = 분리점에서의 순실현가치'를 가정

3) 분리점에서의 순실현가치 = 개별제품의 최종판매가액 - 분리원가

NRV = final sales value - additional processing costs - selling costs

4) NRV가 (−)인 제품은 결합원가를 배분하지 못함

5) 결합원가만이 부가가치가 있고, 분리원가는 부가가치가 없다고 봄

(4) Constant gross margin percentage method

1) '기업전체 매출총이익률 = 개별제품의 매출총이익률'을 가정

2) 개별제품 매출원가 = 개별제품 최종판매가액 × 기업전체 매출원가율

3) 개별제품 결합원가 배분액 = 개별제품 매출원가 − 개별제품 추가원가

4) (−)의 결합원가가 배분될 수도 있음

Example-1

Exxon Mobil Company buys crude oil. Refining this oil results in two products at the split-off point: AA and BB. The joint costs of purchasing and processing the crude oil are $3,000 that generate 1,000 gallons of AA and 500 gallons of BB. AA sells for $4 per gallon and BB sells for $2 per gallon.

- 1,000 gallons of AA are further processed to yield 1,000 gallons of product AAA at additional processing costs of $2,000. Product AAA is sold for $5 per gallon.
- 500 gallons of BB are further processed to yield 500 gallons of product BBB at additional processing costs of $1,000. Product BBB is sold for $6 per gallon.

Calculate how the joint costs of $3,000 would be allocated under the following methods :
(1) Physical-measures (gallons)
(2) Sales value at split-off
(3) NRV
(4) Constant gross-margin percentage

(1) Physical measures

    Joint costs for AA = $3,000 × 1,000 gallons/1,500 gallons = $2,000

    Joint costs for BB = $3,000 × 500 gallons/1,500 gallons = $1,000

(2) Sales value at split−off

    1) Sales value at split−off

        AA = $4 × 1,000 gallons = $4,000

        BB = $2 × 500 gallons = $1,000

    2) Allocation

        Joint costs for AA = $3,000 × $4,000/ $5,000 = $2,400

        Joint costs for BB = $3,000 × $1,000/ $5,000 = $600

(3) NRV

  1) Estimated NRV

    AA = $5 × 1,000 gallons − $2,000 = $3,000

    BB = $6 × 500 gallons − $1,000 = $2,000

  2) Allocation

    Joint costs for AA = $3,000 × $3,000/$5,000 = $1,800

    Joint costs for BB = $3,000 × $2,000/$5,000 = $1,200

(4) Constant gross−margin percentage

  1) Company's gross−margin percentage

    Sales = $5 × 1,000 gallons + $6 × 500 gallons = $8,000

    COGS = $3,000 + $2,000 + $1,000 = $6,000

    gross−margin percentage = (8,000−6,000)/8,000 = 25%

    COGS percentage = 6,000/8,000 = 75%

  2) Allocation

    Joint costs for AA = $5,000 × 75% − $2,000 = $1,750

    Joint costs for BB = $3,000 × 75% − $1,000 = $1,250

> **Example-2**

Exxon Mobil Company buys crude oil. Refining this oil results in two products at the split-off point: AA and BB. The joint costs of purchasing and processing the crude oil are $3,000 that generate 1,000 gallons of AA and 500 gallons of BB. AA sells for $4 per gallon and BB sells for $2 per gallon.

- 1,000 gallons of AA are further processed to yield 900 gallons of product AAA at additional processing costs of $2,000. Product AAA is sold for $5 per gallon.
- 500 gallons of BB are further processed to yield 400 gallons of product BBB at additional processing costs of $1,000. Product BBB is sold for $6 per gallon.

Calculate how the joint costs of $3,000 would be allocated under the following methods :
(1) NRV
(2) Constant gross-margin percentage

(1) NRV
   1) Estimated NRV
      AA = $5 × 900 gallons − $2,000 = $2,500
      BB = $6 × 400 gallons − $1,000 = $1,400
   2) Allocation
      Joint costs for AA = $3,000 × $2,500/$3,900 = $1,923
      Joint costs for BB = $3,000 × $1,400/$3,900 = $1,077

(2) Constant gross−margin percentage
   1) Company's gross−margin percentage
      Sales = $5 × 900 gallons + $6 × 400 gallons = $6,900
      COGS = $3,000 + $2,000 + $1,000 = $6,000
      COGS percentage = 6,000/6,900 = 86.96%
   2) Allocation
      Joint costs for AA = $4,500 × 86.96% − $2,000 = $1,913
      Joint costs for BB = $2,400 × 86.96% − $1,000 = $1,087

2 Byproducts

부산물은 연산품의 제조과정에서 부수적으로 생산되며 연산품에 비하여 판매가치가 현저히 낮기 때문에 연산품과 동일한 원가계산을 할 수는 없다.

부산물의 원가배분 및 회계처리 방법은 다음 두 가지 방법이 있다.

- Time of production (생산기준법)
- Time of sale (판매기준법)

(1) Time of production

1) 부산물을 생산시점에서 부산물의 순실현가치(NRV)로 평가

2) 분리점에서의 부산물 금액 = 부산물의 순실현가치(NRV)

3) 연산품에 배분될 결합원가 = 결합원가 – 부산물의 순실현가치

   joint costs for joint products = joint costs – NRV of byproducts

4) 부산물의 중요성이 큰 경우에 사용

(2) Time of sale

1) 부산물에 결합원가를 배분하기 않고, 결합원가 전액을 모두 연산품에 배분

2) 분리점에서의 부산물 금액 = 0

3) 연산품에 배분될 결합원가 = 결합원가

   joint costs for joint products = joint costs

4) 부산물의 중요성이 작은 경우에 사용

5) 부산물의 판매시점에서 판매이익을 인식하는 방법은 다음 두 가지 방법이 있다.

   ① Other income(영업외수익)으로 인식
   ② COGS(매출원가)에서 차감

> **Example-3**

Exxon Mobil buys crude oil. Refining this oil results in two main products and a by-product. The joint costs of purchasing and processing the crude oil are $3,000.

- First main product is further processed to yield 1,000 gallons of product AAA at additional processing costs of $2,000. Product AAA is sold for $5 per gallon.
- Second main product is further processed to yield 500 gallons of product BBB at additional processing costs of $1,000. Product BBB is sold for $6 per gallon.
- A byproduct is further processed to yield 100 gallons at additional processing costs of $100. The byproduct is sold for $3 per gallon.
- Exxon Mobil has employed the estimated NRV method to allocate joint production costs to the main products.

Calculate how the joint costs of $3,000 would be allocated.

(1) The company account for the byproduct's production by deducting the estimated NRV of the byproduct from the joint costs of the main products

(2) The company account for the byproduct's sales by deducting the NRV of the byproduct from COGS from the main products the joint costs.

(1) Time of production

    1) Estimated NRV

        First main product = $5 × 1,000 gallons − $2,000 = $3,000

        Second main product = $6 × 500 gallons − $1,000 = $2,000

        Byproduct = $3 × 100 gallons − $100 = $200

    2) Allocation

        Joint costs for Byproduct = $200

        Joint costs for First main product = $2,800 × $3,000/$5,000= $1,680

        Joint costs for Second main product = $2,800 × $2,000/$5,000= $1,120

⟨Journal entry⟩

Split—off	First main product	1,680	
	Second main product	1,120	
	Byproduct	200	
	WIP		3,000
Further processing	Byproduct	100	
	Cash		100
Sale	Cash	300	
	Byproduct		300

(2) Time of sales

　1) Estimated NRV ⇨ time of production 자료와 동일

　2) Allocation

　　Joint costs for Byproduct = $0

　　Joint costs for First main product = $3,000 × $3,000/$5,000 = $1,800

　　Joint costs for Second main product = $3,000 × $2,000/$5,000 = $1,200

⟨Journal entry⟩

Split—off	First main product	1,800	
	Second main product	1,200	
	Byproduct	0	
	WIP		3,000
Further processing	Byproduct	100	
	Cash		100
Sale	Cash	300	
	Byproduct		100
	COGS*		200

* COGS대신 other income으로 인식할 수 있다.

만일 부산물이 Third main product 이었다면 다음과 같이 원가배분 및 회계처리를 한다.

Joint costs for First main product = $3,000 \times $3,000/$5,200= $1,731

Joint costs for Second main product = $3,000 \times $2,000/$5,200= $1,154

Joint costs for Third main product = $3,000 \times $200/$5,200= $115

⟨Journal entry⟩

Split–off	First main product Second main product Third main product WIP	1,731 1,154 115	 3,000
Further processing	Third main product Cash	100	 100
Sale	Cash Sales COGS Third main product	300 215	 300 215

3 Case study

정유업체의 정유공정은 다음과 같다.

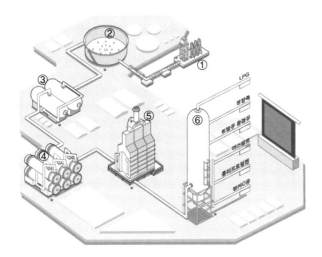

① 원유부두(Crude warf)	대형 유조선으로부터 원유를 하역한다.
② 저장탱크(Crude tank)	원유를 대형탱크에 저장한다.
③ 탈염기(Desalter)	원유 속의 불순물을 제거한다.
④ 열교환기(Exchanger)	원유를 예열 시킨다.
⑤ 가열로(Heater)	원유를 360도까지 가열한다.
⑥ 상압증류탑 (Crude Distillation Unit)	비등점의 차이에 따라 유분을 분리한다. • LPG　　　　　　　　• 방향족 • 휘발유, 등유, 경유　• 아스팔트 • 폴리프로필렌　　　　• 벙커C유

03   Sell or process further decision

관련원가에 대한 논의는 12장 의사결정에서 자세히 설명하고 있다. 연산품을 분리점에서 판매하느냐 또는 추가 가공하여 완제품으로 판매하느냐의 의사결정에서 다음 사항들을 고려하여야 한다.

- Joint cost : 의사결정에 영향을 주지 않은 irrelevant cost (Sunk cost)
- Separable cost : 의사결정에 영향을 주는 relevant cost

앞의 예제-1을 이용하여 의사결정을 하면 다음과 같다.

	Estimated NRV	Sales value at split-off	Incremental profit
Product AA	$3,000	$4,000	(−) 1,000
Product BB	$2,000	$1,000	+ 1,000

Product AA는 순실현가치가 분리점에서의 판매가치보다 $1,000 작기 때문에 추가가공하지 않고 분리점에서 판매하는 것이 $1,000 유리하다.

Product BB는 순실현가치가 분리점에서의 판매가치보다 $1,000 크기 때문에 분리점에서 판매하지 않고 추가가공하는 것이 $1,000 유리하다.

▷ 추가가공 의사결정에서 결합원가는 의사결정에 영향을 주지 않는다.

04 MCQ (Multiple Choice Questions)

01. The principal disadvantages of using the physical quantity method of allocating joint costs are that

a. Costs assigned to inventory may have no relationship to value.

b. Physical quantities may be difficult to measure.

c. Additional processing costs affect the allocation base.

d. Joint costs should not be separated on a unit base.

Questions 2 and 4 are based on the following information.

KIMCPA is a small company that acquires high-grade crude oil from low-volume production wells owned by individuals. The crude oil is processed in a single refinery into Gasoline, Diesel and impure distillates. KIMCPA does not have the technology or capacity to process these products further and sells most of its output each month to major refineries.

There were no beginning inventories on January 1. The production cost and output of KIMCPA for January are as follows:

Crude oil acquired and placed in production	$5,000,000
Direct labor and related costs	2,000,000
Factory overhead	3,000,000

Production and sales

• Gasoline, 300,000 barrels produced; 80,000 barrels sold at $20 each.

• Diesel, 240,000 barrels produced; 120,000 barrels sold at $30 each.

• Distillates, 120,000 barrels produced and sold at $15 each.

02. What is the portion of the joint product costs assigned to Diesel based on physical output?

a. $3,600,000　　　　　　　　　　b. $3,636,364

c. $4,000,000　　　　　　　　　　d. $4,800,000

03. What is the portion of the joint product costs assigned to Gasoline based on relative sales value?

a. $3,600,000　　　　　　　　　　b. $3,636,364

c. $4,000,000　　　　　　　　　　d. $4,800,000

04. What is the portion of the joint product costs assigned to Distillates based on constant gross-margin percentage?

a. $1,000,000　　　　　　　　　　b. $1,636,364

c. $1,200,000　　　　　　　　　　d. $1,800,000

05. (주)백두산화학은 동일한 원재료를 가공하여 두 개의 결합제품 A와 B를 생산한다. 7월중 A와 B의 생산과정에서 발생한 직접재료원가는 ₩140,000, 가공원가는 ₩180,000이었다. 분리점에서 A의 판매가치는 ₩280,000인 반면, B는 추가가공을 거쳐 C라는 제품으로 전환되어 ₩500,000에 판매된다. 추가공정에서는 ₩80,000의 가공원가가 발생한다. 최종판매시점에서 A제품의 매출총이익은 얼마인가? (K-CPA)

a. 120,000　　　　　　　　　　b. 152,000

c. 180,000　　　　　　　　　　d. 200,000

1. 물량기준법은 간단하지만 각 제품의 부가가치를 무시하는 단점이 있다.

정답 : a

2. Joint costs = 5,000,000 + 2,000,000 + 3,000,000 = $10,000,000

   Total units = 300,000 + 240,000 + 120,000 = 660,000 units

   Joint costs for Diesel = $10,000,000 × 240,000 ÷ 660,000 = $3,636,364

정답 : b

3. Total sales value = (300,000 × $20) + (240,000 × $30) + (120,000 × $15)

   = $15,000,000

   Joint costs for Gasoline = $10,000,000 × $6,000,000 ÷ $15,000,000 = $4,000,000

정답 : c

4. Total sales = $15,000,000

   Total product costs = $10,000,000

   COGS percentage = 10,00,000/15,000,000 = 2/3

   Joint costs for Distillates = 120,000 × $15 × 2/3 − 0 = $1,200,000

정답 : c

5. NRV(A) = 280,000

   NRV(B) = 500,000 − 80,000 = 420,000

   A제품에 배분되는 joint cost = 320,000 × 280,000 / 700,000 = 128,000

   A제품 gross profit = 280,000 − 128,000 = 152,000

정답 : b

05 / TBS (Task-Based Simulation)

Problem-1

The KIMCPA Company operates a simple chemical process to convert a single material into three separate items, referred to here as X, Y, and Z. All three end products are
separated simultaneously at a single split-off point. Products X and Y are ready for sale
immediately upon split-off without further processing or any other additional costs.
Product Z, however, is processed further before being sold. There is no available market
price for Z at the split-off point. The selling prices quoted here are expected to remain
the same in the coming year. During 20X1, the selling prices of the items and the total
amounts sold were as follows:

- X—68 tons sold for $1,200 per ton
- Y—480 tons sold for $900 per ton
- Z—672 tons sold for $600 per ton

The total joint manufacturing costs for the year were $580,000. KIMCPA spent an ad-
ditional $200,000 to finish product Z. There were no beginning inventories of X, Y, or
Z. At the end of the year, the following inventories of completed units were on hand: X,
132 tons; Y, 120 tons; Z, 28 tons. There was no beginning or ending work in process.

• Instruction •

Compute the cost of inventories of X, Y, and Z for balance sheet purposes and the cost of
goods sold for income statement purposes as of December 31, 20X1, using the following
joint cost allocation methods:

1. NRV method
2. Constant gross—margin percentage
3. Sales value at split—off method
4. Physical—measure method

Problem-2

LAY'S Company is a producer of potato chips. A single production process at the company yields potato chips as the main product and a byproduct that can also be sold as a snack. Both products are fully processed by the split-off point, and there are no separable costs.

For 20X1, the cost of operations is $500,000. Production and sales data are as follows:

	Production (in pounds)	Sales (in pounds)	Selling price per pound
Potato chips	52,000	42,640	$16
Byproduct	8,500	6,500	$10

There were no beginning inventories on 20X1.

• Instruction •

1. What is the gross margin for LAY'S under the production method and the sales method of byproduct accounting?

2. What are the inventory costs reported in the balance sheet on 20X1, for the main product and byproduct under the two methods of byproduct accounting in instruction 1?

Problem-3

Skippy is a large food-processing company. It processes 150,000 pounds of peanuts in the peanuts department at a cost of $180,000 to yield 12,000 pounds of product A, 65,000 pounds of product B, and 16,000 pounds of product C.

- Product A is processed further in the salting department to yield 12,000 pounds of salted peanuts at a cost of $27,000 and sold for $12 per pound.
- Product B (raw peanuts) is sold without further processing at $3 per pound.
- Product C is considered a byproduct and is processed further in the paste department to yield 16,000 pounds of peanut butter at a cost of $12,000 and sold for $6 per pound.

The company wants to make a gross margin of 10% of revenues on product C and needs to allow 20% of revenues for marketing costs on product C.

· Instruction ·

1. Compute unit costs per pound for products A, B, and C, treating C as a byproduct. Use the NRV method for allocating joint costs. Deduct the NRV of the byproduct produced from the joint cost of products A and B.

2. Compute unit costs per pound for products A, B, and C, treating all three as joint products and allocating joint costs by the NRV method.

Problem-4

(주)한강은 동일 공정에서 3가지 제품 A, B, C를 생산하고 있다. 결합원가는 분리점에서의 상대적 판매가치를 기준으로 배분하고 있다. 이와 관련된 자료는 다음과 같다. 분리점 이후에 C제품 400개에 대하여 총 ₩14,000을 추가로 투입하여 최종제품으로 완성한 다음 단위당 ₩500에 판매하는 경우 C제품의 매출총이익은? (K-CPA)

	A	B	C	합계
생산량	?	?	400	2,000개
결합원가	180,000	?	?	₩360,000
분리점의 판매가치	?	280,000	?	₩800,000

Problem-5

(주)영남은 동일한 원료를 결합공정에 투입하여 주산품 X, Y와 부산품 B를 생산한다. 결합원가는 순실현가치(net realizable value)를 기준으로 제품에 배부한다. 당기에 결합공정에 투입된 총원가는 ₩150,000이고, 주산품 X, Y 및 부산품 B의 분리점에서 순실현가치의 상대적 비율은 6 : 3 : 1 이었다. 주산품 X에 배부된 결합원가가 ₩80,000이었다면, 부산품 B의 순실현가치는 얼마인가? 단, 부산품은 생산된 시점에서 순실현가치로 평가하여 재고자산으로 계상한다. (K-CPA)

PART I

Cost Accounting

Chapter

06

Just-in-time and Value Chain

Just-in-time and Value Chain

01 Just-In-Time(JIT)

1 Just-in-time

(1) JIT (적기생산방식)

- 1970년대 일본의 도요타(Toyota)자동차가 원가절감을 위하여 만든 생산방식

- Demand-pull system

  제조업체가 부품업체로부터 부품을 필요한 시기에 필요한 수량만큼만 공급받아 재고가 없도록 해주는 재고관리 시스템

- Kanban

  Kanban is a card with an inventory number that's attached to a part. A part is only manufactured or ordered if there is a kanban card for it.

(2) Lean production (Lean)

- A manufacturing method used for eliminating waste within the manufacturing system.

- Reduce the waste generated from uneven workloads and overburden in order to increase value and reduce costs.

- Lean is based on the Toyota Production System (TPS)

- Wastes : unnecessary transportation, excess inventory, waiting, defects

- Continual process improvement (Kaizen)

- Identify value from the customer's perspective

(3) Characteristics of JIT

- Reduce inventory level, ideally to zero

- Reduce production cycle time

- Production flexibility using manufacturing cells

- Solving production problems immediately

- A few reliable, quality-oriented suppliers who inspects goods and makes frequent delivery.

- Back-flush costing

- Increase number of orders

(4) Advantages

- Decrease inventory carrying costs

- Decrease defects

- Increase inventory turnover and productivity

- Quickly move from one product to another.

- Spend less money on raw materials

(5) Achilles point in JIT

The success of the JIT production process relies on steady production, high-quality workmanship, no machine breakdowns, and reliable suppliers.

- Suppliers do not deliver goods promptly

- Poorly trained employees

- Unreliable technology and equipment

- Higher manufacturing costs

2 Push system

(1) The push system of inventory control

- Forecasting inventory needs to meet customer demand.
- Produce enough product to meet the forecast demand.
- Sell (= push) the goods to the consumer.

  e.g.) warm jackets get pushed to clothing retailers as summer ends and the fall and winter seasons start.

(2) Materials Requirement Planning (MRP)

- Computer-based information system designed to calculate the materials and components needed to manufacture a product.
- bill of materials + inventory data + master production schedule (MPS)
  → calculate required materials
- MRP is considered a "push" system
- Manufacturing Resource Planning (MRP II) : 1983
- Enterprise Resource Planning (ERP) : 1990

(3) Advantages

- Economies of scale (규모의 경제)
- Decrease stock out costs

(4) Disadvantages

- Forecasts are often inaccurate
- Increase carrying costs
- High inventories and waste
- Bullwhip effect (채찍효과)

3 Pull system

(1) The pull system of inventory control

- Begins with a customer's order.

- Only produce enough product to meet customer's orders.

(2) Just-in-time (JIT system)

- Keep inventory levels to a minimum by only having enough inventor to meet customer demand.

- JIT is considered a "pull" system

(3) Advantages

- Reduce inventory levels

- Decrease carrying costs

- Decrease bullwhip effect

- Waste reduction

(3) Disadvantages

- Ordering dilemmas, such as a supplicr not being able to get a shipment out on time.

- Increase stock out costs and customer dissatisfaction.

- Reduce economies of scale.

4 Supply chain management (SCM)

(1) Supply chain management

- the handling of the entire production flow of a good or service, starting from the raw components all the way to delivering the final product to the consumer.
- ERP and CRM help SCM by connecting firm to suppliers and customers.

(2) ERP (Enterprises Resource Planning)

통합적인 컴퓨터 데이터베이스를 구축해 회사의 자금, 회계, 구매, 생산, 판매 등 모든 업무의 흐름을 효율적으로 자동 조절해주는 전산 시스템

(3) CRM (Customer Relationship Management)

고객과 관련된 기업의 내/외부 자료를 분석, 통합하여 고객 특성에 기초한 마케팅 활동을 계획하고, 지원하며, 평가하는 과정.

5 Back-flush costing

(1) Back-flush costing

역류원가계산(Back-flush costing)는 적시생산시스템(JIT)을 도입한 기업이 사용하는 원가계산방법이다. 전통적인 원가계산방법에서는 원재료의 구입에서부터 제품의 제조 및 판매까지 원가흐름의 순서에 따라 원가를 추적하여 회계처리를 하였다.

적시생산시스템(JIT)에서는 최소한의 재고만 유지되고 구매 및 생산 활동이 빠르게 이루어지므로 모든 제조원가가 거의 대부분 매출원가가 된다. 따라서 원재료 구입부터 제품의 판매까지 순환과정에서 상당수의 회계처리를 생략하여 단순화한 원가계산방법을 역류원가계산(Back-flush costing)이라고 한다.

(2) Accounting for back-flush costing

역류원가계산에 따른 회계처리를 전통적인 회계처리와 비교하면 다음과 같다.

	Traditional costing		Back-flush costing	
Purchase raw materials	Raw material A/P	xxx xxx	Raw and in-process A/P	xxx xxx
Issue raw materials	WIP Raw material	xxx xxx	No entry	
DL incurred	WIP Cash or payable	xxx xxx	Conversion control Cash or payable	xxx xxx
OH incurred	OH control Various accounts	xxx xxx	Conversion control Various accounts	xxx xxx
OH Application	WIP OH allocated	xxx xxx	No entry	
Completion of product	FG WIP	xxx xxx	FG Raw and in-process Conversion control	xxx xxx xxx

(3) Lean accounting

Lean accounting is a costing method that focuses on value streams, as distinguished from individual products or departments, thereby eliminating waste in the accounting process.

If a company makes multiple, related products in a single value stream, it does not compute product costs for the individual products. Instead, it traces many actual costs directly to the value stream. Tracing more costs as direct costs to value streams is possible because companies using lean accounting often dedicate resources to individual value streams.

02 / Value Chain

1 Value-chain analysis

(1) Value chain

The value chain is the sequence of business functions by which a product is made progressively more useful to customers.

가치사슬(Value chain)은 제품의 설계, 개발, 제조, 판매 및 서비스에 있어서 기업이 필요로 하는 활동을 말하며 이를 그림으로 나타내면 다음과 같다.

[그림 6-1]

(2) Supply chain

The parts of the value chain associated with producing and delivering a product or service are referred to as the supply chain. The supply chain describes the flow of goods, services, and information from the initial sources of materials and services to the delivery of products to consumers.

(3) Key success factors

Customers want companies to use the value chain and supply chain to deliver ever-improving levels of performance when it comes to several of the following :

1) Cost and efficiency

2) Quality

3) Timeliness

4) Innovation

5) Sustainability

2 Life-cycle costing

(1) Life-cycle

The product life cycle spans the time from initial R&D on a product to when customer service and support is no longer offered for that product.

Upstream stage	Production	Downstream stage
R&D costs Design costs	DM DL MOH	Marketing costs Distribution costs Customer-service costs

(2) Life-cycle costing

Life-cycle costing tracks and accumulates business function costs across the entire value chain from a product's initial R&D to its final customer service and support.

These life-cycle techniques are particularly important when (a) a high percentage of total life-cycle costs are incurred before production begins and revenues are earned over several years and (b) a high fraction of the life-cycle costs are locked in at the R&D and design stages.

(3) Value engineering

Systematic evaluation of all aspects of the value chain, with the objective of reducing costs and achieving a quality level that satisfies customers.

03   MCQ (Multiple Choice Questions)

01. A company employs a just-in-time (JIT) production system and utilizes backflush accounting. All acquisitions of raw materials are recorded in a raw materials control account when purchased. All conversion costs are recorded in a control account as incurred, while the assignment of conversion costs are from an allocated conversion cost account. Company practice is to record the cost of goods at the time the units are completed using the estimated budgeted cost of the goods. At the end of an accounting period, any minor difference in actual conversion cost incurred in the control account and the budgeted conversion cost assigned to production would be (CMA)

     a. written-off to cost of goods sold.

     b. written-off to finished goods-control.

     c. written-off to raw materials-control.

     d. prorated to work-in-process-control, finished goods-control, and cost of goods sold.

02. Which of the following is not a downstream stage costs in value chain?

     a. Marketing costs   b. Distribution costs

     c. Customer-service costs   d. Manufacturing costs

03. Advertising cost is

	Discretionary cost	Upstream stage cost in value chain
a.	Yes	Yes
b.	Yes	No
c.	No	Yes
d.	No	No

04. Which of the following is not a correct comparison of a just-in-time system with a traditional system? (CMA)

	Traditional	Just-in-Time
a	Longer lead times	Shorter lead times
b	Inventory is an asset	Inventory is a liability
c	Some scrap tolerated	Zero defects desired
d	Lot size based on immediate need	Lot size based on formulas

05. Systematic evaluation of the trade-offs between product functionality and product cost while still satisfying customer needs is the definition of (CMA)

a. activity-based management.

b. theory of constraints.

c. total quality management.

d. value engineering.

• 정답 및 해설

1. JIT에서는 기말재고가 거의 없기 때문에 과소/과대 배부금액은 전액 CGS에 배분한다.

정답 : a

2. 제조원가는 upstream과 downstream의 기준이 된다.

정답 : d

3. 광고비는 고정비 중 재량원가이며 downstream 이다.

정답 : b

4. JIT은 주문생산이므로 lot size based on immediate need 이다.

정답 : d

5. 제품의 요구사항을 유지한 상태에서 원가절감요인 분석을 가치공학이라고 한다.

정답 : d

04 / TBS (Task-Based Simulation)

Problem-1

Galaxy is developing a new touch-screen smartphone to compete in the cellular phone industry. The company will sell the phones at wholesale prices to cell phone companies, which will in turn sell them in retail stores to the final customer. Galaxy has undertaken the following activities in its value chain to bring its product to market:
- Identify customer needs (What do smartphone users want?)
- Perform market research on competing brands
- Design a prototype of the Galaxy smartphone
- Market the new design to cell phone companies
- Manufacture the Galaxy smartphone
- Process orders from cell phone companies
- Package the Galaxy smartphones
- Deliver the Galaxy smartphones to the cell phone companies
- Provide online assistance to cell phone users for use of the Galaxy smartphone
- Make design changes to the smartphone based on customer feedback

During the process of product development, production, marketing, distribution, and customer service, Galaxy has kept track of the following cost drivers:
- Number of smartphones shipped by Galaxy
- Number of design changes
- Number of deliveries made to cell phone companies
- Engineering hours spent on initial product design
- Hours spent researching competing market brands
- Customer-service hours
- Number of smartphone orders processed
- Number of cell phone companies purchasing the Galaxy smartphone
- Machine hours required to run the production equipment
- Number of surveys returned and processed from competing smartphone users

1. Identify each value chain activity listed at the beginning of the exercise with one of the following value—chain categories:
   a. Design of products and processes
   b. Production
   c. Marketing
   d. Distribution
   e. Customer service

2. Use the list of preceding cost drivers to find one or more reasonable cost drivers for each of the activities in Galaxy's value chain.

PART II

Planning & Analysis

Chapter

07

Cost Behavior

Cost Behavior

01 Cost behavior

1 Cost behavior

원가행태(cost behavior)란 생산량이나 작업시간으로 표시되는 조업도(volume)의 증감변동에 따라 총원가가 변화하는 형태를 말한다. 이러한 원가행태에 따라 원가를 분류하면 변동원가(variable cost)와 고정원가(fixed cost)로 나눌 수 있다. 이러한 원가개념을 설명하기 위하여 다음과 같은 원가함수를 생각하여 보자.

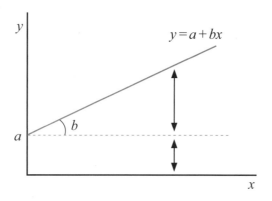

[그림 7-1]

y (dependant variable) : 총원가(total cost)

x (independent variable) : 조업도 (volume)

a (constant coefficient, intercept) : 총 고정원가 (total fixed cost)

b (variable coefficient, slope) : 단위당 변동비(unit variable cost)

2 Variable cost

변농원가는 조업도(volume)의 증감변동에 따라 총원가(total cost : TC)가 비례하여 변동하는 원가로 직접재료원가(DM)과 직접노무원가(DL)이 대표적인 예이다.

$$TC = y = bx$$

변동원가는 조업도가 변동함에도 불구하고 단위당 원가(unit cost : UC)는 일정하다.

$$UC = \frac{y}{x} = b$$

이를 그림으로 나타내면 다음과 같다.

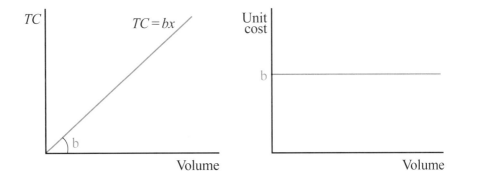

[그림 7-2]

3 Fixed cost

고정원가는 조업도(volume)의 증감변동에도 불구하고 총원가가 일정한 원가로 감가상각비와 임차료가 대표적인 예이다.

$$TC = y = a$$

고정원가는 조업도가 증가하면 단위당 원가는 감소, 조업도가 감소하면 단위당 원가는 증가한다.

$$UC = \frac{y}{x} = \frac{a}{x}$$

이를 그림으로 나타내면 다음과 같다.

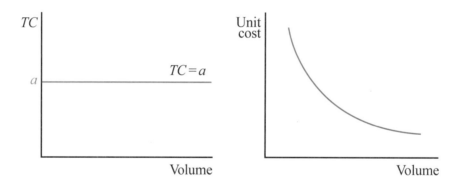

[그림 7-3]

조업도가 변동함에 따른 변동원가와 고정원가의 원가행태를 요약하면 다음과 같다.

Volume	Increase		Decrease	
Cost	Total cost	Unit cost	Total cost	Unit cost
Variable cost	increase	constant	decrease	constant
Fixed cost	constant	decrease	constant	increase

고정원가는 통제목적으로 기초고정원가(committed costs)와 재량원가(discretionary costs)로 구분된다.

(1) Committed costs

기초고정원가는 단기적으로 통제가 불가능한 고정원가로 다음과 같다.

ex depreciation, property taxes, insurance expense, rent expense

(2) Discretionary costs

재량원가는 경영자의 재량에 의하여 발생하는 고정원가를 말하며 다음과 같다.

ex advertising, R&D, training costs

4 Semi-variable cost

준변동원가(semi-variable cost) 또는 혼합원가(mixed cost)는 조업도의 증감변동에 총원가가 고정원가와 변동원가 성격을 모두 가지고 있는 원가로 전기료 등 utility cost가 대표적이 예이다.

$$TC = y = a + bx$$

혼합원가는 조업도가 증가하면 단위당 원가는 감소, 조업도가 감소하면 단위당 원가는 증가한다.

$$UC = \frac{y}{x} = \frac{a}{x} + b$$

이를 그림으로 나타내면 다음과 같다.

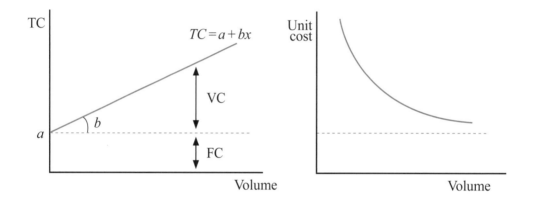

[그림 7-4]

제조간접원가(MOH)는 혼합원가이며 다음과 같이 분류한다.

● 변동제조간접원가(variable manufacturing overhead : VOH)
  제조간접원가 중 변동원가로 제조관련 전기료가 대표적인 예이다.

● 고정제조간접원가(fixed manufacturing overhead : FOH)
  제조간접원가 중 고정원가로 제조관련 감가상각비가 대표적인 예이다.

제품의 추적가능성과 원가행태를 분류하면 다음과 같다.

	Direct or Indirect cost (D or I)	Variable or Fixed cost (V or F)
Direct material	D	V
Direct labor	D	V
Variable overhead	I	V
Fixed overhead	I	F
Selling expense	I	V or F
Administrative expense	I	V or F

- 직접재료원가(DM)와 직접노무원가(DL)는 제품에 추적이 가능한 직접원가(direct cost)이며 조업도에 따라 변동하는 변동원가이다.

- 간접재료원가(IDM)는 제품에 추적이 불가능한 간접원가(indirect cost)이며 조업도에 따라 변동하는 변동원가이므로 변동제조간접원가(VOH)이다.

- 간접노무원가(IDL)는 제품에 추적이 불가능한 간접원가(indirect cost)이며 조업도의 변동에도 불구하고 일정한 고정원가이므로 고정제조간접원가(FOH)이다.

When production levels are expected to increase within a relevant range,

	Increase	Decrease	Constant
Total fixed cost			v
Fixed cost per unit		v	
Total variable cost	v		
Variable cost per unit			v
Total mixed cost	v		
Mixed cost per unit		v	

When production levels are expected to decrease within a relevant range,

	Increase	Decrease	Constant
Total fixed cost			v
Fixed cost per unit	v		
Total variable cost		v	
Variable cost per unit			v
Total mixed cost		v	
Mixed cost per unit	v		

5 Semi-fixed cost

준고정원가(semi-fixed cost)또는 계단원가(step cost)는 일정한 관련범위 내에서는 조업도가 변동함에도 불구하고 총원가가 일정하지만, 그 관련범위를 벗어나면 총원가가 변동하여 새로운 관련범위 내에서는 총원가가 일정한 원가를 말한다.

$$TC = y = a_1 \ \Rightarrow \ TC = y = a_2 \ \Rightarrow \ TC = y = a_3$$

이를 그림으로 나타내면 다음과 같다.

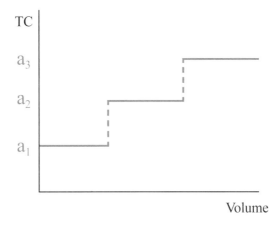

[그림 7-5]

Example-1

AVIS operates car rental agencies at more than 20 airports. Customers can choose from one of three contracts for car rentals of one day or less:

- Contract 1: $50 for the day
- Contract 2: $30 for the day plus $0.20 per mile traveled
- Contract 3: $1 per mile traveled

(1) Express each contract as a linear cost function of the form Y = a + bX
(2) Identify each contract as a variable-, fixed-, or mixed-cost function

(1) Linear cost function

    1) Contract 1 : $Y = \$50$

    2) Contract 2 : $Y = \$30 + 0.20 \cdot X$ (X = mile)

    3) Contract 3 : $Y = \$1 \cdot X$ (X = mile)

(2) Cost function

    1) Contract 1 : fixed cost

    2) Contract 2 : mixed cost

    3) Contract 3 : variable cost

Example-2

Volkswagen Corporation assembles two types of cars (Beetle and Golf). Separate assembly lines are used for each type of car.

Classify each cost item as follows:
(1) Direct or indirect (D or I) costs for the total number of Beetle assembled.
(2) Variable or fixed (V or F) costs depending on how total costs change as the total number of Beetle assembled changes.

A. Cost of tires used on Beetle
B. Salary of factory manager for Volkswagen plant
C. Depreciation cost for Volkswagen plant
D. Cost of lubricant used on the Beetle assembly line
E. Freight costs of Beetle engines shipped from Port of Hamburg to Volkswagen
F. Electricity costs for Beetle assembly line (single bill covers entire plant)
G. Wages paid to temporary assembly-line workers hired in periods of high Beetle production (paid on hourly basis)
H. Annual fire-insurance policy cost for Volkswagen plant.

	Direct or Indirect cost	Variable or Fixed cost
A : DM	D	V
B : FOH	I	F
C : FOH	I	F
D : IDM ⇨ VOH	I	V
E : DM	D	V
F : VOH	I	V
G : DL	D	V
H : FOH	I	F

02 　 Estimating cost function

1 　 Estimating cost function

회계자료 등을 이용하여 특정변수와 원가사이의 관계를 규명하여 원가함수를 추정하고 원가함수를 이용하여 미래원가를 예측하는 방법에는 다음과 같은 4가지 방법이 있다.

- Industrial engineering method (산업공학적 방법)
- Conference method (회의법)
- Account analysis method (계정분석법)
- Quantitative analysis method (통계분석법)

(1) Industrial engineering method (work–measurement method)

1) This method estimates cost functions by analyzing the relationship between inputs and outputs in physical terms. ⇨ "Time-and-motion study"

2) Advantages and disadvantages

① A very thorough and detailed way to estimate a cost function when there is a physical relationship between inputs and outputs.

② It can be time consuming

③ The physical relationships between inputs and outputs are difficult to specify for some items

(2) Conference method

1) This method estimates cost functions on the basis of opinions gathered from various departments of a company (purchasing, manufacturing, and so on).

2) Advantages and disadvantages

① Encourages interdepartmental cooperation

② Cost functions can be developed quickly

③ The accuracy of the cost estimates depends largely on the care and skill of the people.

(3) Account analysis method

1) This method estimates cost functions by classifying various cost accounts as variable, fixed, or mixed.

2) Advantages and disadvantages

① This is widely used because it is reasonably accurate, cost effective, and easy to use.

② The accuracy depends on the accuracy of the qualitative judgments

(4) Quantitative analysis method

1) This method uses a formal mathematical method to fit cost functions to past data observations. ⇨ "Excel"

2) Two techniques : high-low method, regression analysis

3) Advantages and disadvantages

① This is the most rigorous approach to estimate costs.

② Regression analysis requires more detailed information and is therefore more time consuming to implement.

2 Quantitative analysis

Six steps in estimating cost function using quantitative analysis of past data

⟨Step1⟩ Choose the dependent variable

⟨Step2⟩ Identify the cost drivers

⟨Step3⟩ Collect data on the dependent variable and cost drivers

⟨Step4⟩ Plot the data

⟨Step5⟩ Estimate the cost function

⟨Step6⟩ Evaluate the cost driver of the estimate the cost function

⇨ Economic plausibility, Goodness of fit, Significance of independent variable

3 High-low method

고저점법(high-low method)은 최대조업도와 최저조업도의 원가자료를 이용하여 원가를 추정하는 방법이다.

$$TC = y = a + bx$$

b = (최고조업도 총원가 − 최저조업도 총원가) ÷ (최고조업도 − 최저조업도)

a = 최고조업도 총원가 − b × 최고조업도

  = 최저조업도 총원가 − b × 최저조업도

Example-3

UPS Company applied the high-low method of cost estimation to customer order date for the first four months. What is the estimated order filling cost for May?

Month	Orders	Total costs
January	1,200	$3,120
February	1,300	3.185
March	1,800	4,320
April	1,700	3.895
May	2,000	???

최대조업도 : March, 최저조업도 : January

b = ($4,320 − $3,120) ÷ (1,800 − 1,200) = $2 per order

a = $4,320 − $2 × 1800 = $720 or

a = $3,120 − $2 × 1200 = $720

원가함수 : $y = 720 + 2x$

total costs : x = 2,000 ⇨ y=$720 + $2 × 2000 = $4,720

unit cost = $4,720 ÷ 2,000 = $2.36

4 Regression analysis

(1) Regression analysis

회귀분석(regression analysis)은 독립변수(independent variable)가 종속변수(dependent variable)에 미치는 영향을 확인하고자 사용하는 분석방법이다. 회귀분석은 다른 독립변수들을 고정시키고 한 가지 독립변수만을 변화시킬 때 종속변수가 어떻게 변화하는지를 확인한다.

하나의 종속변수와 하나의 독립변수 사이의 관계를 분석할 때 단순회귀분석(simple regression analysis)이라 하고, 하나의 종속변수와 여러 독립변수 사이의 관계를 규명하고자 할 때 다중회귀분석(multiple regression analysis)이라 한다.

(2) Simple regression analysis

Simple regression analysis estimates the relationship between the dependent variable and one independent variable.

단순회귀분석이란 하나의 독립변수로 종속변수와의 관계를 분석하는 것이다. 단순회귀분석의 모형은 독립변수와 종속변수의 관계를 선형으로 가정하여 다음과 같이 나타낸다.

$$Y = a + bX + e$$

Y : 실제 관찰된 종속변수 값, X : 독립변수의 관찰된 값
a : 회귀선의 절편, b : 회귀선의 기울기, e : 잔차 (오차)

$$y = a + bX$$

y : 회귀모형으로 추정된 종속변수의 값

$$e = Y - y$$

e : 잔차(residual)
　　회귀모형에 의하여 추정된 종속변수의 값과 실제 관찰된 종속변수 값과의 차이

(3) Least squares method

최소자승법은 회귀 분석을 시행함에 있어 그 방정식의 계수를 구하기 위해 가장 흔히 사용하는 방법으로 수집된 통계자료에 대해 오차 제곱의 합($\sum (Y - y)^2$)이 최소가 되는 회귀계수 a와 b를 찾는다.

(4) Coefficient of correlation

r로 표현되는 상관계수(coefficient of correlation)는 두 변량 X, Y 사이의 상관관계의 정도를
나타내는 수치이다. 상관계수는 −1에서 +1 사이의 값을 갖는다. 상관관계가 강할수록 1 또는
−1에 가깝고 서로 연관이 없으면 0에 가깝다.

① r = −1 : A perfectly inverse relationship between X and Y

② r = +1 : A perfectly direct relationship between X and Y

③ r = 0 : No liner relationship between X and Y

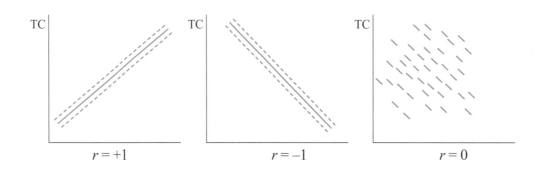

[그림 7−7]

(5) Coefficient of determination

결정계수는 회귀분석에서 추정한 회귀선이 실제 표본을 어느 정도 설명해 주고 있는지를
측정하는 계수를 말한다. 이 값이 1인 경우에는 회귀선이 자료와 완벽한 일치를 보임을 의미
한다. 반대로 결정계수 값이 0인 경우에는 회귀선이 자료의 분포를 전혀 설명하지 못함을 의
미한다. 통계학에서 결정계수는 r로 표현되는 상관계수(coefficient of correlation)를 제곱한 것
과 같기 때문에 r^2으로 표현된다.

(6) Multiple regression analysis

Multiple regression analysis estimates the relationship between the dependent variable and
two or more independent variables.

다중회귀분석은 종속 변수는 하나이고 독립 변수가 2개 이상인 회귀 모델에 대한 분석을 수
행하는 방법이다. 예를 들어, 사람들의 뇌의 크기, 키, 몸무게 값(다중독립 변수)으로 그 사람

의 지능(종속 변수)을 예측하고자 한다면, 이 경우 다중 회귀 분석을 적용할 수 있다.

독립변수가 k개인 다중회귀식은 다음과 같이 구한다.

$$Y = a + b_1 X_1 + b_2 X_2 + .. + b_k X_k + e$$

※ Multicollinearity

Multicollinearity exists when two or more independent variables are highly correlated with each other.
다중공선성(Multicollinearity)문제는 회귀분석에서 독립변수들 간에 강한 상관관계가 나타나는 문제이다

(7) Assumptions of regression analysis

① The relationship is liner within the relevant range.

② The residual terms are unaffected by the level of the cost driver.

③ The residual term for any one observation is not related to the residual term for any other observation.

⇨ Autocorrelation : serial correlation in residuals (violation of this assumption)

④ The residuals are distributed normally around the regression line.

5 Evaluate the cost driver of the estimate the cost function

(1) Economic plausibility

독립변수(independent variable : cost driver)와 종속변수(dependant variable : cost)사이에는 밀접한 관련이 있어야 한다.

(2) Goodness of fit

1) Goodness of fit measures how well the predicted values, y, based on the cost driver, X, match actual cost observations, Y. The regression analysis method computes a measure of goodness of fit, called the coefficient of determination.

2) The coefficient of determination(r^2; 결정계수)

① r^2 measures the percentage of variation in Y explained by X

결정계수는 Y의 변동이 X에 의하여 설명되는 정도를 측정한다.

② $0 \leq r^2 \leq 1$

$r^2 = 0$: implying no explanatory power

$r^2 = 1$: implying perfect explanatory power

(3) Significance of independent variable

1) Significance measures that X results in significant changes in Y.

2) Slope coefficient of the regression line (b)

3) t-value

t-value measures how large the value of the estimated coefficient is relative to its standard error (SE, 표준오차). ($t = \dfrac{b}{SE}$)

일반적으로 t 〉 2인 경우에는 통계적인 유의성이 있다는 것을 의미한다.

4) Confidence interval

test that the coefficient b is significantly different from zero

6 Non-liner cost function

A nonlinear cost function is a cost function for which the graph of total costs is not a straight line within the relevant range.

비선형함수(Non-liner cost function)의 발생원인은 다음과 같다.

1) Quantity discount of materials

2) Step cost

3) Learning-curve effect

7 Learning-curve effect

A learning curve is a function that measures how labor-hours per unit decline as units of production increase because workers are learning and becoming better at their jobs.

학습곡선효과란 동일한 작업을 반복할 경우 능률이 향상되어 생산량이 증가할수록 단위당 노동시간이 체계적으로 감소하는 효과를 말하며, 일반적으로 노동시간과 관련이 있는 원가에서 발생한다. 학습효과의 발생원인으로는 생산설비의 효율적인 이용과 노동자의 숙련도의 증가 등을 들 수 있다.

학습곡선모형은 누적평균시간모형(cumulative average-time learning model)과 증분단위시간모형(incremental unit-time learning model)이 있다.

(1) Cumulative average-time learning model

누적 생산량이 2배가 될 때마다 단위당 평균노동시간이 전 단계의 단위당 평균노동시간보다 일정한 비율(= 1 - 학습률)로 감소하는 모형

(2) Incremental unit-time learning model

누적 생산량이 2배가 될 때마다 증분단위노동시간이 전 단계의 증분단위노동시간보다 일정한 비율(=1 - 학습률)로 감소하는 모형

학습률(learning percentage) 80%를 가정하고 최초 1단위당 소요시간을 100시간으로 한 학습 곡선모형은 다음과 같다.

Cumulative average–time learning model

Cumulative number of units	Cumulative average time per unit (Hours)	Cumulative total time (hours)	Incremental unit-time (hours)
1	100	100	100
2	80	160	60
4	64	256	48

Incremental unit–time learning model

Cumulative number of units	Cumulative average time per unit (Hours)	Cumulative total time (hours)	Incremental unit-time (hours)
1	100	100	100
2	90	180	80
4	77	308	64

03   MCQ (Multiple Choice Questions)

01. Ace Inc. estimates its total materials handling costs at two production levels as follows.

Cost	Gallons
$160,000	80,000
$132,000	60,000

What is the estimated total cost for handling 75,000 gallons? (CMA)

a. $146,000   b. $150,000   c. $153,000   d. $165,000

02. Roberta Johnson is the manager of SleepWell Inn, one of a chain of motels located throughout the United States. An example of an operating cost at SleepWell that is semi-variable is (CMA)

a. the security guard's salary.

b. electricity.

c. postage for reservation confirmations.

d. local yellow pages advertising.

03. Lar Company has found that its total electricity cost has both a fixed component and a variable component within the relevant range. The variable component seems to vary directly with the number of units produced. Which one of the following statements concerning Lar's electricity cost is incorrect? (CMA)

a. The total electricity cost will increase as production volume increases.

b. The total electricity cost per unit of production will increase as production volume increases.

c. The variable electricity cost per unit of production will remain constant as production volume increases.

d. The fixed electricity cost per unit of production will decline as production volume increases.

04. The cost behavior is often expressed as Y = A + B × X. What is the symbol for the independent variable?

a. Y   b. A   c. B   d. X

05. The cost behavior is often expressed as Y = A + B × X. What is the symbol for the dependent variable?

a. Y   b. A   c. B   d. X

06. The cost behavior is often expressed as Y = A + B × X. What is the symbol for the variable coefficient?

a. Y   b. A   c. B   d. X

07. Which one of the following categories of cost is most likely not considered a component of fixed factory overhead?

a. Rent   b. Property taxes

c. Depreciation   d. Power

Questions 8 and 13 are based on the following information

KIMCPA has recently developed two new products, a cleaning unit for laser discs and a tape duplicator for reproducing home movies taken with a video camera.

However, KIMCPA has only enough plant capacity to introduce one of these products during the current year. The company controller has gathered the following data to assist management in deciding which product should be selected for production.

KIMCPA's fixed overhead includes rent and utilities, equipment depreciation and supervisory salaries. Selling and administrative expenses are not allocated to products.

	Tape duplicator	Cleaning unit
Raw materials	$44.00	$36.00
Machining @$12/hr.	18.00	15.00
Assembly @$10/hr.	30.00	10.00
Variable overhead @$8/hr.	36.00	18.00
Fixed overhead @$4/hr.	18.00	9.00
Total costs	$146.00	$88.00
Suggested selling price	$169.95	$99.98
Actual R&D costs	$240,000	$175,000
Proposed advertising costs	$500,000	$350,000

08. For KIMCPA's tape duplicator, the unit costs for raw materials, machining and assembly represent

a. conversion costs

b. separable costs

c. committed costs

d. prime costs

09. The differences between the $99.98 suggested selling prices for KIMCPA's laser disc cleaning unit and its total unit costs of $88.00 represent the unit's

a. contribution margin ratio

b. gross profit

c. contribution margin

d. gross profit margin ratio

10. The total overhead cost of $27.00 for KIMCPA's laser disc cleaning unit is a

a. carrying cost
c. sunk cost

b. discretionary cost
d. mixed cost

11. R&D costs for KIMCPA's two new products are

a. conversion costs
c. relevant costs

b. sunk costs
d. avoidable costs

12. The advertising costs for the products selected by KIMCPA will be

a. discretionary costs
c. committed costs

b. opportunity costs
d. incremental costs

13. The costs included in KIMCPA's fixed overhead are

a. joint costs
c. opportunity costs

b. committed costs
d. prime costs

정답 및 해설

1. b = ($160,000 − $132,000) ÷ (80,000 − 60,000) = $1.4

   $160,000 = a + 80,000 × 1.4에서 a = $48,000

   y = $48,000 + 75,000 × 1.4 = $153,000 　　　　　　　　정답 : c

2. a : 고정원가, b: 준변동원가, c : 변동원가, d : 고정원가 　　　정답 : b

3. 준변동원가의 단위당 원가는 수량이 증가하면 감소한다. 　　　정답 : b

4. Y는 종속변수, X는 독립변수 　　　　　　　　　　　　　　정답 : d

5. Y는 종속변수, X는 독립변수 　　　　　　　　　　　　　　정답 : a

6. A는 상수계수, B는 변수계수 　　　　　　　　　　　　　　정답 : c

7. 전기료는 변동원가 또는 준변동원가다. 　　　　　　　　　　정답 : d

8. machining과 assembly는 직접노무원가(DL)이다. 　　　　　　정답 : d

9. Selling price − manufacturing unit cost = gross profit per unit 　정답 : b

10. 변동원가와 고정원가가 혼합되어 있는 mixed cost다. 　　　　정답 : d

11. R&D는 제조 의사결정 이전에 발생하므로 제조의사결정에 대해서는 sunk cost다.

　　　　　　　　　　　　　　　　　　　　　　　　　　　정답 : b

12. 광고비는 고정원가 중에서 재량원가이다. 　　　　　　　　　정답 : a

13. 공장의 감가상각비는 고정제조간접원가(FOH)이며 계약원가다. 　정답 : b

04 TBS (Task-Based Simulation)

Problem-1

Tesla Motors specializes in producing one specialty vehicle. It is called Model S. Tesla has the following manufacturing costs:

• Plant management costs : $1,200,000 per year

• Cost of leasing equipment : $1,800,000 per year

• Workers'wages : $700 per vehicle produced

• Direct materials costs: Steel, $1,500 per vehicle;

Tires, $125 per tire, each vehicle takes 5 tires (one spare).

• City license, which is charged monthly based on the number of tires used in production:

0–500 tires : $50,000

501–1,000 tires : $74,500

more than 1,000 tires : $200,000

Tesla currently produces 110 vehicles per month.

• Instruction •

1. What is the variable manufacturing cost per vehicle? What is the fixed manufacturing cost per month?

2. What is the total manufacturing cost of each vehicle if 100 vehicles are produced each month? 225 vehicles?

Problem-2

KIMCPA, financial analyst at AIFA Corporation, is examining the behavior of quarterly maintenance costs for budgeting purposes. KIMCPA collects the following data on machine hours worked and maintenance costs for the past 12 quarters:

Quarter	Machine-Hours	Maintenance Costs
1	100,000	$205,000
2	120,000	240,000
3	110,000	220,000
4	130,000	260,000
5	95,000	190,000
6	115,000	235,000
7	105,000	215,000
8	125,000	255,000
9	105,000	210,000
10	125,000	245,000
11	115,000	200,000
12	140,000	280,000

• Instruction •

1. Estimate the cost function for the quarterly data using the high−low method.

2. KIMCPA anticipates that AIFA will operate machines for 100,000 hours in quarter 13. Calculate the predicted maintenance costs in quarter 13 using the high−low method.

PART II

Planning & Analysis

Chapter

08

Cost-volume-profit (CVP) Analysis

Chapter 08 · Cost-volume-profit(CVP) Analysis

01 Basics of CVP analysis

1 Introduction

CVP(cost−volume−profit)분석은 원가. 조업도, 이익을 연계하여 분석하는 기법으로 다음과 같은 경영계획과 의사결정에 유용한 분석도구이다.

- 영업이익 = 0이 되기 위하여 몇 개의 제품을 판매하여야 하는가? (손익분기점)
- 현재의 매출액이 손익분기점과 비교하여 얼마나 안전한가? (안전한계)
- 목표이익을 달성하기 위하여 몇 개를 판매하여야 하는가? (목표이익분기점)

2 Assumptions of CVP

(1) All costs can be classified as either variable or fixed.

모든 원가는 변동원가와 고정원가로 분리할 수 있다.

(2) The behavior of both cost and revenue is linear within the relevant range.

⇨ selling price is constant per unit

⇨ variable cost is constant per unit

⇨ fixed cost is constant in total

관련범위 내에서 원가와 수익의 행태는 선형이다. 따라서 관련범위 내에서 단위당 판매가격, 단위당 변동원가, 총고정원가가 일정하다.

(3) Sales mix remains constant.

복수제품을 생산하는 경우에는 제품의 매출배합은 일정하다.

(4) Inventory levels are fairly constant, with the number of units produced equaling the number of units sold.

재고량은 불변이다. (생산량 = 판매량)

⇨ 이 가정은 전부원가계산(Absorption costing)에서 필요한 가정이며, 변동원가계산(Variable costing)에서는 이 가정은 필요 없다.

3 Terminology of CVP

(1) Abbreviations

- P = Selling price
- UCM = Unit contribution margin
- VC = Variable costs
- TR = Total revenues
- CM = Contribution margin
- NI = Net income
- CM% = Contribution margin percentage

- UVC = Unit variable costs
- Q = Quantity of units sold
- FC = Fixed costs
- TC = Total costs
- OI = Operating income
- t = Income taxe rate

(2) Equation

Net income = Operating income - Income taxes	$NI = OI \times (1 - t)$
Operating income = Total revenues - Total costs	$OI = TR - TC$
Total revenues = Selling price x Quantity of units sold	$TR = P \times Q$
Total costs = Variable costs + Fixed costs	$TC = VC + FC$
Variable costs = Unit variable costs x Quantity of units sold	$VC = UVC \times Q$

(3) Contribution Margin

1) 공헌이익(Contribution margin: CM)이란 총수익에서 총변동비를 차감한 이익이다.

Contribution margin = Total revenues - Variable costs	$CM = TR - VC$
Operating income = Contribution margin - Fixed costs	$OI = CM - FC$

2) 단위당 공헌이익(Unit Contribution margin : UCM)이란 공헌이익을 판매수량으로 나눈 값으로 판매가격에서 단위당 변동비를 차감한 이익을 말한다.

Contribution margin = Unit Contribution margin × Quantity of units sold	$CM = UCM \times Q$
Unit Contribution margin = Selling price − Unit variable costs	$UCM = P - UVC$

3) 공헌이익률(Contribution margin percentage)은 매출액에서 공헌이익이 차지하는 비율을 말한다. 변동비율은 매출액에서 변동원가가 차지하는 비율을 뜻하므로 '공헌이익률 = 1 − 변동비율'을 의미한다.

Contribution margin percentage = Contribution margin ÷ Total revenues	$CM\% = CM \div TR$
Contribution margin percentage = Unit Contribution margin ÷ Selling price	$CM\% = UCM \div P$
Contribution margin = Total revenues × Contribution margin percentage	$CM = TR \times CM\%$

02   The break-even point (BEP)

1   Break even formula

손익분기점(break-even point :BEP)이란 영업활동에 따른 이익이나 손실이 발생하지 않는 점, 즉 영업이익이 0이 되는 점을 말하며 다음과 같이 구할 수 있다.

Operating income = Total revenues − Total costs에서

손익분기점은 Operating income = 0 이므로 ⇨ Total revenues = Total costs

Total revenues : TR = P × Q

Total costs : TC = UVC × Q + FC

⇨ P × Q = UVC × Q + FC

⇨ Q = FC ÷ (P − UVC) = FC ÷ UCM

손익분기점 판매량의 공식을 요약하면 다음과 같다.

$$BEP_Q = \frac{FC}{UCM}$$

손익분기점 판매량은 총고정비를 단위당 공헌이익으로 나눈 값이다.

손익분기점 매출액은 다음과 같이 구한다.

Breakeven revenues = Breakeven quantity × Selling price

$$BEP_S = BEP_Q \times P = \frac{FC}{UCM} \times P = \frac{FC}{\frac{UCM}{P}} = \frac{FC}{CM\%}$$

$$BEP_S = \frac{FC}{CM\%}$$

손익분기점 매출액은 총고정비를 공헌이익률로 나눈 값이다.

2 Graph method

(1) CVP graph

CVP(cost-volume-profit) graph는 조업도의 변동에 따른 총수익과 총비용 및 이익의 변동을 그림으로 나타낸 것이다.

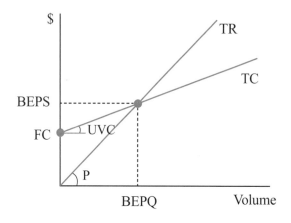

[그림 8-1]

1) Total revenues line

총수익선은 원점에서 출발하며 기울기가 판매가격인 직선이다.

2) Total costs line.

총비용선은 고정원가에서 출발하며, 기울기가 단위당 변동원가인 직선이다.

3) Break-even point

- 총수익선과 총비용선이 만나는 점이 손익분기점이다.
- 손익분기점의 X축 값은 손익분기점 판매량이며, 손익분기점의 Y축 값은 손익분기점 매출액이다.
- 손익분기점 오른쪽에서는 이익이 발생하며, 손익분기점 왼쪽에서는 손실이 발생한다.

(2) PV graph

PV(profit-volume) graph는 조업도의 변동에 따른 이익의 변동을 그림으로 나타낸 것이다.

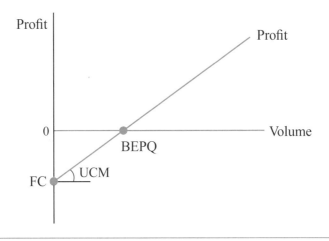

[그림 8-2]

1) Profit line

이익선은 마이너스(-) 고정원가에서 출발하며, 기울기가 단위당 공헌이익인 직선이다.

2) Break-even point

- 이익선의 X축과 만나는 점이 손익분기점이다.
- 손익분기점 오른쪽에서는 이익이 발생하며, 손익분기점 왼쪽에서는 손실이 발생한다.

Example-1

Parker Company manufactures and sells pens. Currently, 40,000 units are sold per year at $15 per unit. Fixed costs are $150,000 per year. Variable costs are $9 per unit.

(1) What is the present breakeven point in units?

(2) What is the present breakeven point in revenues?

(3) What is the current annual operating income?

(4) Compute the new breakeven point in units for each of the following changes:

    1) A 10% increase in fixed costs

    2) A 10% increase in unit variable costs

    3) A 10% increase in selling price

(1) Breakeven point in units

    UCM = P − UVC = $15 − $9 = $6

    BEPQ = $150,000 ÷ $6 = 25,000 units

(2) Breakeven point in revenues

    CM% = $6 ÷ $15 = 40%

    BEPS = $150,000 ÷ 0.40 = $375,000

(3) Operating income

    Operating income = Contribution margin − Fixed costs

            = $6 × 40,000 − $150,000 = $90,000

(4) Breakeven point in units

    1) FC = $150,000 × 1.10 = $165,000

       BEPQ = $165,000 ÷ $6 = 27,500 units

    2) UVC = $9 × 1.10 = $9.9 ⇨ UCM = $15 − $9.9 = $5.1

       BEPQ = $150,000 ÷ $5.1 = 29,412 units

    3) P = $15 × 1.10 = $16.5 ⇨ UCM = $16.5 − $9 = $7.5

       BEPQ = $150,000 ÷ $7.5 = 20,000 units

3 BEP analysis

다른 조건이 일정한 경우, 손익분기점이 감소하면 동일한 판매량에 대해서도 더 많은 이익을 달성할 수 있다. 손익분기점을 감소시키는 방법은 다음과 같다.

Fixed cost	Decrease
UCM	Increase
Price	Increase
UVC	Decrease

만일 학습곡선효과에 의하여 단위당 인건비를 감소하였다면
UVC decrease → UCM increase → BEP decrease의 결과를 가져온다.

이를 PV chart로 그려보면 [그림 8-3]과 같다.

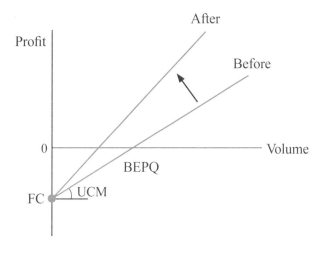

[그림 8-3]

4 Target income analysis

목표이익점(Target income point : TIP)이란 영업활동에 따른 목표이익을 달성하기 위한 판매수량 또는 매출액을 말한다.

Operating income = Total revenues − Total costs

$\Rightarrow$ OI = P × Q − (UVC × Q + FC)

$\Rightarrow$ Q = (FC + OI) ÷ (P− UVC) = (FC + OI) ÷ UCM

목표이익점 판매량의 공식을 요약하면 다음과 같다.

$$TIP_Q = \frac{FC+ OI}{UCM}$$

목표이익점 판매량은 목표영업이익과 총고정비를 더한 값을 단위당 공헌이익으로 나눈 값이다.

목표이익점 매출액은 다음과 같다.

$$TIP_S = \frac{FC+ OI}{CM\%}$$

목표이익점 판매량은 목표영업이익과 총고정비를 더한 값을 공헌이익률로 나눈 값이다.

목표영업이익은 세전이익을 말한다. 세후이익의 목표이익점을 구하기 위해서는 세후이익을 세전이익으로 전환하여 목표이익점을 구한다.

$$OI= \frac{NI}{1- t}$$

Example-2

Parker Company manufactures and sells pens. Currently, 40,000 units are sold per year at $15 per unit. Fixed costs are $150,000 per year. Variable costs are $9 per unit. The income tax rate is 40%.

(1) Compute the units needed to earn the target operating income of $36,000.
(2) Compute the revenues needed to earn the target operating income $36,000.
(3) Compute the units needed to earn the target net income of $36,000.
(5) Compute the revenues needed to earn the target net income $36,000.

(1) Target income point in units
   UCM = P − UVC = $15 − $9 = $6
   TIPQ = ($150,000 + $36,000) ÷ $6 = 31,000 units

(2) Target income point in revenues
   CM% = $6 ÷ $15 = 40%
   TIPS = ($150,000 + $36,000) ÷ 0.40 = $465,000

(3) Target income point in units
   Operating income = $36,000 ÷ (1− 0.40) = $60,000
   TIPQ = ($150,000 + $60,000) ÷ $6 = 35,000 units

(4) Target income point in revenues
   TIPS = ($150,000 + $60,000) ÷ 0.40 = $525,000

Example-3

The Sweet Meal has two restaurants that are open 24 hours a day. Fixed costs for the two restaurants together total $456,000 per year. Service varies from a cup of coffee to full meals. The average sales check per customer is $9.50. The average cost of food and other variable costs for each customer is $3.80. The income tax rate is 30%. Target net income is $159,600.

(1) Compute the revenues needed to earn the target net income.
(2) How many customers are needed to break even?
(3) Compute net income if the number of customers is 145,000

(1) Target income point in revenues
$\quad$ UCM $= 9.50 - 3.80 = \$5.70$
$\quad$ CM% $= \$5.70 \div 9.50 = 0.6 \ (60\%)$
$\quad$ Operating income $= \$159,600 \div (1- 0.30) = \$228,000$
$\quad$ TIPS $= (\$456,000 + \$228,000) \div 0.60 = \$1,140,000$

(2) Breakeven point in units
$\quad$ BEPQ $= \$456,000 \div \$5.70 = 80,000 \ \text{units}$

(3) Forecasting net income
$\quad$ Net income $= (145,000 \times \$5.70 - \$456,000) \times (1-0.3) = \$259,350$

Example-4

Dunkin' Donuts owns and operates six doughnut outlets in and around Seoul City. You are given the following corporate budget data for next year:
- Revenues : $10,400,000
- Fixed costs : $2,100,000
- Variable costs : $7,900,000

Variable costs change based on the number of doughnuts sold. Compute the budgeted operating income for each of the following deviations from the original budget data. (Consider each case independently.)

(1) An 20% increase in contribution margin, holding revenues constant
(2) A 4% increase in fixed costs
(3) A 7% decrease in units sold
(4) A 4% decrease in variable costs

(1) Increase in contribution margin

Contribution margin $= 10,400,000 - 7,900,000 = 2,500,000$

Operating income $=$ Contribution margin $-$ Fixed costs

$\qquad = 2,500,000 \times 1.20 - 2,100,000 = \$900,000$

(2) Increase in fixed costs

Operating income $= 2,500,000 - 2,100,000 \times 1.04 = \$316,000$

(3) Decrease in units sold

Operating income $= 2,500,000 \times 0.93 - 2,100,000 = \$225,000$

(4) Decrease in variable costs

Operating income $= 2,500,000 + 7,900,000 \times 0.04 - 2,100,000 = \$716,000$

03   CVP analysis

1   Margin of safety

안전한계(margin of safety ; M/S)란 예상 또는 실제 판매량(매출액)이 손익분기점의 판매량(매출액)을 초과하는 판매량(매출액)을 의미한다.

> Margin of safety = Current revenues − Breakeven revenues
>
> Margin of safety in units = Current sales units − Breakeven units

안전한계는 현 상황에서 손실을 발생시키지 않으면서 허용할 수 있는 판매량(매출액)의 최대감소폭을 나타내기 때문에 기업의 안전성을 측정하는 지표이다.

안전한계율(margin of safety percentage: M/S%)은 안전한계 매출액을 매출액으로 나눈 값이다.

> Margin of safety percentage = Margin of safety ÷ Current revenues

안전한계율은 현재의 매출액에서 몇 %가 감소하면 손실이 발행하는지를 보여주는 비율이다.

Example-5

Parker Company manufactures and sells pens. Currently, 40,000 units are sold per year at $15 per unit. Fixed costs are $150,000 per year. Variable costs are $9 per unit.

(1) Compute the margin of safety in units.
(2) Compute the margin of safety in dollars.
(3) Compute the margin of safety percentage.

(1) Margin of safety in units

BEPQ = $150,000 ÷ $6 = 25,000 units

Margin of safety in units = 40,000 − 25,000 = 15,000 units

(2) Margin of safety in dollars

BEPS = $150,000 ÷ 0.40 = $375,000

Current revenues = 40,000 × $15 = $600,000

Margin of safety in dollars = $600,000 − $375,000 = $225,000

(3) Margin of safety percentage

M/S percentage = $225,000 ÷ $600,000 = 0.375 (37.5%)

2 Multi-products

여러 종류의 제품을 판매하는 경우의 복수제품 CVP분석은 복수제품간의 제품배합(Sales mix)이 일정하다는 가정 하에서 진행된다. 제품배합은 판매량 배합과 매출액 배합으로 표현할 수 있는데 일반적으로 제품배합은 판매량 배합을 의미한다.

Sales mix is the quantities (or proportion) of various products that constitute a company's total unit sales.

판매량 배합은 총 판매량에서 각 제품이 판매량이 차지하는 상대적 비율을 의미한다.

복수제품의 CVP분석은 다음 절차에 의하여 계산한다.

(Step-1) Compute WACM (weighted-average contribution margin)

(Step-2) Compute BEP for total quantity

(Step-3) BEP for each product = BEP for total quantity × sales mix

Example-6

AIFA Company has three product lines of products(A, B, and C) with units contribution margins of $5, $3, and $2, respectively. The president foresees sales of 30,000 units in the coming period, consisting of 9,000 units of A, 15,000 units of B, and 6,000 units of C. The company's fixed costs for the period are $68,000

(1) What is the company's breakeven point in units, assuming that the given sales mix is maintained?
(2) If the sales mix is maintained, what is the operating income when 30,000 units are sold?

(1) Breakeven point in units

Sales mix of product A = 9,000 / 30,000 = 30%

Sales mix of product B = 15,000 / 30,000 = 50%

Sales mix of product C = 6,000 / 30,000 = 20%

Step 1〉 WACM = (0.3 × $5) + (0.5 × $3) + (0.2 × $2) = $3.40

Step 2〉 BEP for total quantity = $68,000 ÷ $3.40 = 20,000 units

Step 3〉 BEP for product A = 20,000 × 0.3 = 6,000 units

BEP for product B = 20,000 × 0.5 = 10,000 units

BEP for product C = 20,000 × 0.2 = 4,000 units

(2) Forecasting operating income

Operating income = 30,000 × $3.40 − $68,000 = $34,000

3 Operating leverage

Operating leverage describes the effects that fixed costs have on changes in operating income as changes occur in units sold and contribution margin.

영업 레버리지(operating leverage)란 매출액의 증감률이 고정원가로 인하여 확대되어 영업이익에 반영되는 효과를 말한다.

매출이 변동할 때 변동원가는 동일 비율로 변동하므로 공헌이익은 항상 매출과 동일비율로 변동하지만 고정원가는 일정하게 발생하므로 영업이익의 증가율은 매출의 증가율보다 더 커지게 되는데 이를 영업레버리지라고 한다.

결국 영업 레버리지는 변동원가와 고정원가의 상대적인 비율에 따라 결정되므로 기업의 원가구조와 밀접한 관련이 있으며 이를 요약하면 다음과 같다.

Industry	Cost structure		CM ratio	Operating leverage
	Fixed costs	Unit variable costs		
Capital-intensive	High	Low	High	High
Labor-intensive	Low	High	Low	Low

Degree of operating leverage (DOL) is the change in operating income resulting from a percentage change in sales.

영업 레버리지의 크기는 영업 레버리지도(DOL:degree of operating leverage)로 측정할 수 있다. 영업레버리지도는 매출액의 변화율에 대한 영업이익의 변화율 정도를 측정한 지표로 다음과 같이 계산한다.

$$\text{DOL} = \text{영업이익 변화율} \div \text{매출액 변화율} = \frac{CM}{OI}$$

영업 레버리지도(DOL)이 5인 경우 매출액이 1% 증가한다면 영업이익은 5%증가하고, 매출액이 1% 감소한다면 영업이익은 5% 감소한다. 따라서 영업 레버리지도가 클수록 매출에 대한 영업이익의 민감도가 큰 것이다.

Example-7

Parker Company manufactures and sells pens. Currently, 40,000 units are sold per year at $15 per unit. Fixed costs are $150,000 per year. Variable costs are $9 per unit.

(1) Calculate the degree of operating leverage at sales of 40,000 units
(2) Calculate the degree of operating leverage at sales of 26,000 units

(1) Degree of operating leverage

Contribution margin = 40,000 × $6 = $240,000

Operating income = $240,000 − $150,000 = $90,000

DOL = 240,000 / 90,000 = 2.67

(2) Degree of operating leverage

Contribution margin = 26,000 × $6 = $156,000

Operating income = $156,000 − $150,000 = $6,000

DOL = 156,000 / 6,000 = 26

4 Sensitivity analysis

Sensitivity analysis is a "what-if" technique managers use to examine how an outcome will change if the original predicted data are not achieved or if an underlying assumption changes.

민감도 분석(Sensitivity analysis)이란 하나의 독립변수가 변화할 경우에 종속변수가 어떻게 영향을 받는가를 분석하는 기법이다. 민감도 분석을 이용한 CVP분석이란 아래의 독립 변수들의 변화에 대한 손익분기점의 변화나 손익에 미치는 효과를 분석하는 것이다.

① Sales units

② Sales price

③ Sales mix

④ Unit variable cost

⑤ Total Fixed cost

민감도 분석은 다른 독립변수를 상수로 고정시킨 상태에서 특정 독립변수가 종속변수에 미치는 영향을 분석하기 때문에 독립변수들 간의 상호작용을 무시하며, 확률을 고려하지 않는다는 문제점이 있다.

04 MCQ (Multiple Choice Questions)

01. Associated Supply, Inc. is considering introducing a new product that will require a $250,000 investment of capital. The necessary funds would be raised through a bank loan at an interest rate of 8%. The fixed operating costs associated with the product would be $122,500 while the contribution margin percentage would be 42%. Assuming a selling price of $15 per unit, determine the number of units (rounded to the nearest whole unit), Associated would have to sell to generate earnings before interest and taxes (EBIT) of 32% of the amount of capital invested in the new product. (CMA)

    a. 35,318 units.   b. 32,143 units.

    c. 25,575 units.   d. 23,276 units.

02. Specialty Cakes Inc. produces two types of cakes, a round cake and a heart-shaped cake. Total fixed costs for the firm are $92,000. Variable costs and sales data for these cakes are presented below.

	Round Cake	Heart-shape Cake
Selling price per unit	$12	$20
Variable cost per unit	$8	$15
Budgeted sales (units)	10,000	15,000

How many cakes will be required to reach the breakeven point? (CMA)

    a. 8,000 round cakes and 12,000 heart-shaped cakes.

    b. 9,000 round cakes and 11,000 heart-shaped cakes.

    c. 10,000 round cakes and 10,000 heart-shaped cakes.

    d. 23,000 round cakes and 18,400 heart-shaped cakes.

03. Romashka, Inc. plans on introducing a new product. The marketing manager forecasts a unit selling price of $500. The variable cost per unit is estimated to be $100 per unit. In addition, there is a total of $110,000 fixed indirect manufacturing cost and $150,000 in fixed operating costs associated with these units. What quantity will the company have to sell to break even? (CMA)

a. 220 units.   b. 275 units.

c. 520 units.   d. 650 units.

Questions 4 through 8 are based on the following information.

The following data are KIMCPA's unit costs of a product.

Selling price	$60.00
Manufacturing costs	
Direct materials	$20
Direct labor	15
Variable overhead	5
Selling & Administration costs	
Variable	$5

The company's annual fixed costs are $900,000 and it has a 40% tax rate.

---

04. What is KIMCPA's annual break-even point in units?

a. 50,000 units   b. 60,000 units

c. 61,667 units   d. 70,000 units

05. If KIMCPA sold 6,000 units of product per month, what amount would an annual after-tax income for KIMCPA be?

a. $72,000   b. $108,000

c. $120,000   d. $180,000

06. What total dollar amount must KIMCPA sell to achieve after-tax operating income of $150,000 for the year?

    a. $3,600,000   b. $4,200,000

    c. $4,600,000   d. $4,800,000

07. If variable conversion costs increased by 25% and all other variables remained the same, what would KIMCPA's contribution margin per unit be?

    a. $5   b. $10

    c. $15   d. $20

08. How many products must KIMCPA sell to earn an annual margin of safety of $100,000?

    a. 50,000 units   b. 60,000 units

    c. 61,667 units   d. 70,000 units

09. In calculating the breakeven point for a multi-product company, which of the following assumptions are commonly made when absorption costing is used?

    Ⅰ. Sales volume equals production volume.

    Ⅱ. Variable costs are constant per unit.

    Ⅲ. A given sales mix is maintained for all volume changes.

    a. Ⅰ and Ⅱ   b. Ⅰ and Ⅲ

    c. Ⅱ and Ⅲ   d. Ⅰ, Ⅱ and Ⅲ

10. In calculating the breakeven point for a multi-product company, which of the following assumptions are commonly made when variable costing is used?

Ⅰ. Sales volume equals production volume.

Ⅱ. Variable costs are constant per unit.

Ⅲ. A given sales mix is maintained for all volume changes.

a. Ⅰ and Ⅱ

b. Ⅰ and Ⅲ

c. Ⅱ and Ⅲ

d. Ⅰ, Ⅱ and Ⅲ

11. The breakeven point in units increases when unit costs

a. increase and sales price remains unchanged.

b. decrease and sales price remains unchanged.

c. remain unchanged and sales price increases.

d. decrease and sales price increases.

· 정답 및 해설

1. TIPQ = (250,000 × 0.32 + 122,500) ÷ (0.42 × $15) = 32,143 units

   정답 : b

2. WACM = ($4 × 10,000 ÷ 25,000) + ($5 × 15,000 ÷ 25,000) = $4.60
   BEPQ = $92,000 ÷ $4.60 = 20,000 units
   Round cake = 20,000 × 0.40 = 8,000 units

   정답 : a

3. BEPQ = ($100,000 + $150,000) ÷ ($500 − $100) = 650 units

   정답 : d

4. BEPQ = $900,000 ÷ ($60 − $45) = 60,000 units

   정답 : b

5. NI = (6,000 × 12 × $15 − $900,000) × (1−0.4) = $108,000

   정답 : b

6. TIP$ = ($900,000 + $150,000 ÷ 0.60) ÷ ($15 ÷ $60) = $4,600,000

   정답 : c

7. Variable conversion cost = DL + VOH = 15 + 5 = 20
   20 × 25% = 5가 증가하며 UCM = 15 − 5 = $10

   정답 : b

8. TIPQ = BEPQ + $100,000 ÷ $60 = 61,667 units

   정답 : c

9. 전부원가계산에서는 판매량과 생산량이 일정하다는 가정은 필요하다.　　정답 : d

10. 변동원가계산에서는 판매량과 생산량이 일정하다는 가정은 필요없다.　　정답 : c

11. increase in unit cost ⇨ decrease in UCM ⇨ increase in BEPQ
    increase in price ⇨ increase in UCM ⇨ decrease in BEPQ

    정답 : a

05 / TBS (Task-Based Simulation)

Problem-1

Skechers Company, a manufacturer of famous shoes, had a steady growth in sales for the past 5 years. However, increased competition has led KIM, the president, to believe that an aggressive marketing campaign will be necessary next year to maintain the company' present growth. To prepare for next year' marketing campaign, the company' controller has prepared and presented KIM with the following data for the current year, 20X1:

⟨Variable cost (per unit)⟩

Direct materials	$ 3.00
Direct manufacturing labor	8.00
Variable overhead (manufacturing, marketing, distribution, and customer service)	7.50
Total variable cost per unit	$ 18.50

⟨Fixed costs⟩

Manufacturing	$ 20,000
Marketing, distribution, and customer service	194,500
Total fixed costs	$214,500

Selling price	$ 35.00
Expected sales, 22,000 units	$770,000
Income tax rate	40%

• Instruction •

1. What is the projected net income for 20X1?

2. What is the break even point in units for 20X1?

3. KIM has set the revenue target for 20X2 at a level of $875,000 (or 25,000 bowls). He believes an additional marketing cost of $16,500 for advertising in 20X2, with all other costs remaining constant, will be necessary to attain the revenue target. What is the net income for 20X2 if the additional $16,500 is spent and the revenue target is met?

4. What is the break even point in revenues for 20X2 if the additional $16,500 is spent for advertising?

5. If the additional $16,500 is spent, what are the required 20X2 revenues for 20X2 net income to equal 20X1 net income?

6. At a sales level of 25,000 units, what maximum amount can be spent on advertising if a 20X2 net income of $108,450 is desired?

Problem-2

LEVI'S Co. sells blue jeans wholesale to major retailers across the country. Each pair of jeans has a selling price of $30 with $21 in variable costs of goods sold. The company has fixed manufacturing costs of $1,200,000 and fixed marketing costs of $300,000. Sales commissions are paid to the wholesale sales reps at 5% of revenues. The company has an income tax rate of 25%.

• Instruction •

1. How many jeans must LEVI'S Co. sell in order to break even?

2. How many jeans must the company sell in order to reach:
   (1) a target operating income of $450,000?
   (2) a net income of $450,000?

3. How many jeans would LEVI'S Co. have to sell to earn the net income of $450,000 if (consider each requirement independently).
   (1) The contribution margin per unit increases by 10%
   (2) The selling price is increased to $32.50
   (3) The company outsources manufacturing to an overseas company increasing variable costs per unit by $2.00 and saving 60% of fixed manufacturing costs.

Problem-3

Starbucks Company has three product lines of mugs– -A, B, and C– -with contribution margins of $5, $4, and $3, respectively. The president foresees sales of 168,000 units in the coming period, consisting of 24,000 units of A, 96,000 units of B, and 48,000 units of C. The company's fixed costs for the period are $405,000.

• Instruction •

1. What is the company's breakeven point in units, assuming that the given sales mix is maintained?

2. If the sales mix is maintained, what is the total contribution margin when 168,000 units are sold? What is the operating income?

3. What would operating income be if the company sold 24,000 units of A, 48,000 units of B, and 96,000 units of C? What is the new breakeven point in units if these relationships persist in the next period?

4. Comparing the breakeven points in requirements 1 and 3, is it always better for a company to choose the sales mix that yields the lower breakeven point?

TurboTax has total budgeted revenues for 20X1 of $618,000, based on an average price of $206 per tax return prepared. The company would like to achieve a margin of safety percentage of at least 45%. The company's current fixed costs are $327,600, and variable costs average $24 per customer.

· Instruction ·

Consider each of the following separately.

1. Calculate TurboTax's breakeven point and margin of safety in units.

2. Which of the following changes would help TurboTax achieve its desired margin of safety?
   (1) Average revenue per customer increases to $224.
   (2) Planned number of tax returns prepared increases by 15%
   (3) TurboTax purchases new tax software that results in a 5% increase to fixed costs but e-files all tax returns, which reduces mailing costs an average $2 per customer.

Problem-5

Sunglass Hut operates a kiosk at the local mall, selling sunglasses for $20 each. Sunglass Hut currently pays $800 a month to rent the space and pays two full-time employees to each work 160 hours a month at $10 per hour. The store shares a manager with a neighboring mall and pays 50% of the manager's annual salary of $40,000 and benefits equal to 20% of salary. The wholesale cost of the sunglasses to the company is $5 a pair.

• Instruction •

1. How many sunglasses does Sunglass Hut need to sell each month to break even?

2. If Sunglass Hut wants to earn an operating income of $4,500 per month, how many sunglasses does the store need to sell?

3. If the store's hourly employees agreed to a 15% sales−commission−only pay structure, instead of their hourly pay, how many sunglasses would Sunglass Hut need to sell to earn an operating income of $4,500?

4. Assume Sunglass Hut pays its employees hourly under the original pay structure, but is able to pay the mall 8% of its monthly revenue instead of monthly rent. At what sales levels would Sunglass Hut prefer to pay a fixed amount of monthly rent, and at what sales levels would it prefer to pay 8% of its monthly revenue as rent?

Problem-6

Mohawk Industries is holding a 2-week carpet sale at a local warehouse store. Mohawk Industries plans to sell carpets for $1,000 each. The company will purchase the carpets from a local distributor for $400 each, with the privilege of returning any unsold units for a full refund. The local warehouse store has offered Carmel Rugs two payment alternatives for the use of space.

- Option 1: A fixed payment of $17,400 for the sale period
- Option 2: 20% of total revenues earned during the sale period

Assume Mohawk Industries will incur no other costs.

• Instruction •

1. Calculate the breakeven point in units for (a) option 1 and (b) option 2.

2. At what level of revenues will Mohawk Industries earn the same operating income under either option?
   a. For what range of unit sales will Mohawk Industries prefer option 1?
   b. For what range of unit sales will Mohawk Industries prefer option 2?

3. Calculate the degree of operating leverage at sales of 87 units for the two rental options.

Problem-7

㈜한지는 제품 A와 제품 B를 생산·판매한다. ㈜한지는 변동원가계산방법을 사용하며 당기 예상판매 및 예상원가 자료는 다음과 같다.

매출배합이 일정하다고 가정하고 손익분기점을 달성하기 위한 제품A의 판매수량은 각각 얼마인가? (K-CPA)

구분	제품 A	제품 B	합 계
판매수량	300개	700개	1,000개
총매출액	₩ 30,000	₩ 42,000	₩ 72,000
총변동원가	₩ 15,000	₩ 21,000	₩ 36,000
총고정원가			₩ 21,600

Problem-8

㈜경진은 한 가지 제품만을 생산하며 매월 생산한 제품은 당해 월에 모두 판매한다. ㈜경진의 법인세율은 40%의 단일세율이며, 20X1년도 1월과 2월의 원가자료는 다음과 같다.

㈜경진의 20X1년 1월과 2월의 당기순이익이 각각 ₩60,000과 ₩72,000이라면, 1월과 2월의 제품 매출액의 차이는 얼마인가? (K-CPA)

구분	1월	2월
제품 단위당 판매가격	₩ 500	₩ 450
제품 단위당 변동비	300	270
총 고정비	500,000	600,000

100실 규모의 호텔을 운영하는 영산호텔의 연간 고정비용은 ₩120,000,000이고, 객실의 1일 임대료는 ₩50,000, 임대객실 1실 당 평균변동비용은 ₩10,000이다. 1년 365일 무휴인 영산호텔이 손익분기에 도달하기 위한 객실임대율(점유율)은 얼마인가? 단, 객실임대는 1일 단위로 한다. (K-CPA)

(주)남천은 위성라디오를 제조하는 회사이다. 울산에 있는 공장의 연간 생산능력은 50,000단위이다. 최근에 (주)남천은 판매가격 ₩21,000에 40,000단위를 판매하고 있다. 이 제품의 원가구조는 다음과 같다.

단위당 변동제조원가	₩9,000
고정제조원가	₩160,000,000
단위당 변동마케팅원가	₩2,000
고정마케팅원가	₩120,000,000

제조부서에서는 새로운 사양을 추가하기 위해서 제조공정을 변화시킬 것을 제안했다. 제조공정의 변화는 고정제조원가를 ₩20,000,000 증가시키고 단위당 변동제조원가를 ₩400 증가시키게 된다. 현재 판매량인 40,000단위를 기준으로 할 때, (주)남천이 제조공정의 변화 후에도 최소한 기존의 영업이익을 유지하기 위해서는 단위당 판매가격을 얼마로 해야 하는가? (K-CPA)

PART **II**

Planning & Analysis

Chapter

09

Variable and Absorption Costing

Variable and Absorption Costing

01   Variable and absorption costing

1   Variable and absorption costing

제품원가계산은 제품원가를 구성하는 구성요소에 따라 전부원가계산(absorption costing :AC)과 변동원가계산(variable costing :VC)으로 구분할 수 있다.

(1) Variable costing

Variable costing is a method of inventory costing in which all variable manufacturing costs (direct and indirect) are included as inventoriable costs. All fixed manufacturing costs are excluded from inventoriable costs and are instead treated as costs of the period in which they are incurred.

변동원가계산(VC)은 변동제조원가(DM + DL + VOH)만을 제품원가에 포함시키고, 고정제조간접원가(FOH)는 기간비용으로 처리하는 방법으로 'direct costing'이라고도 한다. 따라서 변동원가계산(VC)에서는 고정제조간접원가(FOH)가 판매비 및 관리비와 더불어 기간비용으로 처리된다. 이 방법은 주로 의사결정 및 성과평가 등 내부관리목적으로 이용된다.

(2) Absorption costing

Absorption costing is a method of inventory costing in which all variable manufacturing costs and all fixed manufacturing costs are included as inventoriable costs. That is, inventory "absorbs"all manufacturing costs.

전부원가계산 또는 흡수원가계산(AC)은 모든 제조원가(DM + DL + VOH + FOH)를 제품원가에 포함시키는 방법으로, 'full costing'이라고도 하며, 회계기준(GAAP)에서 인정하는 원가계산방식으로, 외부보고용 재무제표를 작성 할 내에는 이 방법에 따라야 한다.

(3) Comparing variable costing and absorption costing

변동원가계산과 전부원가계산의 차이를 요약하면 다음과 같다.

	Variable costing	Absorption costing
Purpose	Internal reporting	External reporting
Product cost	DM + DL + VOH	DM + DL + VOH + FOH
Period cost	FOH Selling & Administration	Selling & Administration
Advantages	Relevant for decision making	GAAP & IRS에서 인정한다.
Disadvantages	GAAP & IRS에서 인정하지 않는다.	Not relevant for decision making

(4) Job order costing and process costing

변동원가계산(VC)과 전부원가계산(AC)은 고정제조간접원가(FOH)를 기간비용처리하거나 제품원가에 포함시키는 제품원가 구성요소의 차이이므로 개별원가계산(job order costing) 및 종합원가계산(process costing)에서 모두 적용이 가능하다

2 Income statement

변동원가계산(VC)과 전부원가계산(AC)은 고정제조간접원가(FOH)에 대한 회계처리가 다르기 때문에 손익계산서의 양식도 차이가 있다. 두 방법의 손익계산서를 비교하면 다음과 같다.

Absorption costing		Variable costing	
Sales	xxx	Sales	xxx
CGS	(xxx)	Variable manufacturing costs	(xxx)
Gross Profit	xxx	**Manufacturing contribution margin**	xxx
S&A expense	(xxx)	Variable S&A	(xxx)
Operating Income	xxx	**Contribution Margin**	xxx
		Fixed manufacturing overhead	(xxx)
		Fixed S&A	(xxx)
		Operating Income	xxx

전부원가계산(AC)에 의한 손익계산서는 전통적인 손익계산서(conventional income statement)라고도 하는데 비용을 매출원가, 판매비와 관리비와 같이 그 기능(function)에 따라 분류한다. 이 손익계산서는 판매량의 변동이 비용에 미치는 영향을 쉽게 파악할 수 없기 때문에 계획 및 의사결정 등에 이용하기가 어렵다.

변동원가계산(VC)에 의한 손익계산서는 비용을 원가행태(cost behavior)에 따라 분류하므로 비용을 변동원가와 고정원가로 구분하여 표시하게 되며, 공헌이익(contribution margin)이 표시되므로 공헌이익 손익계산서(contribution income statement)라고도 한다. 이 손익계산서는 판매량의 변동이 비용에 미치는 영향을 쉽게 파악할 수 있기 때문에 계획 및 의사결정 등에 유용하다.

3 Throughput costing

Throughput costing, which is also called super-variable costing, is an extreme form of variable costing in which only direct material costs are included as inventoriable costs. All other costs are costs of the period in which they are incurred.

초변동원가계산(throughput costing or super-variable costing)은 직접재료원가(DM)만을 제품원가에 포함시키고, 나머지 원가는 모두 기간비용으로 처리하는 방법이다.

02 **Operating income**

1 **Income statement for one year**

The basis of the difference between variable costing and absorption costing is how fixed manufacturing costs are accounted for. If inventory levels change, operating income will differ between the two methods because of the difference in accounting for fixed manufacturing costs.

변동원가계산(VC)은 고정제조간접원가(FOH)를 기간비용으로 처리하기 때문에 발생시점에서 손익계산서에 비용으로 보고되며, CVP분석에서 계산된 영업이익은 변동원가계산(VC)의 영업이익이다. 전부원가계산(AC)은 고정제조간접원가(FOH)를 제품원가에 포함시키기 때문에 제품이 판매된 시점에서 손익계산서에 비용으로 보고된다.

따라서 생산수량과 판매수량이 다르면 두 방법의 영업이익도 달라진다. 재고자산의 수량이 증가하는 경우(생산량 〉 판매량), 전부원가계산에서는 고정제조간접원가(FOH)의 일부가 기말재고에 포함되어 다음 기간으로 비용처리가 이연된다. 그러나 변동원가계산에서는 고정제조간접원가(FOH)는 모두 비용으로 인식된다. 따라서 재고자산의 수량이 증가하면 전부원가계산의 영업이익이 변동원가계산의 영업이익보다 더 크다. 이를 요약하면 다음과 같다.

Quantity	Operating income
sales = production (no changes in inventory)	VC = AC
sales < production (Increases in inventory)	VC < AC
sales > production (Decreases in inventory)	VC > AC

VC : variable costing, AC :absorption costing

if sales < production (Increases in inventory)

OI under AC = OI under VC + ending inventory units x FOH per unit

or

OI under AC = OI under VC + FOH per unit x (production units − sales units)

Example-1

Tesla Motors assembles and sells motor vehicles.

Actual data relating to 20X1 are as follows:

⟨Units data⟩

- Production : 10,000 units
- Sales : 8,000 units
- Sales price per unit : $60

⟨Variable costs⟩

- Manufacturing cost per unit : $35
- Selling and administrative cost per unit : $6

⟨Fixed costs per month⟩

- Manufacturing costs : $100,000
- Selling and administrative costs: $30,000

Prepare income statements for 20X1under variable costing and absorption costing.

(1) Variable costing

Sales revenue = 8,000 × 60 = $480,000

UVC = 35 + 6 = $41 ⇨ VC = 8,000 × 41 = $328,000

CM = 480,000 − 328,000 = $152,000

FC = 100,000 + 30,000 = $130,000

OI = 152,000 − 130,000 = $22,000

(2) Absorption costing

Sales revenue = 8,000 × 60 = $480,000

FOH per unit = 100,000 ÷ 10,000 = $10

CGS per unit = 35 + 10 = $45 ⇨ CGS = 8,000 × 45 = $360,000

GM(gross margin) = 480,000 − 360,000 = $120,000

S&A expense = 8,000 × 6 + 30,000 = $78,000

OI = 120,000 − 78,000 = $42,000

(3) Income difference

    1) OI under VC $= 8,000 \times (60 - 41) - 130,000 = \$22,000$

    2) OI under AC $= 22,000 + 2,000 \text{ units} \times \$10 = \$42,000$ or

       OI under AC $= 22,000 + \$100,000 \times 2,000 \text{ units} \div 10,000 \text{ units} = \$42,000$

• Income statement of 20X1

Absorption Costing		Variable Costing	
Sales	$480,000	Sales	$480,000
Cost of goods sold	(360,000)	Variable costs	(328,000)
Gross Profit	$120,000	Contribution Margin	$152,000
S&A expense	(78,000)	Fixed costs	(130,000)
Operating Income	$42,000	Operating Income	$22,000

• Balance sheet of 20X1

기말재고자산의 금액은 다음과 같다.

AC의 기말재고자산 $= 2,000 \text{ units} \times \$45 = \$90,000$

VC의 기말재고자산 $= 2,000 \text{ units} \times \$35 = \$70,000$

2 Income statement for multi-years

기초재고자산과 기말재고자산이 있는 경우 전부원가계산(AC)의 영업이익과 변동원가계산(VC) 의 영업이익 차이 조정은 다음과 같다.

$$\text{OI under AC} = \text{OI under VC} + \text{ending inventory units} \times \text{FOH per unit}$$
$$- \text{beginning inventory units} \times \text{FOH per unit}$$

기초재고와 기말재고의 단위당 고정제조간접원가(FOH per unit)가 동일한 경우 두 방법의 영업 이익 차이 조정은 다음의 식을 사용할 수도 있다.

$$\text{OI under AC} = \text{OI under VC} + \text{FOH per unit} \times (\text{production units} - \text{sales units})$$

> **Example-2**

The following questions refer to Example-1.
Actual data relating to 20X2 are as follows:

⟨**Units data**⟩

- Production : 10,000 units
- Sales : 11,000 units
- Sales price per unit : $60

⟨**Variable costs**⟩

- Manufacturing cost per unit : $35
- Selling and administrative cost per unit : $6

⟨**Fixed costs per month**⟩

- Manufacturing costs : $100,000
- Selling and administrative costs: $30,000

Prepare income statements for 20X2under variable costing and absorption costing.

(1) Variable costing

Sales revenue = $11,000 \times 60 = \$660,000$

UVC = $35 + 6 = \$41 \Rightarrow VC = 11,000 \times 41 = \$451,000$

CM = $660,000 - 451,000 = \$209,000$

FC = $100,000 + 30,000 = \$130,000$

OI = $209,000 - 130,000 = \$79,000$

(2) Absorption costing

Sales revenue = $11,000 \times 60 = \$660,000$

FOH per unit = $100,000 \div 10,000 = \$10$

CGS per unit = $35 + 10 = \$45 \Rightarrow CGS = 11,000 \times 45 = \$495,000$

GM(gross margin) = $660,000 - 495,000 = \$165,000$

S&A expense = $11,000 \times 6 + 30,000 = \$96,000$

OI = $165,000 - 96,000 = \$69,000$

(3) Income difference

    1) OI under VC = $11,000 \times (60 - 41) - 130,000 = \$79,000$

    2) OI under AC = $79,000 + 1,000 \text{ units} \times \$10 - 2,000 \text{ units} \times \$10 = \$69,000$ or

       OI under AC = $79,000 + \$10 \times (10,000 \text{ units} - 11,000 \text{ units}) = \$69,000$

- **Income statement of 20X2**

Absorption Costing		Variable Costing	
Sales	$660,000	Sales	$660,000
Cost of goods sold	(495,000)	Variable costs	(451,000)
Gross Profit	$165,000	Contribution Margin	$209,000
S&A expense	(96,000)	Fixed costs	(130,000)
Operating Income	$69,000	Operating Income	$79,000

- **Balance sheet of 20X1**

기말재고자산의 금액은 다음과 같다.

AC의 기말재고자산 = 1,000 units × $45 = $45,000

VC의 기말재고자산 = 1,000 units × $35 = $35,000

※ 기말재고금액의 크기 : 전부원가계산(AC) > 변동원가계산(VC)

3 Normal costing

실제원가계산(actual costing)이 아닌 정상원가계산(normal costing)을 하는 경우 전부원가계산 (AC)에서는 고정제조간접원가(FOH)를 제품원가로 계산하기 위하여 예정배부율에 의한 배부액 으로 제품원가를 계산하며, 배부금액과 실제발생액이 차이가 발생하는 고정제조간접원가(FOH) 의 배부차이가 발생한다. 이러한 고정제조간접원가(FOH)의 배부차이를 "조업도 차이(production-volume variance)"라고 한다.

$$\text{Production- volume variance} = \text{Budgeted FOH} - \text{FOH allocated}$$

변동원가계산(VC)에서는 고정제조간접원가(FOH)를 기간비용으로 인식하므로 배부차이가 발 생하지 않는다. 따라서 정상원가계산(normal costing)을 하는 경우 두 방법의 영업이익 차이 조정 에 조업도 차이(production - volume variance)를 고려하여야 한다.

4 Break-even analysis

변동원가계산(VC)의 손익분기점(BEP)은 CVP분석의 손익분기점이다. 전부원가계산(AC)의 손 익분기점(BEP)은 CVP분석의 손익분기점을 다음과 같이 수정하여야 한다.

$$\text{BEPQ} = \{\text{FC} + \text{FOH per unit} \times (\text{BEPQ} - \text{Units produced})\} \div \text{UCM}$$

03   MCQ (Multiple Choice Questions)

Questions 1 and 2 are based on the following information.

Consider the following situation for AIFA Corporation for the prior year.

- The company produced 1,000 units and sold 900 units, both as budgeted.
- There were no beginning or ending work-in-process inventories and no beginning finished goods inventory.
- Budgeted and actual fixed costs were equal, all variable manufacturing costs are affected by volume of production only, and all variable selling costs are affected by sales volume only.
- Budgeted per unit revenues and costs were as follows.

	Per Unit
Sales price	$100
Direct materials	30
Direct labor	20
Variable manufacturing costs	10
Fixed manufacturing costs	5
Variable selling costs	12
Fixed selling costs	4
Fixed administrative costs	2

01. The operating income for AIFA for the prior year using absorption costing was (CMA)

    a. $13,600   b. $14,200

    c. $15,300   d. $15,840

02. Assuming that AIFA uses variable costing, the operating income for the prior year was (CMA)

a. $13,600   b. $14,200

c. $14,800   d. $15,300

03. Which one of the following is an advantage of using variable costing? (CMA)

a. Variable costing complies with the U.S. Internal Revenue Code.

b. Variable costing complies with generally accepted accounting principles.

c. Variable costing makes cost-volume relationships more easily apparent.

d. Variable costing is most relevant to long-run pricing strategies.

04. Which one of the following is the best reason for using variable costing? (CMA)

a. Fixed factory overhead is more closely related to the capacity to produce than to the production of specific units.

b. All costs are variable in the long term.

c. Variable costing is acceptable for income tax reporting purposes.

d. Variable costing usually results in higher operating income than if a company uses absorption costing.

05. Dawn Company has significant fixed overhead costs in the manufacturing of its sole product, auto mufflers. For internal reporting purposes, in which one of the following situations would ending finished goods inventory be higher under direct (variable) costing rather than under absorption costing? (CMA)

a. If more units were produced than were sold during a given year.

b. If more units were sold than were produced during a given year.

c. In all cases when ending finished goods inventory exists.

d. None of these situations.

1. Total fixed cost = ($5 × 1000units) + ($6 × 900 units) = $10,400

   UVC = 30 + 20 + 10 + 12 = 72

   UCM = 100 − 72 = 28

   Operating income (VC) = 900 × 28 − 10,400 = $14,800

   Operating income (AC) = 14,800 + $5,000 × 10% = $15,300

   정답 : c

2. 1번의 풀이를 참조

   정답 : c

3. 변동원가계산은 단기적 의사결정에 매우 유용하다.

   정답 : c

4. FOH는 수요량이 아닌 공급량 기준으로 재고자산 원가에 배분

   정답 : a

5. 재고자산은 항상 전부원가가 변동원가 보다 크다.

   정답 : d

04 TBS (Task-Based Simulation)

Problem-1

LG Corporation manufactures and sells 50-inch television sets and uses standard costing. Actual data relating to January, February, and March 20X1 are as follows:

⟨Units data⟩

	January	February	March
Beginning inventory	0	100	100
Production	1,400	1,400	1,400
Sales	1,300	1,400	1,425

⟨Variable costs⟩

Manufacturing cost per unit : $950

Selling and administrative cost per unit : $725

⟨Fixed costs per month⟩

Manufacturing costs : $490,000

Selling and administrative costs: $120,000

The selling price per unit is $3,500. The budgeted level of production used to calculate the budgeted fixed manufacturing cost per unit is 1,400 units. Any production- volume variance is written off to cost of goods sold in the month in which it occurs.

• Instruction •

1. Prepare income statements for LG Corporation in January, February, and March 20X1 under (a) variable costing and (b) absorption costing.

2. Prepare a numerical reconciliation of the difference between operating income for each month under variable costing and absorption costing.

Problem-2

LG Corporation manufactures and sells 50-inch television sets and uses standard costing. Actual data relating to January, February, and March 20X1 are as follows:

<Units data>

	January	February	March
Beginning inventory	0	100	100
Production	1,400	1,375	1,430
Sales	1,300	1,375	1,455

⟨Variable costs⟩

Manufacturing cost per unit : $950
Selling and administrative cost per unit : $725

⟨Fixed costs per month⟩

Manufacturing costs : $490,000
Selling and administrative costs: $120,000

The selling price per unit is $3,500. The budgeted level of production used to calculate the budgeted fixed manufacturing cost per unit is 1,400 units. Any production- volume variance is written off to cost of goods sold in the month in which it occurs.

• Instruction •

1. Prepare income statements for LG Corporation in January, February, and March 20X1 under (a) variable costing and (b) absorption costing.

2. Prepare a numerical reconciliation of the difference between operating income for each month under variable costing and absorption costing.

Problem-3

Flow Snowboard manufactures a specialized snowboard made for the advanced snow-boarder. Flow Snowboard began 20X1 with an inventory of 240 snowboards. During the year, it produced 900 boards and sold 995 for $750 each. Fixed production costs were $280,000, and variable production costs were $325 per unit. Fixed advertising, marketing, and other general and administrative expenses were $112,000, and variable shipping costs were $15 per board. Assume that the cost of each unit in beginning inventory is equal to 20X1 inventory cost.

• Instruction •

1. Prepare an income statement assuming Flow Snowboard uses variable costing.

2. Prepare an income statement assuming Flow Snowboard uses absorption costing. Whistler uses a denominator level of 1,000 units. Production—volume variances are written off to cost of goods sold.

3. Prepare a numerical reconciliation of the difference between operating income for 20X1 under variable costing and absorption costing.

Problem-4

20X1년 초에 설립된 ㈜동건은 제품원가계산 목적으로 전부원가계산을, 성과평가목적으로는 변동원가계산을 사용한다. 20X2년도 기초제품 수량은 2,000단위이고 기말제품 수량은 1,400단위이었으며, 제품 단위당 원가는 20X1년도에 ₩10(이 중 50%는 변동비)이고 20X2년도에 ₩12(이 중 40%는 변동비)이었다. 20X2년도 전부원가계산에 의한 영업이익은 변동원가계산에 의한 영업이익과 비교하여 어떠한 차이가 있는가? 단, 회사의 원가흐름가정은 선입선출법(FIFO)이다. (K-CPA)

Problem-5

다음은 ㈜동양금속의 제조원가와 생산 및 판매량에 관한 자료이다.

〈제조간접원가〉
- 단위당 변동원가 : ₩1,000
- 고정원가   : ₩3,000,000

〈생산 및 판매량〉
- 기초제품재고량 : 2,000개
- 생산량   : 18,000개
- 판매량   : 19,000개

고정제조간접원가 배부율을 계산하기 위한 기준조업도는 20,000개이라면, 변동원가계산에 의한 순이익이 ₩6,000,000일 때 전부원가계산에 의한 순이익은 얼마인가? 단, 고정제조간접원가 배부율은 기초제품과 당기제품에 동일하게 적용된다. (K-CPA)

Chapter

10

Planning and Budgeting

Planning and Budgeting

01 Strategy and Planning

1 Introduction

기업은 미래의 불확실성에 대처하기 위하여 사전에 계획(planning)을 수립한다. 이때 기업의 계획을 화폐가치로 표현한 것을 예산편성(budgeting)이라고 한다. 예산편성은 기업의 전략(strategy)와 통합하여야 유용하다. 전략, 계획 및 예산편성의 관계를 그림으로 나타내면 다음과 같다.

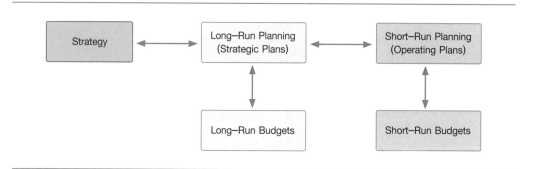

[그림 10-1] Strategy, Planning, and Budgets

2 Strategy

전략이란 경쟁우위 확보를 위한 체계적인 경영활동으로 환경적응능력을 촉진하고 전사적인 관점에서 경영자원을 통합하는 이론이다. 경영전략은 다음과 같은 절차로 이루어진다.

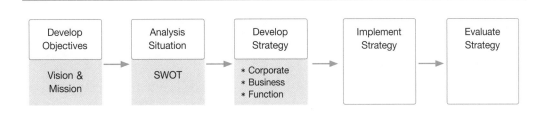

[그림 10-2]

(1) SWOT analysis

SWOT분석은 기업의 내부환경을 분석하여 강점과 약점을 발견하고 외부환경을 분석하여 기회와 위협을 찾아내어 전략적 대안을 개발하는 기법을 말한다.

Internal abilities	Strength	경쟁우위요인
	Weakness	제약요인
External situations	Opportunity	기술개발, 정부지원
	Threat	경쟁자, 정부규제

SWOT분석은 일반적으로 다음과 같은 SWOT Matrix를 이용한다.

	Strength	Weakness
Opportunity	강점을 이용하여 기회를 이용	기회를 이용하여 약점을 보완
Threat	강점을 이용하여 위기를 극복	위기극복을 위하여 약점 보완

(2) Types of strategy

전략은 위계에 따라 다음 3가지 유형으로 구분된다.

1) Corporate level

전사적 수준의 전략이란 여러 개의 사업부를 가지고 있는 기업의 본부에서 수립하는 전략으로 주로 기업이 어떤 사업을 해야 하는지를 결정하는 것을 추구하는 전략이다.

2) Business level

사업부 수준의 전략이란 전략적 사업단위(SBU : strategic business unit)수준의 전략으로 기업의 각 사업 영역에서 어떻게 경쟁해야 하는지 결정하는 전략이다. 이 전략은 주로 제품시장을 놓고 경쟁자와 실제로 경쟁하기 위한 전략을 의미하기 때문에 '경쟁전략(competitive strategy)'이라고 한다.

3) Functional level

기능 수준의 전략이란 사업부 수준의 전략을 지원하는 전략으로 사업부에 속해있는 기능부서들의 전략을 의미한다.

(3) Corporate strategy

전사적 수준의 전략은 수직적 통합, 수평적 통합, 다각화 등으로 구분된다.

1) Vertical integration

수직적 통합은 기업이 전후방의 가치사슬(value chain)중에 어디까지를 내부 활동의 범위로 통합할 것인가를 결정하는 전략으로 전방통합과 후방통합의 두 가지로 구분할 수 있다.

전방통합(forward integration)은 원료를 공급하는 기업이 생산기업을 통합하거나, 제품을 생산하는 기업이 유통채널을 가진 기업을 통합하는 것을 말한다. 후방통합(backward integration)은 유통기업이 생산기업을 통합하거나, 생산기업이 원재료 공급기업을 통합하는 것을 말한다.

2) Horizontal integration

수평적 통합은 경쟁력을 강화하거나 또는 경쟁의 정도를 줄이기 위하여 같은 산업내의 기업을 통합하는 것을 말한다.

3) Diversification

다각화 전략이란 기존의 사업과는 다른 새로운 사업 영역에 진출하여 기업의 성장을 꾀하는 방법이다.

(4) Business strategy

마이클 포터(M. Porter)는 경쟁전략(competitive strategy)으로 원가우위전략, 차별화 전략, 집중화 전략을 제시하였다.

1) Cost leadership strategy

원가우위전략은 경쟁기업보다 더 낮은 원가로 재화 또는 서비스를 생산함으로써 경쟁자들을 능가하는 전략이다. 원가 우위를 확보하기 위해서는 대규모의 자본투자로 생산 공정을 자동화하여 인건비를 절감하거나 규모의 경제를 활용하여 원가를 인하한다.

2) Differentiation strategy

차별화 전략은 비싼 가격에도 불구하고 구입을 유도하는 독특한 요인으로 경쟁우위를 확보하려는 전략이다. 브랜드 파워, 혁신적 기술, 마케팅 능력, 기초연구 능력, 관리 능력 등으로 차별화한다.

3) Focus strategy

집중화 전략은 특정 고객, 특정 제품, 특정 지역 등 한정된 영역에 기업 경영자원을 집중하는 전략이다. 이 전략은 세분화된 고객 중 어느 특정 층을 겨냥하여 비용우위나 차별화를 통해 집중적으로 공략한다.

(5) Five competitive forces

마이클 포터(M. Porter)는 기업의 경쟁적 환경 및 경쟁적 우위를 결정하는 요인을 다음과 같이 5가지로 제시하였다.

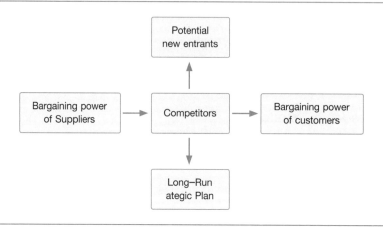

[그림 10-3]

1) Competition in the industry : 산업 내 경쟁기업과의 경쟁강도

2) Potential of new entrants into the industry : 신규 진입자의 위협

3) Power of suppliers : 공급자와의 교섭력

4) Power of customers : 구매자와의 교섭력

5) Threat of substitute products : 대체제의 위협

3 Planning

(1) Planning and control

계획(planning)은 기업이 미래의 불확실성에 효율적으로 대처하기 위하여 사전에 수립한 것을 말하며, 예산(budget)은 계획의 한 도구이다. 계획(planning)은 영향을 미치는 범위에 따라서 전략적 계획과 운영적 계획으로 구분한다.

통제(control)는 기업이 수립한 계획(planning)을 각 부문이나 관리자가 제대로 수행하고 있는지를 평가하고, 중대한 차이가 발생하였을 경우 적절한 조치가 취해지도록 하는 것을 말한다.

Planning과 Control의 차이를 요약하면 다음 그림과 같다.

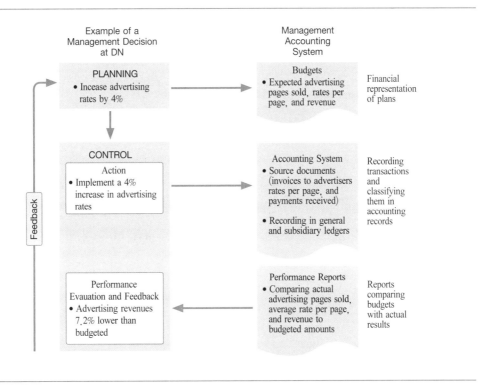

[그림 10-4]

(2) Strategic planning

전략적 계획은 기업의 목표를 효과적으로 달성하기 위하여, 비교적 장기간에 걸쳐 수립되는 전체적인 계획으로 다음과 같은 특징이 있다.

- 최고경영층의 수준에서 수립되는 계획.
- 조직전반에 영향을 미치는 계획.
- 장기적 계획 (Long-term planning)
- Budgeting : Capital budgeting (자본예산)

(3) Operational planning

운영적 계획은 전략적 계획을 수립한 다음에 이를 시행해 나가는 과정에서 기존의 자원을 최대한으로 활용할 수 있도록 하는 계획으로 다음과 같은 특징이 있다.

- 중간경영층이나 하위경영층 수준에서 수립되는 계획.
- 전략적 계획을 실행하기 위한 구체적, 반복적 활동.
- 단기적 계획 (Short-term planning)
- Budgeting : Master budgeting (종합예산)

(4) MBO (Management By Objectives)

목표관리(MBO)는 현대 경영학을 창시한 피터 드러커(P. Drucker)가 1954년에 제창한 경영관리방식의 하나로, 달성해야 할 일의 목표를 설정하고, 그 목표달성을 위해 노력하여, 목표와도 대비하여 결과의 업적을 평가한다. 이 방법은 종업원의 참여과정을 통하여 상사와 함께 목표를 작성하고 그 성과를 평가함으로써 목표와 책임을 명확화하고, 개인적 특성보다는 성과결과에 초점을 둔다.

02 / Budgets

1 Budgets

(1) Functions of budgets

A budget is the quantitative expression of a proposed plan of action by management for a specified period and an aid to coordinate what needs to be done to implement that plan.

예산(budget)은 미래에 대한 경영계획을 화폐가치로 계량화하여 표현한 것으로, 기업경영의 목표와 계획을 반영하여야 한다. 예산(budget)의 유용성은 다음과 같다.

1) The budget is a planning tool

예산을 수립함으로써 미래에 대한 계획수립이 더 용이해진다.

2) The budget is a control tool

예산과 실제성과를 비교함으로써 조직 구성원의 성과평가를 할 수 있다.

3) The budget is a motivation tool

예산이 확정되면 조직 구성원은 자신에게 주어진 역할이 무엇인지를 알 수 있다.

4) The budget is a communication tool

예산을 편성하는 과정에서 기업 내 모든 부문 사이에 계획이 서로 전달되므로 부문 상호간에 의사소통을 가능하게 한다.

(2) Adverse effect of budgets

예산(budget)은 다음과 같은 부작용이 있다.

1) 각 계층의 경영자들에게 심적 부담을 준다.

2) 기업의 장기적 목표달성에 악영향을 미칠 수 있다.

3) 각 계층의 경영자에게 성과를 조작할 수 있는 유인을 제공한다.

※ Budgetary slack

The practice of underestimating revenues and overestimating expenses to make budgetary targets more easily achievable.

예산슬랙은 달성 가능한 목표치를 의도적으로 낮추는 것이다.

2 Types of budgets

(1) Static budget (Fixed budget)

Static budget is based on only one level of output.

고정예산은 조업도의 변화를 고려하지 않고 하나의 조업도만을 기준으로 편성한 예산으로 성과평가 목적으로 이용하기에는 부적합하다.

(2) Flexible budget

A series of budget that are prepared for a range of activity levels.

변동예산은 관련범위 내에서의 조업도의 변화에 따른 신축적으로 편성되는 예산으로 실제 조업도 수준에 있어서의 예산원가와 실제원가를 비교할 수 있기 때문에 성과평가 목적으로 유용하다.

⇨ 고정예산과 변동예산의 성과평가는 13장에서 자세히 다룰 것이다.

(3) Master budget

종합예산은 기업 전체를 대상으로 하여 보통 1년을 단위로 작성한 예산이다.

(4) Departmental budget

부문예산은 기업 전체의 차원이 아닌 기업 내의 특정 부문에 대한 예산이다.

(5) Capital budget

자본예산은 장기계획에 근거한 기업의 총괄적인 투자에 대한 예산이다.

(6) Rolling budget (Continuous budget)

갱신예산은 일정기간에 일성한 예산을 편성한 후 일부의 기간이 경과함에 따라 지나간 기간에 대한 예산을 탈락시키고 새로운 기간에 대한 예산을 포함하여 항상 일정기간의 예산이 유지되도록 하는 예산이다. 예산기간 말에 조직구성원이 근시안적으로 행동하는 것을 방지할 수 있다.

🔅 4-quarter rolling budget : 3개월이 경과하면 1년 예산수립

(7) Incremental budget

증분예산은 전통적인 예산수립 방법으로 기존예산의 증분을 하여 미래의 예산을 수립하는 것으로 과거의 비능률이 미래의 예산에도 포함되는 문제점이 있다.

(8) Zero-based budget

영기준예산은 과거의 예산에 일정비율을 증가하거나 감소하는 예산이 아닌 예산을 원점에서 새로 수립하는 방법으로 과거의 예산에 편성된 비능률을 배제할 수 있는 장점이 있지만 예산편성에 많은 시간이 비용이 든다.

(9) Kaizen budgeting

Kaizen은 생산 공정을 지속적으로 개선(improvement)해야 한다는 일본식 경영의 대표적인 기업이다. Kaizen budgeting은 이러한 Kaizen의 기본개념을 예산편성에 반영하는 방법이다.

(10) Activity-based budgeting(ABB)

활동기준예산은 활동기준원가(ABC)의 기본개념을 예산편성에 적용하여 활동을 중심으로 예산을 편성하는 방법이다. 특히 간접원가를 활동을 중심으로 재분류하여 활동별로 원가동인을 적용하여 예산편성을 한다.

(11) Life-cycle budgeting

수명주기예산은 연구개발(R&D)에서부터 판매 및 관리활동에 이르는 제품의 가치사슬의 모든 원가에 대하여 예산을 수립하는 방법을 말한다.

3 Budgetary process

(1) Authoritative budgeting

중앙집권적 예산편성이란 하위관리자와 의사소통 없이 최고경영자가 독단적으로 예산을 편성하여 하위관리자에게 통보하는 방식을 말한다. 이 방법은 예산편성과정의 시간을 단축시켜주고 예산슬랙의 가능성을 감소시키는 장점이 있지만 하위 경영자의 동기부여가 어렵고 목표가 과도하게 높을 경우 최고경영자에 대한 불신을 초래하는 단점이 있다.

(2) Participative budgeting

참여적 예산편성이란 모든 계층의 관리자가 예산편성에 적극적으로 참여하고 상호 의사소통을 통하여 예산을 편성하는 방식을 말한다. 이 방법은 조직의 모든 구성원으로 하여금 기업 전체의 목표달성을 위해 협조하고 동기부여가 되는 장점이 있지만 예산편성과정이 복잡하고 의견조율을 하는데 많은 시간이 소요되며, 예산슬랙이 발생할 가능성이 높은 단점이 있다.

03　Master Budget

1　Master budget

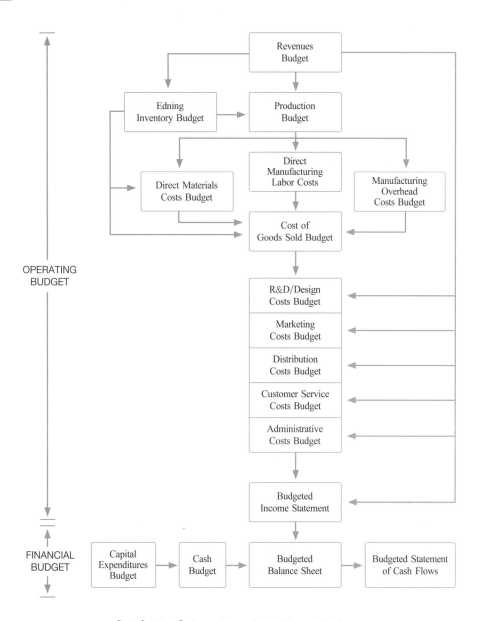

[그림 10-6] Overview of the Master Budget

The master budget expresses management' operating and financial plans for a specified period, usually a fiscal year, and it includes a set of budgeted financial statements.

종합예산(master budget)은 기업의 영업부문과 재무부문을 대상으로 1년 단위로 편성되는 단기예산이다. 종합예산은 회계연도 초에 기업이 달성해야 할 목표를 구체적으로 나타낸 고정예산(fixed budget)으로 'comprehensive budget'이라고도 한다.

종합예산은 영업예산 (operating budget)과 재무예산 (financial budget)으로 구성된다. 단, 재무예산 중 자본예산은 종합예산에서 제외된다.

Operating budget	Financial budget
• Revenue budget • Production budget • DM, DL, MOH costs budget • Ending inventories budget • Cost of goods sold budget • R&D, Selling, Administration budget • Budgeted Income Statement	• Cash budget • Capital budget • Budgeted Balance Sheet • Budgeted Statement of Cash Flow

2 Operating budget

(1) Operating budget

영업예산은 판매, 생산, 구매 등 기업의 주요 영업활동에 대한 예산을 말하며, 판매예산에서 출발하여 예산 손익계산서의 작성으로 마무리 된다. 영업예산은 다음과 같은 단계를 거쳐 편성된다.

① Revenue budget

② Production budget

③ Direct material costs budget

④ Direct labor costs budget

⑤ Manufacturing overhead costs budget

⑥ Ending inventories budget

⑦ Cost of goods sold budget

⑧ R&D, Selling, Administration budgets

⑨ Develop budgeted income statement

(2) Revenue budget

판매예산은 종합예산(master budget)편성의 출발점으로 판매예측을 통하여 판매수량을 예측하고, 매출액을 예측하는 예산으로 다음과 같이 계산한다.

1) Budget sales in units (판매수량) : 판매예측 (sales forecast)

2) Revenue budget = Budget sales in units × Selling price

(3) Production budget (in units)

생산예산은 목표생산량을 결정하는 예산으로 다음과 같이 계산한다.

Budget production in units (목표생산량)

= Budget sales in units + Target ending FG − Beginning FG

⇨ 기말제품재고량(Target ending FG)은 재고정책에 의하여 결정된다. 이때 재고정책은 '다음기 판매량의 일정비율'로 제시된다.

(4) Direct material costs budget

직접재료원가 예산은 목표생산량을 생산할 때 발생할 것으로 예상되는 직접재료원가에 대한 예산으로 다음과 같이 계산한다.

1) DM 투입수량 = Budget production in units × DM per unit

2) DM 투입금액 = DM 투입수량 × cost per unit

3) DM 구입수량 = DM 투입수량 + Target ending RM − Beginning RM

4) DM 구입금액 = DM 구입수량 × cost per unit

▷ 기말원재료 재고정책은 '다음 기 생산에 필요한 수량의 일정비율'로 제시.

(5) Direct labor costs budget

직접노무원가 예산은 목표생산량을 생산할 때 발생할 것으로 예상되는 직접노무원가에 대한 예산으로 다음과 같이 계산한다.

Direct labor costs budget

= Budget production in units × DL hours per unit × Hourly wage rate

(6) Manufacturing overhead costs budget

제조간접비원가 예산은 목표생산량을 생산할 때 발생할 것으로 예상되는 제조간접원가에 대한 예산으로 변동제조간접원가와 고정제조간접원가로 구분하여 편성하는 것이 바람직하다.

- Variable manufacturing overhead costs budget

  = Budget production in units × DL hours per unit × Hourly VOH rate

- Fixed manufacturing overhead costs budget : 목표생산량과 관계없이 일정하게 발생

(7) Ending inventories budget

기말재고예산은 기말재고로 계획된 제품 및 원재료의 금액을 나타내는 예산으로 다음과 같이 계산한다.

1) Unit cost of FG = DM per unit + DL per unit + MOH per unit

2) RM ending inventories budget

   = Target ending RM in units x unit cost of RM

3) FG ending inventories budget

= Target ending FG in units x unit cost of FG

(8) Cost of goods sold budget

매출원가예산은 예산판매량에 대한 원가를 산정하는 방법으로 다음과 같이 계산한다.

CGS budget

= Beginning FG + DM used budget + DL budget + MOH budget − Ending FG budget

(9) R&D, Selling, Administration budgets

비제조원가예산은 예산기간 중 비제조활동에서 발생할 것으로 예상되는 연구개발비, 판매비 및 관리비에 대한 예산이다. 판매량의 변동에 비례하는 변동판매관리비와 판매량과 관계없이 일정하게 발생하는 고정판매관리비로 구분하여 편성하는 것이 바람직하다.

(10) Develop budgeted income statement

예산손익계산서는 영업예산(operating budget)의 마지막 단계로서 판매예산(1단계), 매출원가예산(7단계), 판매비와관리비예산(8단계)을 기초로 작성한다.

Example-1

AIFA Company has prepared a sales budget of 43,000 finished units for a 3-month period. The company has an inventory of 11,000 units of finished goods on hand at December 31 and has a target finished goods inventory of 19,000 units at the end of the succeeding quarter.

It takes 4 gallons of direct materials to make one unit of finished product. The company has an inventory of 66,000 gallons of direct materials at December 31 and has a target ending inventory of 56,000 gallons at the end of the succeeding quarter.

How many gallons of direct materials should AIFA Company purchase during the 3 months ending March 31?

(1) Revenue budget

Budget sales in units = 43,000 units

(2) Production budget

Budget production in units = 43,000 + 19,000 − 11,000 = 51,000 units

(3) Direct material budget

DM usage budget = 51,000 × 4 = 204,000 gallons

DM purchase budget = 204,000 + 56,000 − 66,000 = 194,000 gallons

3　Financial budget

(1) Financial budget

　　재무예산(financial budget)은 영업활동을 수행하기 위하여 필요한 투자 및 재무활동에 대한 예산이다. 재무예산은 현금예산(cash budget)과 자본예산(capital budget)으로 구성되며, 예산 대차대조표 및 예산 현금흐름표의 작성으로 마무리된다.

　　종합예산 중 재무예산은 다음과 같은 단계를 거쳐 편성된다.

① Cash budget

② Develop budgeted balance sheet

③ Develop budgeted statement of cash flows

(2) Cash budget

　　현금예산은 예산기간 중에 영업활동 및 투자/재무활동이 현금유입과 현금유출에 미치는 영향을 예측하는 예산으로 재무예산의 일부이다. 현금예산의 주요 구성항목은 다음과 같다.

---

1) Beginning cash balance

2) Cash receipts

3) Cash available for needs (before any financing) = 1) + 2)

4) Cash disbursements

5) Minimum ending cash balance desired

6) Total cash needed = 4) + 5)

7) Cash excess (deficiency) = 3) − 6)

8) Financing

9) Ending cash balance = 7) + 8)

---

2) Cash receipts

　　현금유입의 구성요소는 다음과 같다.

① Collections of accounts receivable

② Cash sales

③ Miscellaneous recurring sources, such as rental or royalty receipts

4) Cash disbursements

현금유출액의 구성요소는 다음과 같다.

① Direct material purchases

② Direct manufacturing labor and other wage and salary outlays

③ Other costs ⇨ depreciation does not require a cash outlay.

④ Other disbursements ⇨ outlays for PPE and long-term investments.

⑤ Income tax payments

(3) Develop budgeted balance sheet

예산 대차대조표는 예산기간 말의 재무상태를 나타내며, 예산기간 초의 재무상태에 지금까지 편성한 각종 예산들을 반영하여 작성한다.

(4) Develop budgeted statement of cash flows

예산 현금흐름표는 예산기간 중에 현금유입과 현금유출을 영업활동, 투자활동, 재무활동으로 구분하여 작성한다.

(5) Capital budget

자본예산은 장기계획에 근거한 기업의 투자계획이므로 1년 이하를 대상으로 하는 종합예산의 범주 내에는 포함되지 않는다.

Example-2

Health Foods Inc. has decided to start a cash budgeting program to improve overall cash management. Information gathered from the past year reveals the following cash collection trends.

- 40% of sales are on credit
- 50% of credit sales are collected in month of sale
- 30% of credit sales are collected first month after sale
- 15% of credit sales are collected second month after sale
- 5% of credit sales result in bad debts

Gross sales for the last five months were as follows.

January	$220,000
February	240,000
March	250,000
April	230,000
May	260,000

Based on this information, the expected cash receipts for March, April and May would be (CMA)

(1) Cash receipts for March

$(220,000 \times 0.4 \times 0.15) + (240,000 \times 0.4 \times 0.30) + (250,000 \times 0.6) + (250,000 \times 0.4 \times 0.50) = \$242,000$

(2) Cash receipts for April

$(240,000 \times 0.4 \times 0.15) + (250,000 \times 0.4 \times 0.30) + (230,000 \times 0.6) + (230,000 \times 0.4 \times 0.50) = \$228,400$

(3) Cash receipts for May

$(250,000 \times 0.4 \times 0.15) + (230,000 \times 0.4 \times 0.30) + (260,000 \times 0.6) + (260,000 \times 0.4 \times 0.50) = \$250,600$

4 Sales forecasting

판매예측은 생산계획의 수립에 필수적인 기초 자료로서 주로 판매실적과 시장정보에 의존한다. 판매예측방법은 정량적 방법(quantitative technique)과 정성적 방법(qualitative technique)으로 구분된다.

정성적 예측방법(qualitative technique)은 실무자, 전문가 등의 판단에 의존적인 방법이며, 정량적 예측 방법(quantitative technique)은 과거에 대한 정보, 과거의 시계열 자료 등 수치적인 자료를 이용하여 예측하는 방법이다.

Quantitative technique	Qualitative technique
• Time-series analysis • Casual forecasting • Markov technique	• Management judgment • Sales-force polling • Customer surveys • Delphi technique

(1) Management judgment

예측과 관련 있는 상위 경영자의 의견을 모아 예측하는 방법으로 장기계획 및 제품개발에 이용된다.

(2) Sales-force polling

특정 시장에 정통한 판매원이나 거래점의 의견을 종합하여 수요를 예측하는 방법이다.

(3) Customer surveys

소비자의 의견조사 내지 시장조사를 통해 시장 및 수요예측을 하는 방법, 시간과 비용이 많이 들지만 비교적 정확하다.

(4) Delphi technique

예측대상 전문가그룹을 대상으로 여러 차례 질문지를 돌려 그들의 답변을 정리하고, 이 결과를 전문가에게 알려 주는 과정을 반복하여 의견을 수렴하는 방법이다. 시간과 비용이 많이 들지만 예측에 불확실성이 많거나 과거자료가 불충분할 때 사용하는 방법이다.

(5) Time-series analysis

시계열 예측기법은 과거의 수요를 분석하여 시간에 따른 수요의 패턴을 파악하고 이의 연장선상에서 미래의 수요를 예측하는 방법이다. 시계열자료는 일반적으로 장기적 추세(trend), 계절적 변동(seasonality), 순환변동(cycle), 우연변동(random fluctuation)의 4가지 요소의 조합으로 설명될 수 있다고 가정하고 있다. 시계열 예측기법에는 이동평균(moving average)법, 지수평활(exponential smoothing)법, 최소자승법(least square method) 등이 있다.

1) Moving average method

이동평균법은 시계열 예측기법 중 가장 쉽게 적용될 수 있는 방법으로 시계열에서 가장 최근의 일정기간의 자료를 단순 평균하여 예측치를 산정한다. 이동평균법은 시계열 자료에 추세, 순환 변동, 계절적 변동이나 급격한 변화가 없고 우연 변동만 존재하는 경우에 수요 예측에 유용하게 적용될 수 있다

2) Exponential smoothing

지수평활법은 가장 최근 데이터에 가장 큰 가중치가 주어지고 시간이 지남에 따라 가중치가 기하학적으로 감소되는 가중치 이동 평균 예측 기법으로, 최소의 자료로 단기예측활동에 유용하게 활용할 수 있는 예측기법이다.

(6) Casual forecasting

인과형 예측기법은 수요에 영향을 주는 환경 요인들을 파악하고 수요와 이 요인들 간의 인과관계를 파악함으로써 미래의 수요를 예측하는 기법이다. 이 방법은 수요를 종속변수로 하고 수요에 영향을 주는 요인들을 독립변수로 하며 GNP, 경쟁업체의 판매정책, 출생률 등 기업 외적환경 변화와 관련된 요인들과 광고나 판촉활동, 품질, 신용정책 등 기업 내적요인들이 모두 모형에 반영될 수 있다. 인과형 예측기법으로는 회귀분석(regression analysis)등이 있다.

(7) Markov technique

마르코프 분석은 러시아의 수학자 마르코프(1856~1922)가 도입한 확률 과정을 이용한 기법이다. 이 방법은 어떤 시스템의 미래 움직임을 예측하기 위하여 그 시스템의 현재 행태를 분석하는 절차이다. 예들 들면 어느 병원에서 환자의 회복에 관한 과거 자료가 있으면 환자의 미래 상태를 예측할 수 있으며, 고객의 과거 상표 교체 정보와 제품의 현재 시장점유율을 알고 있으면 예컨대 1년 후와 같은 특정 시기의 또는 먼 장래의 제품별 시장점유율을 예측할 수 있다.

04 MCQ (Multiple Choice Questions)

01. In the budgeting and planning process for a firm, which one of the following should be completed first? (CMA)

a. Sales budget.

b. Financial budget.

c. Cost management plan.

d. Strategic plan.

02. The type of budget that is available on a continuous basis for a specified future period by adding a month, quarter, or year in the future as the month, quarter, or year just ended is deleted, is called a (CMA)

a. rolling budget.

b. kaizen budget.

c. activity-based budget.

d. flexible budget.

03. Parker Company pays each member of its sales staff a salary as well as a commission on each unit sold. For the coming year, Parker plans to increase all salaries by 5% and to keep unchanged the commission paid on each unit sold. Because of increased demand, Parker expects the volume of sales to increase by 10%. How will the total cost of sales salaries and commissions change for the coming year? (CMA)

a. Increase by 5% or less.

b. Increase by more than 5% but less than 10%.

c. Increase by 10%.

d. Increase by more than 10%.

04. Which one of the following best describes tactical profit plans? (CMA)

    a. Detailed, short-term, broad responsibilities, qualitative.

    b. Broad, short-term, responsibilities at all levels, quantitative.

    c. Detailed, short-term, responsibilities at all levels, quantitative.

    d. Broad, long-term, broad responsibilities, qualitative.

05. When compared to static budgets, flexible budgets (CMA)

    a. offer managers a more realistic comparison of budget and actual fixed cost items under their control.

    b. provide a better understanding of the capacity variances during the period being evaluated.

    c. encourage managers to use less fixed costs items and more variable cost items that are under their control.

    d. offer managers a more realistic comparison of budget and actual revenue and cost items under their control.

06. All of the following are advantages of top-down budgeting as opposed to participatory budgeting, except that it (CMA)

    a. increases coordination of divisional objectives.

    b. reduces the time required for budgeting.

    c. may limit the acceptance of proposed goals and objectives.

    d. facilitates implementation of strategic plans.

07. Which one of the following best describes the order in which budgets should be prepared when developing the annual master operating budget? (CMA)

    a. Production budget, direct material budget, revenue budget.

    b. Production budget, revenue budget, direct material budget.

    c. Revenue budget, production budget, direct material budget.

    d. Revenue budget, direct material budget, production budget.

08. Which one of the following statements is correct concerning a flexible budget cost formula? Variable costs are stated (CMA)

    a. per unit and fixed costs are stated in total.

    b. in total and fixed costs are stated per unit.

    c. in total and fixed costs are stated in total.

    d. per unit and fixed costs are stated per unit.

09. Hannon Retailing Company prices its products by adding 30% to its cost. Hannon anticipates sales of $715,000 in July, $728,000 in August, and $624,000 in September. Hannon's policy is to have on hand enough inventory at the end of the month to cover 25% of the next month's sales. What will be the cost of the inventory that Hannon should budget for purchase in August? (CMA)

    a. $509,600.   b. $540,000.

    c. $560,000.   d. $680,000.

10. Streeter Company produces plastic microwave turntables. Sales for the next year are expected to be 65,000 units in the first quarter, 72,000 units in the second quarter, 84,000 units in the third quarter, and 66,000 units in the fourth quarter. Streeter usually maintains a finished goods inventory at the end of each quarter equal to one half of the units expected to be sold in the next quarter. However, due to a work stoppage, the finished goods inventory at the end of the first quarter is 8,000 units less than it should be. How many units should Streeter produce in the second quarter? (CMA)

a. 75,000 units.   b. 78,000 units.

c. 80,000 units.   d. 86,000 units.

11. Maker Distributors has a policy of maintaining inventory at 15% of the next month's forecasted sales. The cost of Maker's merchandise averages 60% of the selling price. The inventory balance as of May 31 is $63,000, and the forecasted dollar sales for the last four months of the year are as follows.

June	$700,000
July	600,000
August	650,000
September	800,000

What is the budgeted dollar amount of Maker's purchases for July? (CMA)

a. $355,500   b. $360,000

c. $364,500   d. $399,000

12. Tidwell Corporation sells a single product for $20 per unit. All sales are on account, with 60% collected in the month of sale and 40% collected in the following month. A partial schedule of cash collections for January through March of the coming year reveals the following receipts for the period.

	Cash Receipts		
	January	February	March
December receivables	$32,000		
From January sales	54,000	$36,000	
From February sales		66,000	$44,000

Other information includes the following.
- Inventories are maintained at 30% of the following month's sales.
- Assume that March sales total is $150,000.

The number of units to be purchased in February is (CMA)

a. 3,850 units.   b. 4,900 units.

c. 6,100 units.   d. 7,750 units.

13. Albert Hathaway recently joined Brannen University as the chief information officer of the University Computing Services Department. His assigned task is to help reduce the recurrent problem of cost overruns due to uncontrolled computer usage by the user community, while at the same time not curtailing the use of information technology for research and teaching. To ensure goal congruence, which one of the following algorithms should be used to allocate the cost of the University Computing Services Department to other departments within the university? (CMA)

a. Actual rate times actual hours of computer usage.

b. Actual rate times budgeted hours of computer usage.

c. Budgeted rate times actual hours of computer usage.

d. Budgeted rate times budgeted hours of computer usage.

14. When preparing a performance report for a cost center using flexible techniques, the planned cost column should be based on the

    a. budgeted amount in the original budget prepared before the beginning of the year.
    b. actual amount for the same period in the preceding year.
    c. budget adjusted to the actual level of activity for the period being reported.
    d. budget adjusted to the planned level of activity for the period being reported.

15. Which one of the following items is the last schedule to be prepared in the normal budget preparation process?

    a. Cash budget.   b. Cost of goods sold budget.
    c. Manufacturing overhead budget.   d. Selling expense budget.

16. Which one of the following budgeting methodologies would be most appropriate for a firm facing a significant level of uncertainty in unit sales volumes for next year?

    a. Top-down budgeting.   b. Life-cycle budgeting.
    c. Static budgeting.   d. Flexible budgeting.

17. Which of the following forecasting methods is based on qualitative approach?

    a. Exponential smoothing   b. Delphi technique
    c. Markov technique   d. Moving average

• 정답 및 해설

1. budget과 plan중에서는 plan을 먼저 실행한다. 정답 : d

2. 연속적으로 예산을 편성하는 것을 rolling budget이라고 한다. 정답 : a

3. Salary는 고정비로 5%가 증가, commission은 변동비로 10%가 증가하였으며 혼합원
   가는 5%와 10% 사이에서 증가한다.

   정답 : b

4. 전술은 전략과는 달리 상세하고 단기적이다. 정답 : c

5. 변동예산은 고정비 보다는 변동비를 현실적으로 예산과 비교한다.

   정답 : d

6. c는 top-down budgeting의 단점이다. 정답 : c

7. 판매예산 ⇨ 생산예산 ⇨ 제조예산 ⇨ 원재료 투입 예산 ⇨ 원재료 구입 예산

   정답 : c

8. 변동비는 단위당 원가로, 고정비는 총원가로 분석한다.

   정답 : a

9. Purchase = $\{(728{,}000 \times 0.75) + (624{,}000 \times 0.25)\} \div 1.30 = \$540{,}000$

   정답 : b

10. Production = $(72{,}000 + 84{,}000) \times 1/2 + 8{,}000 = 86{,}000$

   정답 : d

11. Purchase = $\{(600{,}000 \times 0.65) + (650{,}000 \times 0.35)\} \times 0.60 = \$364{,}500$

   정답 : c

12. Purchase $-$ {(110,000 × 0.7) + (150,000 × 0.3)} ÷ 20 = 6,100 units

정답 : c

13. 변동예산금액 = 실제 사용시간 × 예산 배부율

정답 : c

14. 변동예산의 budgeted amount = 실제 조업도 × 예산 변동비 + 예산 고정비

정답 : c

15. 현금예산은 종합예산의 마지막 단계이다.

정답 : a

16. 불확실이 클수록 수량오차가 크기 때문에 변동예산이 바람직하다.

정답 : d

17. 델파이기법은 전문가를 대상으로 조사하는 방법으로 대표적인 비계량적 방법이다.

정답 : b

05 / TBS (Task-Based Simulation)

Problem-1

Honda Motor Co. in Japan has a division that manufactures two-wheel motorcycles. Its budgeted sales for Goldwing in 20X1 is 915,000 units. Honda's target ending inventory is 70,000 units, and its beginning inventory is 115,000 units. The company' budgeted selling price to its distributors and dealers is $4,050 per motorcycle. Honda buys all its wheels from an outside supplier. No defective wheels are accepted. The company' target ending inventory is 72,000 wheels, and its beginning inventory is 55,000 wheels. The budgeted purchase price is $180 per wheel.

• Instruction •

1. Compute the budgeted revenues in dollar.
2. Compute the number of motorcycles that Honda should produce.
3. Compute the budgeted purchases of wheels in units and in dollar.

Problem-2

Cyrus Company manufactures and sells two products: Thingone and Thingtwo.

In July 20X1, Cyrus' budget department gathered the following data to prepare budgets for 20X2:

⟨20X2 projected sales⟩

Product	Units	Price
Thingone	62,000	$172
Thingtwo	46,000	$264

⟨20X2 inventories in units⟩

Product	January 1, 20X2	December 31, 20X2
Thingone	21,000	26,000
Thingtwo	13,000	14,000

The following direct materials are used in the two products:

⟨Amount used per unit⟩

DM	Unit	Thingone	Thingtwo
A	pound	5	6
B	pound	3	4

Projected data for 20X2 for direct materials are:

DM	Purchase price	January 1, 20X2	December 31, 20X2
A	$11	37,000 lb.	40,000 lb.
B	6	32,000 lb.	35,000 lb.

Projected direct manufacturing labor requirements and rates for 20X2 are:

Product	Hours per unit	Rate per hour
Thingone	3	$11
Thingtwo	4	$14

Manufacturing overhead is allocated at the rate of $19 per direct manufacturing labor-hour.

• Instruction •

Based on the preceding projections and budget requirements for Thingone and Thingtwo, prepare the following budgets for 20X2:

1. Revenues budget (in dollars)
2. Production budget (in units)
3. Direct material purchases budget (in quantities)
4. Direct material purchases budget (in dollars)
5. Direct manufacturing labor budget (in dollars)
6. Manufacturing overhead cost budgets (in dollars)
7. Budgeted finished goods inventory at December 31, 20X2 (in dollars)
8. Cost of goods sold budget
9. Budgeted income statement (ignore income taxes)

Problem-3

KIMCPA Company has been accumulating data in order to prepare an annual profit plan. Details regarding KIMCPA's sales for the first 6 months of the coming year are as follows: (CMA)

⟨Estimated monthly sales⟩

January	$600,000
February	650,000
March	700,000
April	625,000
May	720,000
June	800,000

⟨Type of monthly sales⟩

Cash sales	20%
Credit sales	80%

⟨Collection pattern for cedit sales⟩

Month of sales	30%
One month following sale	40%
Second month following sale	25%

KIMCPA's cost of goods sold averages 40% of the sales value. KIMCPA's objective is to maintain a target inventory equal to 30% of the next month's sales in units. Purchases of merchandise for resale are paid for in the month following purchase.

The variable operating expenses (other than CGS) are 10% of sales and are paid for in the month of following the sale. The annual fixed operating expenses are presented below. All of these are incurred uniformly throughout the year and paid monthly except for insurance and property taxes. Insurance is paid quarterly in January, April, July and October. Property taxes are paid twice a year in April and October.

⟨Annual fixed operating costs⟩

Advertizing	$720,000
Depreciation	420,000
Insurance	180,000
Property taxes	240,000
Salaries	1,080,000

· Instruction ·

1. Prepare the budgeted income statement for April

2. Prepare the budgeted balance sheet related to operating budget as of April 30.

3. Prepare the statement of cash flow related to operating budget for April.

Sherpa Company makes two pet carriers, the Cat-allac and the Dog-eriffic. They are both made of plastic with metal doors, but the Cat-allac is smaller. Information for the two products for the month of April is given in the following tables:

[Input Prices]

⟨Direct materials⟩

Plastic	$ 5 per pound
Metal	$ 4 per pound

⟨Direct manufacturing labor⟩

$10 per direct manufacturing labor-hour

[Input Quantities per Unit of Output]

	Cat-allac	Dog-eriffic
Direct materials		
Plastic	4 pounds	6 pounds
Metal	0.5 pounds	1 pound
Direct manufacturing labor-hours	3 hours	5 hours
Machine-hours (MH)	11 MH	19 MH

[Inventory Information, Direct Materials]

	Plastic	Metal
Beginning inventory	290 pounds	70 pounds
Target ending inventory	410 pounds	65 pounds
Cost of beginning inventory	$1,102	$217

Sherpa accounts for direct materials using a FIFO cost flow assumption.

[Sales and Inventory Information, Finished Goods]

	Cat-allac	Dog-eriffic
Expected sales in units	530	225
Selling price	$ 205	$ 310
Target ending inventory in units	30	10

Beginning inventory in units	10	25
Beginning inventory in dollars	$1,000	$4,650

Sherpa uses a FIFO cost flow assumption for finished goods inventory.

Sherpa uses an activity-based costing system and classifies overhead into three activity pools: Setup, Processing, and Inspection.

Activity rates for these activities are $105 per setup-hour, $10 per machine-hour, and $15 per inspection-hour, respectively. Other information follows:

[Cost-Driver Information]

	Cat-allac	Dog-eriffic
Number of units per batch	25	9
Setup time per batch	1.50 hours	1.75 hours
Inspection time per batch	0.5 hour	0.7 hour

Non-manufacturing fixed costs for March equal $32,000, half of which are salaries. Salaries are expected to increase 5% in April. The only variable non-manufacturing cost is sales commission, equal to 1% of sales revenue.

• Instruction •

Prepare the following for April:

1. Revenues budget
2. Production budget in units
3. Direct material usage budget and direct material purchases budget
4. Direct manufacturing labor cost budget
5. Manufacturing overhead cost budgets for each of the three activities
6. Budgeted unit cost of ending finished goods inventory and ending inventories budget
7. Cost of goods sold budget
8. Non−manufacturing costs budget
9. Budgeted income statement (ignore income taxes)

K-store, a chain of small neighborhood convenience stores, is preparing its activity-based budget for January 20X1. K-store, has three product categories: soft drinks (35% of cost of goods sold [COGS]), fresh snacks (25% of COGS), and packaged food (40% of COGS). The following table shows the four activities that consume indirect resources at the K-store, the cost drivers and their rates, and the cost-driver amount budgeted to be consumed by each activity in January 20X1.

〈Ordering activity〉

- Cost driver : number of purchasing orders
- January 20X1 budgeted cost driver rate : $45
- January 20X1 budgeted amount of cost driver used :
  soft drinks : 14, fresh snacks : 24, packaged food : 14

〈Delivery activity〉

- Cost driver : number of deliveries
- January 20X1 budgeted cost driver rate : $41
- January 20X1 budgeted amount of cost driver used :
  soft drinks : 12, fresh snacks : 62, packaged food : 19

〈Shelf stocking activity〉

- Cost driver : hours of stocking time
- January 20X1 budgeted cost driver rate : $10.50
- January 20X1 budgeted amount of cost driver used :
  soft drinks : 16, fresh snacks : 172, packaged food : 94

〈Customer support activity〉

- Cost driver : number of items sold
- January 20X1 budgeted cost driver rate : $0.09
- January 20X1 budgeted amount of cost driver used :
  soft drinks : 4,600, fresh snacks : 34,200, packaged food : 10,750

1. What is the total budgeted indirect cost at the K–store in January 20X1?
2. What is the total budgeted cost of each activity at the K–store for January 20X1?
3. What is the budgeted indirect cost of each product category for January 20X1?
4. Which product category has the largest fraction of total budgeted indirect costs?

Pricing

Pricing

---

1 Pricing

(1) Major factors that affect pricing decisions

가격은 제품의 수요(demand)와 공급(supply)에 의하여 결정되며, 수요와 공급에 영향을 주는 고객, 경쟁기업, 원가이다.

- Customers
- Competitors
- Costs

(2) Time horizon

가격의사결정에서 고려하는 기간에 따라 다음과 같이 구분한다.

1) Short-run pricing: Less than one year
2) Long-run pricing: More than one year

장기적 가격결정(long-run pricing)은 우선 고려원인에 따라 다음과 같이 구분한다.

1) Market-based (시장기준 가격결정)
2) Cost-plus based (원가기준 가격결정)

(3) Short-run pricing

단기적 가격결정은 특별주문(one-time special order) 수락여부에 따른 가격결정으로 의사결정과 관련이 있는 관련원가(relevant cost)를 고려하여 가격을 결정한다. 자세한 내용은 12장에서 후술한다.

2 Cost-plus pricing

Cost-plus pricing adds a markup component to the cost base.

원가기준 가격결정은 기준원가(cost)를 먼저 결정하고 적절한 이익을 가산하여 판매가격(price)을 결정하는 방법으로 다음과 같은 순서로 결정된다.

[그림 11-1]

이 방법은 덜 경쟁적인 시장에 적용되며, 간편하고 이해하기 쉬우므로 실무에서 널리 사용하고 있으나 고객(customers)이나 경쟁자(competitors)를 덜 고려한다는 문제점이 있다.

장기적인 관점에서는 고정원가를 통제가능한 원가로 보기 때문에 원가기준 가격결정의 기준원가는 고정원가를 포함한 단위당 총원가(full cost)를 의미한다.

$$Price = Full\ cost + Mark\text{-}up$$

이익가산액(mark-up)은 기업의 목표 투자수익률(target rate of return on investment : ROI)을 반영하여 결정된다. 투자수익률(ROI)는 다음과 같이 계산된다.

$$ROI = \frac{Operating\ income}{Average\ investment}$$

Example-1

Annual sales: 10,000 units

Investment : $100,000

Target ROI: 15%

Cost data:

⟨Variable costs⟩

Manufacturing cost per unit : $3

Selling and administrative cost per unit : $2.50

⟨Fixed costs⟩

Manufacturing costs : $20,000

Selling and administrative costs: $10,000

What was the full cost per unit? What was the selling price?

(1) Full cost per unit

Full cost per unit = $3 + $2.50 + $30,000/10,000 units = $8.50/unit

(2) Mark-up

ROI = 15%이므로 Operating income = $100,000 × 15% = $15,000

Mark-up per unit = $15,000 ÷ 10,000 = $1.50/unit

(3) Price = $8.50/unit + $1.50/unit = $10.00/unit

3 Market-based pricing

Market-based pricing starts with a target price, which is the estimated price for a product or service that potential customers are willing to pay.

시장기준 가격결정은 가격(price)을 시장상황에 맞추어 먼저 결정하고 원가(cost)를 나중에 결정하는 방법이다. 시장기준 가격결정은 다음과 같은 순서로 결정된다.

[그림 11-2]

매우 경쟁적인 시장(competitive market)에서는 기업이 판매가격에 영향력을 행사하기 어려우므로 원가기준 가격결정을 적용하기 어렵기 때문에 이 때에는 시장기준 가격결정을 사용하여야 한다.

(1) Target pricing

고객(customers)이나 경쟁자(competitors)를 우선적으로 고려하여 결정한 가격을 목표가격(target price)이라고 한다. 목표가격은 아래의 결정요인을 고려한다.

1) 고객의 욕구 및 수용가능성(customer needs and perceptions of product value)

2) 경쟁회사 분석(competitor analysis)

(2) Target costing

목표가격에서 목표이익을 확보할 수 있는 원가수준을 목표원가 (target cost)라고 하며 다음과 같이 계산한다.

$$\text{Target cost} = \text{Target price} - \text{Target operating income per unit}$$

(3) Value engineering

Value engineering is a systematic evaluation of all aspects of the value chain, with the objective of reducing costs and achieving a quality level that satisfies customers.

가치공학은 목표원가를 달성하는 방법으로 제품설계변경, 공정변경 등과 같은 공학적 방법을 이용하여 보다 낮은 원가로 동일한 기능을 달성할 수 있도록 제품의 기능을 분석하는 기법을 말한다.

※ **Locked-in costs (= designed-in costs)**

costs that have not yet been incurred but will be incurred in the future based on decisions that have already been made.

Example-2

Annual sales: 10,000 units

Investment : $100,000

Cost data:

⟨Variable costs⟩

Manufacturing cost per unit : $3

Selling and administrative cost per unit : $2.50

⟨Fixed costs⟩

Manufacturing costs : $20,000

Selling and administrative costs: $10,000

In response to competitive pressures, Company must reduce the price to $9 in order to achieve sales of 10,000 units. If Company wants to maintain a 15% ROI, what is the target cost per unit?

(1) Target price = $9.00/unit

(2) Target operating income per unit

ROI = 15%이므로 Operating income = $100,000 × 15% = $15,000

Target operating income per unit = $15,000 ÷ 10,000 = $1.50/unit

(3) Target cost = $9 ⇨ $1.50 = $7.50/unit

(4) Value engineering

Full cost = $8.50 ⇨ Target cost = $7.50

가치사슬(value chain)분석을 통하여 $1.00/unit을 절감하여야 한다.

4 Non-cost factors in pricing decisions

(1) Price discrimination

Charging different customers different prices for the same products or services.
가격차별은 동일한 상품을 구입자에 따라 다른 가격으로 판매하는 것을 말한다.

(2) Peak-load pricing

Charging a higher price for the same products or services when the demand exceeds the physical limit of the capacity to produce.
최대부하가격은 최대수요를 낮추기 위하여 일시적으로 가격을 높이는 것이다.

(3) Predatory pricing

Company deliberately prices below its costs in an effort to drive competitors out of the market and restrict supply and then raises prices rather than enlarge demand.

(4) Dumping

Under U.S. laws, dumping occurs when a non-U.S. company sells a product in the United States at a price below the market value in the country where it is produced, and this lower price materially injures or threatens to materially injure an industry in the United States..

(5) Collusive pricing

Companies in an industry conspire in their pricing and production decisions to achieve a price above the competitive price and so restrain trade.

(6) Anti-trust laws

- the Sherman Act
- the Clayton Act
- the Federal Trade Commission Act
- Robinson-Patman Act,

02 Transfer pricing

1 Transfer price

In a decentralized organization, much of the decision-making power resides in its individual subunits. A transfer price is the price one subunit (department or division) charges for a product or service supplied to another subunit of the same organization.

분권화된 조직(decentralized organization)에서는 각 사업부를 이익중심점이나 투자중심점으로 운영한다. 대체가격(transfer price)이란 분권화 된 두 사업부 간의 재화 및 용역 판매 시 부담 시켜야 할 가격이다.

대체가격(transfer price)이 얼마로 결정되는가에 따라 회사전체의 이익은 영향을 받지 않지만 각 사업부의 이익은 영향을 받는다. 대체가격(transfer price)은 공급사업부(selling subunit)의 수익과 구매사업부(buying subunit)의 원가에 영향을 미친다.

공급사업부(selling subunit)는 유리한 성과평가를 위해서는 대체가격을 높게 책정하려고 하지만, 구매사업부(buying subunit)는 유리한 성과평가를 위해서는 대체가격을 낮게 책정하려고 하기 때문에 이해상충의 문제가 발생한다.

In a well designed transfer-pricing system, managers focus on maximizing the performance of their subunits and in doing so optimize the performance of the company as a whole.

바람직한 대체가격결정(transfer pricing)은 각 사업부의 성과를 극대화하면서 동시에 회사전체의 성과를 최적화시키는 것이다.

2 Criteria for evaluating transfer price

(1) Goal congruence

목표일치성 기준은 각 사업부 경영자가 각 사업부의 목표뿐만 아니라 기업전체의 목표가 최대가 되도록 대체가격을 결정하여야 한다는 기준으로 가장 중요한 기준이다. 목표일치성 기준이 준수된다면 준최적화 현상은 발생하지 않는다.

※ Sub-optimal decisions (준최적화, 부문최적화)

Decisions that are in their own best interest but that may be inefficient from the standpoint of the organization as a whole.

(2) Performance evaluation

성과평가기준은 각 사업부 경영자에 대한 성과평가가 공정(fair)하게 될 수 있도록 대체가격을 결정되어야 한다는 기준이다.

(3) Autonomy

자율성 기준은 사업부 경영자에게 내부거래와 외부거래를 선택 할 수 있는 자율성이 주어져야 한다는 기준으로 자율성은 분권화의 본질이다. 하지만 자율성으로 인하여 준최적화 현상이 발생할 가능성이 있다.

(4) Fiscal Management

재정관리기준은 국세청, 관세청과 같은 정부기관이 기업이 미칠 수 있는 불리한 영향을 최소화 하도록 대체가격을 결정하는 기준으로 다국적 대체가격(multinational transfer price)에서 매우 중요한 기준이다. 다국적 대체가격결정에서는 다양한 세금(income taxes, payroll taxes, customs duties, tariffs, sales taxes, environment-related taxes)들을 고려하여 가장 유리하도록 대체가격이 결정되어야 한다.

3 Transfer pricing methods

(1) Market-based transfer price

시장가격기준은 각 사업부를 독립적인 실체로 보고 대체가격을 시장가격으로 정하는 방법이다. ⇨ TP(transfer price) = Market price

(2) Cost-based transfer price

원가기준은 시장가격을 신뢰할 수 없는 경우에 사용하는 방법으로 대체가격을 원가로 결정하는 방법이다. 이때 원가는 전부원가를 기준으로 하는 방법과 변동원가를 기준으로 하는 방법이 있다. ⇨ TP(transfer price) = Cost

이 방법은 공급사업부가 대체가격에서 이익을 얻을 수 없기 때문에 공급사업부의 성과평가를 공정하게 할 수 없기 때문에 원가에 이익을 가산하여 대체가격을 결정하기도 한다. ☒ TP(transfer price) = Cost + Mark-up

(3) Negotiated transfer price

협상가격기준은 각 사업부 간에 협의된 협상가격을 대체가격으로 정하는 방법으로 자율성이 최대한 보장되며, 목표일치성을 달성할 수 있다.

(4) Dual transfer price

이중대체가격기준은 목표일치성이 달성될 수 있도록 공급사업부와 구매사업무의 대체가격을 각각 달리 적용하는 방법이다.

Example-3

Tesco Petroleum has two divisions. Each operates as a profit center. The Production Division manages the production of crude oil from a petroleum field. The Refining Division manages a refinery that processes crude oils into gasoline. The operating data for two divisions are as follows:

	The Production Division	The Refining Division
Finished Goods	Crude Oil	Gasoline
Variable costs per unit	$2	$5
Fixed costs per unit	6	9
Full costs per unit	8	14
Market price to outside parties	13	52

Consider the division operating income resulting from four transfer-pricing methods.
Method A: Market-based TP
Method B: Cost-based TP at full costs
Method C: Cost-based TP at variable costs
Method D: Negotiated TP $16

(1) The Production Division

	Method A	Method B	Method C	Method D
Revenue	13	8	2	16
VC	2	2	2	2
FC	6	6	6	6
Operating income	5	0	(6)	8

(2) The Refinery Division

	Method A	Method B	Method C	Method D
Revenue	52	52	52	52
Transfer-in cost	13	8	2	16
VC	5	5	5	5
FC	9	9	9	9
Operating income	25	30	36	22

4 The range of feasible transfer prices

목표일치성이 달성되도록 공급사업부와 구매사업부가 수용 할 수 있는 대체가격의 범위는 다음과 같다.

(1) Minimum transfer price

공급사업부(selling subunit)는 가능한 한 높은 가격으로 대체가격을 결정하려고 하기 때문에 공급사업부가 수용할 수 있는 최소대체가격은 다음과 같이 결정한다.

$$\text{Minimum TP} = \text{Incremental costs} + \text{Opportunity costs}$$

Incremental costs = 변동원가 증가분 + 고정원가 증가분
Opportunity costs = 기존 정규시장의 이익감소
　　　　　　　　+ 유휴생산능력(excess capacity)의 대체적 용도의 이익 상실

(2) Maximum transfer price

구매사업부(buying subunit)는 가능한 한 낮은 가격으로 대체가격을 결정하려고 하기 때문에 구매사업부가 수용할 수 있는 최대대체가격은 다음과 같이 결정한다.

$$\text{Maximum TP} = \text{Min} [①, ②]$$

① = 외부구입가격 + 구매사업부의 원가증가액
② = 중간제품의 순실현가치(NRV)

Alpha Division of Samsung Electronics Co. produces semiconductor chips, 20% of which are sold to Beta Division and the remainder to outside customers. Two divisions are treated as profit centers. Alpha Division's estimated cost data are as follows:

	Beta	Outsiders
Sales	?	$800,000
Variable costs	(90,000)	(360,000)
Fixed costs	(30,000)	(120,000)
Gross margin	?	$320,000
Unit sales	2,000	8,000

Alpha has an opportunity to sell the 2,000 units to an outside customer at a price of $70 per unit. Beta can purchase its requirements from an outside supplier at a price of $80 per unit.

(1) If Alpha's full capacity is 15,000 units, what is the natural bargaining range for the two division?
(2) If Alpha's full capacity is 10,000 units, what is the natural bargaining range for the two division?

(1) Bargaining range for the two division
    UVC = $90,000 ÷ 2,000 = $45
    최대조업도가 15,000개이므로 기존 정규시장의 이익감소은 없다.
    Minimum TP = $45 + 0 = $45
    Maximum TP = $80 + 0 = $80

(2) Bargaining range for the two division
    최대조업도가 10,000개이므로 기존 정규시장의 2,000개 이익감소가 있다.
    기존 정규시장 이익감소 단위당 원가 = ($70 − $45) × 2,000 ÷ 2,000 = $25
    Minimum TP = $45 + $25 = $70
    Maximum TP = $80 + 0 = $80

03 | MCQ (Multiple Choice Questions)

01. Finn Products, a start-up company, wants to use cost-based pricing for its only product, a unique new video game. Finn expects to sell 10,000 units in the upcoming year. Variable costs will be $65 per unit and annual fixed operating costs (including depreciation) amount to $80,000. Finn's balance sheet is as follows.

Assets		Liabilities & Equity	
Current assets	$100,000	Accounts payable	$ 25,000
Plant & equipment	425,000	Debt	200,000
		Equity	300,000

If Finn wants to earn a 20% return on equity, at what price should it sell the new product? (CMA)

a. $75.00.   b. $78.60.

c. $79.00.   d. $81.00.

02. Which one of the following is an incorrect description of transfer pricing? (CMA)

a. It measures the value of goods or services furnished by a profit center to other responsibility centers within a company.

b. If a market price exists, this price may be used as a transfer price.

c. It measures exchanges between a company and external customers.

d. If no market price exists, the transfer price may be based on cost.

1. $10,000 \times (P - 65) - 80,000 = 300,000 \times 20\%$에서 P = $79   정답 : c

2. TP는 외부거래가 아닌 내부거래의 가격이다.   정답 : c

04 TBS (Task-Based Simulation)

Problem-1

The new CEO of AIFA Manufacturing has asked for a variety of information about the operations of the firm from last year. The CEO is given the following information, but with some data missing:

Total sales revenue	?
Number of units produced and sold	500,000 units
Selling price	?
Operating income	$180,000
Total investment in assets	$2,250,000
Variable cost per unit	$4.00
Fixed costs for the year	$2,500,000

• Instruction •

1. Find (a) total sales revenue, (b) selling price, (c) rate of return on investment, and (d) markup percentage on full cost for this product.

2. The new CEO has a plan to reduce fixed costs by $225,000 and variable costs by $0.30 per unit while continuing to produce and sell 500,000 units. Using the same markup percentage as in requirement 1, calculate the new selling price.

3. Assume the CEO institutes the changes in requirement 2 including the new selling price. However, the reduction in variable cost has resulted in lower product quality resulting in 5% fewer units being sold compared with before the change. Calculate operating income (loss).

Problem-2

Skittles makes candy bars for vending machines and sells them to vendors in cases of 30 bars. Although Skittles makes a variety of candy, the cost differences are insignificant, and the cases all sell for the same price.

Skittles has a total capital investment of $15,000,000. It expects to produce and sell 300,000 cases of candy next year. Skittles requires a 10% target return on investment.

Expected costs for next year are:
Variable production costs : $4.00 per case
Variable marketing and distribution costs : $1.00 per case
Fixed production costs : $300,000
Fixed marketing and distribution costs : $400,000
Other fixed costs : $200,000

Skittles prices the cases of candy at full cost plus markup to generate profits equal to the target return on capital.

• Instruction •

1. What is the target operating income?

2. What is the selling price Skittles needs to charge to earn the target operating income? Calculate the markup percentage on full cost.

3. Skittles' closest competitor has just increased its candy case price to $16, although it sells 36 candy bars per case. Skittles is considering increasing its selling price to $15 per case. Assuming production and sales decrease by 4%, calculate Skittles 'return on investment. Is increasing the selling price a good idea?

Problem-3

LG Company manufactures and sells television sets. Its assembly division (AD) buys television screens from the screen division (SD) and assembles the TV sets. The SD, which is operating at capacity, incurs an incremental manufacturing cost of $65 per screen. The SD can sell all its output to the outside market at a price of $100 per screen, after incurring a variable marketing and distribution cost of $8 per screen. If the AD purchases screens from outside suppliers at a price of $100 per screen, it will incur a variable purchasing cost of $7 per screen. LG's division managers can act autonomously to maximize their own division' operating income.

• Instruction •▶

1. What is the minimum transfer price at which the SD manager would be willing to sell screens to the AD?

2. What is the maximum transfer price at which the AD manager would be willing to purchase screens from the SD?

3. Now suppose that the SD can sell only 70% of its output capacity of 20,000 screens per month on the open market. Capacity cannot be reduced in the short run. The AD can assemble and sell more than 20,000 TV sets per month.
   (1) What is the minimum transfer price at which the SD manager would be willing to sell screens to the AD?
   (2) From the point of view of LG's management, how much of the SD output should be transferred to the AD?

Problem-4

㈜대덕은 A사업부와 B사업부를 운영하고 있다. A사업부는 매년 B사업부가 필요로 하는 부품 1,000개를 단위당 ₩2,000에 공급한다. 동 부품의 단위당 변동원가는 ₩1,800이며 단위당 고정원가는 ₩200이다. 다음연도부터 A사업부가 부품단위당 공급가격을 ₩2,200으로 인상할 계획을 발표함에 따라, B사업부도 동 부품을 외부업체로부터 단위당 ₩2,000에 구매하는 것을 고려하고 있다. B사업부가 외부업체로부터 부품을 단위당 ₩2,000에 공급받는 경우 A사업부가 생산설비를 다른 생산활동에 사용하면 연간 ₩150,000의 현금운영원가가 절감된다. A사업부가 부품을 B사업부에 공급하는 경우, 대체가격(transfer price)의 최소가격과 최대가격은 얼마인가? (K-CPA)

Texas Instruments Company manufactures telecommunications equipment at its plant in Scranton, Pennsylvania. The company has marketing divisions throughout the world. A Texas Instruments marketing division in Hamburg, Germany, imports 100,000 broadband routers from the United States.

The following information is available:
- U.S. income tax rate on the U.S. division' operating income : 35%
- German income tax rate on the German division' operating income : 40%
- German import duty : 15%
- Variable manufacturing cost per router : $275
- Full manufacturing cost per router : $400
- Selling price (net of marketing and distribution costs) in Germany : $575

Suppose the United States and German tax authorities only allow transfer prices that are between the full manufacturing cost per unit of $400 and a market price of $475, based on comparable imports into Germany. The German import duty is charged on the price at which the product is transferred into Germany. Any import duty paid to the German authorities is a deductible expense for calculating German income taxes.

1. Calculate the after-tax operating income earned by the United States and German divisions from transferring 100,000 broadband routers (a) at full manufacturing cost per unit and (b) at market price of comparable imports. (Income taxes are not included in the computation of the cost-based transfer prices.)

2. Which transfer price should the Texas Instruments Company select to minimize the total of company import duties and income taxes? Remember that the transfer price must be between the full manufacturing cost per unit of $400 and the market price of $475 of comparable imports into Germany.

Chapter

Decision Making

Chapter 12 Decision Making

01 Decision making rules

1 Types of decision making

의사결정은 단기적 의사결정과 장기적 의사결정으로 구분되며, 이 장에서는 단기적 의사결정에 대하여 살펴본다. 단기적 의사결정은 1년 이내의 상황에 대한 의사결정으로 화폐의 시간가치(time value of money)를 고려하지 않기 때문에 이익의 크기는 중요하지만 이익의 발생시점은 무시한다.

장기적 의사결정은 1년 이상의 상황에 대한 의사결정으로 자본예산이 대표적인 예이다. 장기적 의사결정은 화폐의 시간가치를 고려하므로, 현금흐름의 크기와 발생시점 모두 중요하다.

2 Decision making process

단기적 의사결정과정은 다음과 같다.

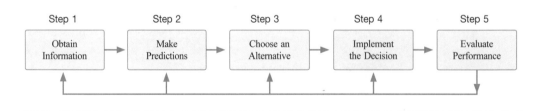

Step 1	Step 2	Step 3	Step 4	Step 5
Obtain Information	Make Predictions	Choose an Alternative	Implement the Decision	Evaluate Performance

[그림 12-1]

3 Decision making rules

(1) Relevant costs and relevant revenues

Relevant costs are expected future costs and relevant revenues are expected future revenues that differ among the alternative courses of action being considered. Costs and revenues that are not relevant are called irrelevant.

관련원가(relevant costs)와 관련수익(relevant revenues)은 의사결정과 관련이 있으며, 고려 중인 대체적 대안들 사이에 차이가 나는 미래현금지출원가 및 미래현금수익을 말한다. 의사 결정과 관련이 없는 원가와 수익을 비관련수익과 비관련원가라고 한다.

(2) Opportunity costs

기회비용은 특정 대안을 채택하기 위하여 포기하는 이익을 말한다. 포기하는 대안이 여러 개라면, 이 대안들의 이익 중 가장 큰 것이 기회비용이 된다. 기회비용은 회계장부에 기록되 지 않지만 의사결정을 할 때에는 반드시 고려되어야 하는 관련원가(relevant costs)이다. 의사 결정분석에서 고려해야 하는 기회비용의 대표적인 유형은 유휴생산능력(excess capacity)의 대체적 용도를 통한 이익 상실분이다.

(3) Sunk costs

매몰원가는 의사결정시점 이전에 이미 발생한 원가로 의사결정에 영향을 미치지 않는 원가 로서 비관련원가(irrelevant costs)이다. 일반적으로 고정원가는 의사결정분석에서 매몰원가로 비관련원가가 되지만 의사결정형태에 따라서 관련원가가 될 수 있다.

(4) Incremental approach

증분접근법(incremental approach)은 각 대안 간에 차이가 나는 증분수익(관련수익)과 증분 비용(관련원가)을 구하고 증분수익에서 증분비용을 차감하여 계산된 증분이익으로 의사결정 을 하는 방법이다. 총수익과 총비용을 구하여 이익을 계산하는 총액접근법 (total approach)은 시간이 많이 소요되기 때문에 의사결정분석에서는 주로 증분접근법을 사용한다.

Relevant cost	Irrelevant cost
Variable costs*	Fixed costs*
Avoidable costs	Unavoidable costs
Opportunity costs	Sunk costs

* 모든 변동원가와 고정원가가 해당되는 것은 아님

4 Qualitative factors

의사결정을 할 때는 양적 요소(quantitative factors)와 질적 요소(qualitative factors)를 동시에 고려하여야 한다. 양적 요소는 화폐금액을 측정이 가능한 재무적 요소(financial factors)와 수치로는 표현될 수 있지만 화폐금액으로 측정이 불가능한 비재무적 요소(non-financial factors)로 구분될 수 있다.

Quantitative	Financial	DM, DL, MOH, S&A costs
	Non-financial	cycle time, product development time
Qualitative		customer satisfaction, quality of products

5 Types of short-term decision making

단기의사결정 유형은 다음과 같다.

(1) Special orders: 일회성 특별주문의 수락 결정

(2) Make or buy: 외부구입 또는 자가제조의 결정

(3) Sell or process further: 분리점에서 판매 또는 추가가공의 결정

(4) Closing a department: 제품의 생산중단여부 결정

(5) Sale of obsolete inventory: 진부화된 재고의 판매결정

(6) Scarce resource: 제한된 자원의 사용결정

02 Types of decision making

1 Special orders

특별주문(one-time-only special order)은 대량 구매이지만 기존의 판매가격보다 낮은 가격으로 공급해 달라는 경우가 많다. 이 경우 다음 사항은 반드시 고려하여야 한다.

- 특별주문의 수락이 기존시장을 교란시키는지의 여부
- 유휴생산능력(excess capacity)이 존재하는 지의 여부
▷ 유휴생산능력이 존재하지 않는다면 유휴생산능력의 대체적 용도를 통한 이익 상실분인 기회비용을 반드시 고려하여야 한다.

2 Make or buy

기업은 부품이나 제품을 직접 제조하지만 필요에 따라 외부에서 구입할 것인가를 고민하기도 한다. 자가 제조(insourcing) 또는 외부구입(outsourcing) 의사결정에서 다음사항은 반드시 고려하여야 한다.

- 외부에서 구입하는 경우 발생하는 유휴생산능력을 임대나 다른 제품의 생산의 용도로 이용할 수 있는가?
- 신규 공급업자의 안정적인 공급능력과 품질관리 (질적 요소)

3 Sell or process further

결합제품을 분리점에서 판매하느냐 또는 추가 가공하여 완제품으로 판매하느냐의 의사결정에서 다음 사항들을 고려하여야 한다.

- Joint costs : 의사결정에 영향을 주지 않은 비관련원가(irrelevant cost)
- Separable costs : 의사결징에 영향을 주는 관련원가(relevant cost)

Example-1

Spalding Company manufactures basketballs for NBA.

Expected annual volume is 10,000 units per year.

Normal selling price is $40/unit.

⟨Variable costs⟩

Manufacturing cost per unit : $20

Selling and administrative cost per unit : $3

⟨Fixed costs per year⟩

Manufacturing costs : $100,000

Selling and administrative costs: $30,000

A customer wants to place a one-time special order for 5,000 units at $28 each.

(1) Spalding's full capacity per year is 15,000 units.

(2) Spalding's full capacity per year is 12,000 units.

(1) With excess capacity

고정원가는 의사결정과 관련 없는 비관련원가이므로 증분원가에 포함하지 않는다.
총생산능력이 15,000개로 유휴생산능력이 있으므로 기회비용을 고려하지 않는다.

1) Incremental revenues = 5,000 units × $28 = $140,000

2) Incremental costs = 5,000 units × ($20 + $3) = $115,000

3) Incremental profit = 140,000 − 115,000 = +$25,000 ⇨ Accept

(2) Without excess capacity

총생산능력이 12,000개로 유휴생산능력이 없기 때문에 기회비용을 고려하여야 한다.
5,000개의 특별주문을 수락하면 기존의 판매분 3,000개를 포기하여야 하므로 유휴생
산능력의 대체적 용도를 통한 이익 상실분은 3,000개에 대한 공헌이익으로 계산한다.

1) Incremental revenues = 5,000 units × $28 = $140,000

2) Opportunity costs = 3,000 units × ($40 − $23) = $51,000

3) Incremental costs = $115,000 + $51,000 = $166,000

4) Incremental profit = 140,000 − 166,000 = −$26,000 ⇨ Reject

Example-2

Harley-Davidson Company manufactures motor scooters.
The following data are annual costs in producing 25,000 ignition switches.

Prime cost	$125,000
Variable manufacturing overhead	40,000
Fixed manufacturing overhead	85,000
Total manufacturing costs	$250,000

Instead of making its own switches, Harley-Davidson might purchase the switches from a supplier at a price of $8 per unit. If Harley-Davidson would purchase the switches from the supplier, $10,000 of its fixed overhead costs will be eliminated.

(1) Opportunity cost of existing capacity = 0
(2) Opportunity cost of existing capacity = $30,000

(1) Without opportunity costs

고정원가 $85,000에서 $10,000는 회피 가능하므로 외부구입 의사결정의 관련수익으로 계산한다.

1) Incremental revenues = 125,000 + 40,000 + 10,000 = $175,000

2) Incremental costs = 25,000 units × $8 = $200,000

3) Incremental profit = 175,000 − 200,000 = −$25,000 ⇨ Reject

(2) With opportunity costs

기존설비를 다른 대체적인 용도에 사용하여 획득할 수 있는 기회비용 $30,000은 외부구입 의사결정의 관련수익으로 계산한다.

1) Incremental revenues = 175,000 + 30,000 = $205,000

2) Incremental costs = 25,000 units × $8 = $200,000

3) Incremental profit = 205,000 − 200,000 = +$5,000 ⇨ Accept

Example-3

Exxon Mobil Company buys crude oil. Refining this oil results in two products at the split-off point: AA and BB. The joint costs of purchasing and processing the crude oil are $3,000 that generate 1,000 gallons of AA and 500 gallons of BB. AA sells for $4 per gallon and BB sells for $2 per gallon.

- 1,000 gallons of AA are further processed to yield 1,000 gallons of product AAA at additional processing costs of $2,000. Product AAA is sold for $5 per gallon.
- 500 gallons of BB are further processed to yield 500 gallons of product BBB at additional processing costs of $1,000. Product BBB is sold for $6 per gallon.

Prepare an analysis to show whether it is more profitable for Exxon Mobil to sell the two products at the split-off point or to process it further.

(1) Product AA

    1) Incremental revenues = 1,000 gallons × ($5 − $4) = $1,000

    2) Incremental costs = $2,000

    3) Incremental profit = 1,000 − 2,000 = −$1,000 ⇨ Reject

    Product AA는 추가가공하지 않고 분리점에서 판매하는 것이 $1,000 유리하다.

(2) Product BB

    1) Incremental revenues = 1,000 gallons × ($6 − $4) = $2,000

    2) Incremental costs = $1,000

    3) Incremental profit = 2,000 − 1,000 = +$1,000 ⇨ Accept

    Product BB는 분리점에서 판매하지 않고 추가가공하는 것이 $1,000 유리하다.

⇨ 추가가공 의사결정에서 결합원가($3,000)는 의사결정에 영향을 주지 않는다.

4 Closing a department

기업이 현재 판매하고 있는 제품 중에 손실이 발생하는 제품이 있다면 이 제품을 계속 생산할 것인가 아니면 생산을 중단할 것인가를 결정하여야 한다. 제품의 생산을 중단할 경우 고정원가는 일부가 계속 발생할 수 있기 때문에 감소되는 고정원가를 정확히 계산하여야 한다.

Example-4

KIMCPA manufactures two product models.

	Product A	Product B	Total
Sales	$300,000	$100,000	$400,000
VC	210,000	90,000	300,000
CM	90,000	10,000	100,000
FC	40,000	30,000	70,000
Operating income	$50,000	$(20,000)	30,000

If product B line is closed, $5,000 of fixed costs would be eliminated. Calculate the increase or decrease in operating income if KIMCPA closes product B line.

제품의 생산을 중단한다면 변동원가 및 고정원가 감소분은 증분수익으로 계산하며, 매출액 감소분은 증분원가로 계산한다.

1) Incremental revenues = 90,000 + 5,000 = $95,000

2) Incremental costs = $100,000

3) Incremental profit = 95,000 − 100,000 = −$5,000 ⇨ Reject

제품B의 생산을 중단하면 영업이익이 $5,000 감소하므로 제품B는 계속 생산 및 판매하는 것이 유리하다.

5 Scarce resource

자원이 제한되어 있는 경우 어떤 제품을 얼마나 생산하느냐에 대한 의사결정과정으로 공헌이익을 최대화 하는 방향으로 의사결정으로 한다.

• 제한된 자원이 하나인 경우 (단일 제약조건)

⇨ 제한된 제품단위당 공헌이익(UCM of limited resource)이 가장 큰 제품 선택

• 제한된 자원이 여러 개인 경우 (복수 제약조건)

⇨ 선형계획법(linear programming)에 의하여 최적 솔루션을 찾는다.

Example-5

KIMCPA manufactures product X and Y. Relevant data consist of the following:

	Product X	Product Y
CM per unit	$50	$60
Machine hours required per unit	2	3

Only 600 machine-hours are available daily for assembling product X and Y. Additional capacity cannot be obtained in the short run. Which product must KIMCPA decide to make in order to maximize net income?

1) UCM of limited resource (X) = $50 ÷ 2 = $25
2) UCM of limited resource (Y) = $60 ÷ 3 = $20

단위당 공헌이익(UCM)이 큰 제품Y보다는 제한된 제품단위당 공헌이익(UCM of limited resource)이 큰 제품X를 우선 제조하는 것이 최적이다.

제한된 기계시간 600시간의 총공헌이익은 다음과 같다.

Product X: 600 machine-hours ÷ 2 × $50 = $15,000

Product Y: 600 machine-hours ÷ 3 × $60 = $12,000

For the US CPA

03   Decision making under uncertainty

미래의 상황이 불확실한 가운데 최적의 대안을 선택하는 것을 불확실성하의 의사결정(decision making under uncertainty)이라고 하며 다음의 순서로 최적 대안을 선택한다.

(Step 1) Identify a choice criterion. (의사결정의 목적 결정)

(Step 2) Identify the set of alternative actions that can be taken. (모든 대안 열거)

(Step 3) Identify the set of events that can occur. (모든 상황 열거)

(Step 4) Assign a probability to each event that can occur. (각 상황에 확률 부여)

(Step 5) Identify the set of possible outcomes. (각 대안의 각 상황별 성과 계산)

(Step 6) Implementation of chosen action (최적대안 선택)

※ Expected value criteria

기대가치기준이란 각 대안별로 성과의 기대가치(expected value)를 계산하고 그 중 기대가치가 가장 큰 대안을 선택하는 것이다.

An expected value is the weighted average of the outcomes, with the probability of each outcome serving as the weight.

기대가치는 특정 대안을 선택할 경우 특정상황에서 얻게 될 성과와 특정 상황이 발생할 확률을 곱한 후 이들을 모두 합하여 계산한다.

Example-6

KIMCPA can purchase each package from suppliers for $120 per package and predicts he can charge $200 per package. At that price, he is reasonably confident that he will be able to sell at least 30 packages and possibly as many as 60 packages. KIMCPA, on the basis of past experience, assesses a 60% chance that he will sell 30 units and a 40% chance that he will sell 60 units.

Suppose AIFA offers KIMCPA three rental alternatives:
- Option 1: $2,000 fixed fee
- Option 2: $800 fixed fee plus 15% of revenues

(Step 1) Identify a choice criterion.

KIMCPA's choice criterion is to maximize expected operating income

(Step 2) Identify the set of alternative actions that can be taken.

A1 = $2,000 fixed fee   A2 = $800 fixed fee plus 15% of revenues

(Step 3) Identify the set of events that can occur

X1 = 30 units   X2 = 60 units

(Step 4) Assign a probability to each event that can occur

P(X1) = 0.60   P(X2) = 0.40

(Step 5) Identify the set of possible outcomes

Operating income (A1, X1) = ($200 − $120) × 30 − $2,000 = $400

Operating income (A1, X2) = ($200 − $120) × 60 − $2,000 = $2,800

Operating income (A2, X1) = ($200 × 85% − $120) × 30 − $800 = $700

Operating income (A2, X2) = ($200 × 85% − $120) × 60 − $800 = $2,200

(Step 6) Implementation of chosen action

E(A1) = ($400 × 0.60) + ($2,800 × 0.40) = $1,360

E(A2) = ($700 × 0.60) + ($2,200 × 0.40) = $1,300

⇨ To maximize expected operating income, KIMCPA should select action A1

04　MCQ (Multiple Choice Questions)

01. The following are the operating results of the two segments of Parklin Corporation.

	Segment A	Segment B	Total
Sales	$10,000	$15,000	$25,000
Variable costs of goods sold	4,000	8,500	12,500
Fixed costs of goods sold	1,500	2,500	4,000
Gross margin	4,500	4,000	8,500
Variable selling and administrative	2,000	3,000	5,000
Fixed selling and administrative	1,500	1,500	3,000
Operating income (loss)	$1,000	$(500)	$500

Fixed costs of goods sold are allocated to each segment based on the number of employees. Fixed selling and administrative expenses are allocated equally. If Segment B is eliminated, $1,500 of fixed costs of goods sold would be eliminated. Assuming Segment B is closed, the effect on operating income would be (CMA)

a. an increase of $500.

c. a decrease of $2,000.

b. an increase of $2,000.

d. a decrease of $2,500.

Questions 2 through 8 are based on the following information.

The following are Parker's unit costs of manufacturing and marketing a high-style pen at a level of 20,000 units per month:

⟨Selling price⟩ $6.00

⟨Manufacturing costs⟩

Direct materials $1.00
Direct labor   1.20
Variable overhead   0.80
Fixed overhead   0.50

⟨Marketing costs⟩

Variable   1.50
Fixed   0.90

02. In an inventory of 10,000 units of the high-style pen presented on the balance sheet, the unit cost used is (CMA)

a. $3.00   b. $3.50

c. $4.00   d. $5.00

03. The pen is usually produced and sold at the rate of 240,000 units per year. Marketing research estimates that unit sales could be increased by 10% if prices were cut to $5.80. Assuming the implied cost-behavior pattern to be continued, this action would (CMA)

a. decrease operating income by a net of $7,200

b. decrease operating income by a net of $48,000

c. decrease operating income by a net of $16,800

d. A loss of $26,400 would result.

04. A cost contract with the government for 5,000 units of the pens calls for the reimbursement of all manufacturing costs and plus a fixed fee of $1,000. No variable marketing costs are incurred on the government contract. You are required to compare the following two alternatives:

Sales each month to	Alternative A	Alternative B
Regular customers	15,000 units	15,000 units
Government	0	5,000 units

Operating income under alternative B is greater than alternative A by (CMA)

a. $1,000   b. $2,500

c. $3,500   d. $300

05. A cost contract with the government for 5,000 units of the pens calls for the reimbursement of all manufacturing costs and plus a fixed fee of $1,000. No variable marketing costs are incurred on the government contract. You are required to compare the following two alternatives:

Sales each month to	Alternative A	Alternative B
Regular customers	20,000 units	15,000 units
Government	0	5,000 units

Operating income under alternative B relative to that under alternative A by (CMA)

a. $4,000 less   b. $3,000 greater

c. $6,500 less   d. $500 greater

06. The company wants to enter a foreign market in which price competition is keen. The company seeks a one-time-only special order for 10,000 units on a mini-mum-unit-price basis. It expects that shipping costs for this order will amount to only $0.75 per unit, but the fixed costs of obtaining the contract will be $4,000. The company incurs no variable marketing costs other than shipping costs. The selling price to break even is (CMA)

    a. $3.50   b. $4.15   c. $4.25   d. $5.00

07. The company has an inventory of 1,000 units of pens that must be sold immediately at reduced prices. Otherwise the inventory will be worthless. The minimum selling price is (CMA)

    a. $1.50   b. $4.00   c. $4.50   d. $3.00

08. A proposal is received from an outside supplier who will make and ship these pens directly to the KIMCPA's customers as sales orders are forwarded. The marketing fixed costs will be unaffected but its variable marketing costs will be slashed by 20%. KIMCPA's plant will be idle but its fixed manufacturing costs will continue at 50%. How much per unit would the company be able to pay the supplier without decreasing operating income? (CMA)

    a. $4.75   b. $3.95   c. $2.95   d.$3.55

09. ㈜성도는 연간 최대생산량이 10,000단위인 생산설비를 보유하고 있으며, 당기에 제품 단위당 ₩500의 판매가격에 8,000단위의 제품을 판매할 수 있을 것으로 예상하고 있다. 현재의 생산설비에 의한 ㈜성도의 제품 단위당 변동제조원가는 ₩300이다. ㈜성도가 당기에 예상판매량을 1,000단위 줄이고 제품 3,000단위를 판매할 수 있는 특별주문을 고려한다면, 이러한 특별주문 제품의 단위당 최저판매가격은 얼마인가? 단, ㈜성도가 판매하는 모든 제품의 변동판매관리비는 단위당 ₩80이다. (K−CPA)

    a. 400   b. 420   c. 450   d. 500

• 정답 및 해설

1. 사업부 B를 제거한다면 회피 가능한 수익 및 비용
$$15,000 - 8,500 - 1,500 - 3,000 = 2,000$$

정답 : c

2. 재무제표에 보고되는 원가는 전부원가이므로
$$1 + 1.20 + 0.80 + 0.50 = 3.50$$

정답 : b

3. UVC $= 1 + 1.20 + 0.80 + 1.50 = 4.50$
TFC $= (0.50 + 0.90) \times 20,000 \text{ units} = \$28,000$
가격할인 의사결정을 한다면
증분수익 $= 24,000 \text{ units} \times \$5.80 = \$139,200$
증분원가 $= (24,000 \text{ units} \times \$4.50) + (240,000 \text{ units} \times 0.20) = \$156,000$
증분이익 $= 139,200 - 156,000 = (-) 16,800$

정답 : c

4. 기회비용이 없는 의사결정
증분수익 $= (5,000 \text{ units} \times 3.50) + \$1,000 = \$18,500$
증분원가 $= 5,000 \text{ units} \times 3.00 = \$15,000$
증분이익 $= 18,500 - 15,000 = +3,500$

정답 : c

5. 기회비용이 5,000개 있는 의사결정
증분수익 $= (5,000 \text{ units} \times 3.50) + \$1,000 = \$18,500$
증분원가 $= (5,000 \text{ units} \times 3.00) + (5,000 \text{ units} \times 1.50) = \$22,500$
증분이익 $= 18,500 - 22,500 = (-) 4,000$

정답 : a

6. 해외진출 관련원가
변동비 $= 10,000 \times (3.00 + 0.75) = 37,500$
고정비 $= 4,000$
최소가격 $= (37,500 + 4,000) \div 10,000 \text{ units} = \$4.15$

정답 : b

7. 진부화 재고자산의 관련원가는 변동판매비이다.

정답 : a

8. 외부구입 관련원가

변동비 = 3.00 + 1.50 × 20% = 3.30

고정비 = 0.50 × 50% = 0.25

최대가격 = 3.30 + 0.25 = \$3.55

정답 : d

9. 단위당 변동원가 = 300 + 80 = 380

기회비용 = 1,000개 × (500 − 380) = 120,000

증분수익 = 3,000개 × P

증분비용 = 3,000개 × 380 + 120,000 = 1,260,000

증분수익 > 증분원가 → P > 420

정답 : b

05　TBS (Task-Based Simulation)

Problem-1

Advanced Circuitry International (ACI) makes 5,200 units of a circuit board, CB76, at a cost of $280 each. Variable cost per unit is $190 and fixed cost per unit is $90. Peach Electronics offers to supply 5,200 units of CB76 for $260. If ACI buys from Peach it will be able to save $10 per unit in fixed costs but continue to incur the remaining $80 per unit.

• Instruction •

Should ACI accept Peach' offer?

Problem-2

The Dalton Company manufactures slippers and sells them at $12 a pair. Variable manufacturing cost is $5.00 a pair, and allocated fixed manufacturing cost is $1.25 a pair. It has enough idle capacity available to accept a one-time-only special order of 5,000 pairs of slippers at $6.25 a pair. Dalton will not incur any marketing costs as a result of the special order.

• Instruction •

What would the effect on operating income be if the special order could be accepted without affecting normal sales?

Problem-3

Rawlings Corporation produces baseball bats for kids that it sells for $36 each. At capacity, the company can produce 50,000 bats a year.

The costs of producing and selling 50,000 bats are as follows:

⟨Cost per Bat⟩

Direct materials : $13

Direct manufacturing labor : $5

Variable manufacturing overhead : $2

Fixed manufacturing overhead : $6

Variable selling expenses : $3

Fixed selling expenses : $2

• Instruction •

1. Suppose Rawlings is currently producing and selling 40,000 bats. At this level of production and sales, its fixed costs are the same as given in the preceding table. MLB Corporation wants to place a one-time special order for 10,000 bats at $23 each. Rawlings will incur no variable selling costs for this special order. Should Rawlings accept this one-time special order? Show your calculations.

2. Now suppose Rawlings is currently producing and selling 50,000 bats. If Rawlings accepts MLB's offer it will have to sell 10,000 fewer bats to its regular customers.

   (1) On financial considerations alone, should Rawlings accept this one-time special order? Show your calculations.

   (2) On financial considerations alone, at what price would Rawlings be indifferent between accepting the special order and continuing to sell to its regular customers at $36 per bat.

   (3) What other factors should Rawlings consider in deciding whether to accept the one-time special order?

Problem-4

The Sacramento Company manufactures Part No. 498 for use in its production line. The manufacturing cost per unit for 30,000 units of Part No. 498 is as follows:

⟨Cost per unit⟩

Direct materials : $5

Direct manufacturing labor : $22

Variable manufacturing overhead : $8

Fixed manufacturing overhead allocated : $15

Total manufacturing cost per unit : $50

The Counter Company has offered to sell 30,000 units of Part No. 498 to Sacramento for $47 per unit. Sacramento will make the decision to buy the part from Counter if there is an overall savings of at least $30,000 for Sacramento. If Sacramento accepts Counter' offer, $8 per unit of the fixed overhead allocated would be eliminated. Furthermore, Sacramento has determined that the released facilities could be used to save relevant costs in the manufacture of Part No. 575.

• Instruction •

For Sacramento to achieve an overall savings of $30,000, the amount of relevant costs that would have to be saved by using the released facilities in the manufacture of Part No. 575 would be?

Problem-5

The Snack Shack is a take-out food store at a popular beach resort. Susan Sexton, owner of the Snack Shack, is deciding how much refrigerator space to devote to four different drinks. Pertinent data on these four drinks are as follows:

	Cola	Lemonade	Punch	Orange Juice
Selling price per case	$18.80	$20.75	$26.90	$39.30
Variable cost per case	$13.80	$16.25	$20.10	$30.10
Cases sold per foot of shelf space per day	7	12	24	6

Sexton has a maximum front shelf space of 12 feet to devote to the four drinks. She wants a minimum of 1 foot and a maximum of 6 feet of front shelf space for each drink.

• Instruction •

1. Calculate the contribution margin per case of each type of drink.

2. A coworker of Sexton' recommends that she maximize the shelf space devoted to those drinks with the highest contribution margin per case. Do you agree with this recommendation? Explain briefly.

Problem-6

Sanchez Corporation runs two convenience stores, one in Connecticut and one in Rhode Island. Operating income for each store in 20X1 is as follows:

	Connecticut Store	Rhode Island Store
Revenues	$1,070,000	$ 860,000
Cost of goods sold	750,000	660,000
Lease rent (renewable each year)	90,000	75,000
Labor costs (paid on an hourly basis)	42,000	42,000
Depreciation of equipment	25,000	22,000
Utilities (electricity, heating)	43,000	46,000
Allocated corporate overhead	50,000	40,000
Operating income (loss)	$ 70,000	$ (25,000)

The equipment has a zero disposal value. In a senior management meeting, Maria Lopez, the management accountant at Sanchez Corporation, makes the following comment, "Sanchez can increase its profitability by closing down the Rhode Island store or by adding another store like it."

• Instruction •

1. By closing down the Rhode Island store, Sanchez can reduce overall corporate overhead costs by $44,000. Calculate Sanchez' operating income if it closes the Rhode Island store. Is Maria Lopez' statement about the effect of closing the Rhode Island store correct? Explain.

2. Calculate Sanchez' operating income if it keeps the Rhode Island store open and opens another store with revenues and costs identical to the Rhode Island store (including a cost of $22,000 to acquire equipment with a one-year useful life and zero disposal value). Opening this store will increase corporate overhead costs by $4,000. Is Maria Lopez' statement about the effect of adding another store like the Rhode Island store correct? Explain.

Problem-7

Walmart Corporation, an international retail giant, is considering implementing a new business-to-business (B2B) information system for processing merchandise orders. The current system costs Walmart $1,000,000 per month and $45 per order. Walmart has two options, a partially automated B2B and a fully automated B2B system. The partially automated B2B system will have a fixed cost of $5,000,000 per month and a variable cost of $35 per order. The fully automated B2B system has a fixed cost of $11,000,000 per month and $20 per order.

Based on data from the past two years, Walmart has determined the following distribution on monthly orders:

Monthly number of orders	Probability
300,000	0.15
400,000	0.20
500,000	0.40
600,000	0.15
700,000	0.10

• Instruction •

1. Prepare a table showing the cost of each plan for each quantity of monthly orders.

2. What is the expected cost of each plan?

Problem-8

㈜아리수는 휴대폰에 장착되는 전지를 생산한다. 회사는 현재 생산시설용량(월 8,000 직접노무시간)의 75%를 가동하고 있다. 최근 회사는 ㈜한국전자로부터 개당 ₩700에 5,000개의 전지를 1개월 안에 납품해 달라는 특별주문을 받았다. 전지의 개당 제조원가는 다음과 같다.

직접재료원가	₩200
직접노무원가(개당 0.5 직접노무시간)	300
제조간접원가	200
개당 제조원가	₩700

㈜아리수의 직접재료원가와 직접노무원가는 변동원가이다. 제조간접원가 중 변동제조간접원가는 직접노무시간당 ₩240이다. ㈜아리수는 향후 수개월동안 월 6,000 직접노무시간(8,000 직접노무시간 × 75%)의 조업도를 유지하기에 충분한 경상주문을 받아 놓고 있다. 경상주문품의 판매가격은 개당 ₩1,000이다. (K−CPA)

• Instruction •

1. ㈜아리수가 5,000개의 특별주문을 수락할 경우, 일부 경상주문을 포기함으로 인한 기회비용(opportunity cost)은 얼마인가?

2. ㈜아리수가 5,000개의 특별주문을 수락할 경우 증분손익은 얼마인가?

Responsibility Accounting

Responsibility Accounting

01   Decentralization

1   Decentralization

기업의 규모가 커지면서 기업의 조직은 부문화가 되는데 이때 각 부문의 의사결정권한을 얼마나 부여할 것인가에 대한 결정에 따라 집권화와 분권화로 구분된다.

- Centralization (집권화) : 최고 경영자가 대부분의 의사결정을 행사하는 것
- Decentralization (분권화) : 부문경영자에게 의사결정권한을 부여하여 의사결정의 자율성을 갖는 것

Decentralization is an organizational structure that gives managers at lower levels the freedom to make decisions. Autonomy is the degree of freedom to make decisions.

2   Benefits of decentralization

(1) It leads to quicker decision making

분권화를 실시하는 기업은 하부경영자가 상부경영자에게 보고하는 절차가 생략되기 때문에 빠른 의사결정이 가능해진다.

(2) It increases motivation

하부경영자들은 더 많은 권한(authority)과 책임(responsibility)을 가지고 의사결정을 하므로 동기부여가 된다.

(3) It aids management development and learning

하부경영자는 미래의 상부경영자가 될 것이므로 현재의 경첩은 좋은 능력개발과 교육이 된다.

(4) It creates greater response to local needs

지역 사업부를 책임지고 있는 경영자는 그 사업부가 위치하고 있는 지역에 대해서 잘 알고 있기 때문에 적시에 적절한 대응을 할 수 있다.

(5) It sharpens the focus of managers

분권화는 사업부별로 보다 집중적인 경영관리를 가능하게 한다.

3 Costs of decentralization

(1) It leads to suboptimal decision making

하부 경영자는 기업 전체의 입장보다는 자신의 입장에서 의사결정을 하는 등 기업전체의 목표와 일치하지 않는 목표불일치 (goal in-congruence) 의사결정의 문제가 발생한다. (준최적화 또는 부문최적화 현상)

(2) It increases the cost of gathering information

각 사업부문마다 필요한 정보를 수집하면서 정보수집비용의 증가한다.

(3) It results in duplication of activities

기업전체로 볼 때 여러 사업부문에서 동일한 활동이 수행되는 중복현상이 발생한다.

02 / Responsibility accounting

1 Responsibility accounting

분권화가 되면 권한을 부여받은 내용에 따라 책임을 지게 된다. 이를 위하여 기업은 기업 내에 여러 책임중심점(responsibility center)을 설정하여 계획을 수립하고 성과평가를 함으로써 책임중심점의 관리자에 대한 평가를 하는데 이를 책임회계(responsibility accounting)이라고 한다.

Responsibility accounting is a system that measures the plans, budgets, actions, and actual results of each responsibility center. A responsibility center is a part, segment, or subunit of an organization whose manager is accountable for a specified set of activities.

2 Responsibility center

책임중심점은 권한과 책임의 범위에 따라 4가지 유형으로 분류된다.

(1) Cost center (원가중심점)

1) Manager is responsible for costs only

⇨ 원가의 발생에 대하여만 책임을 지고 판매수익이나 이익에 대해서는 책임을 지지 않는다.

2) Example: production department (제조부문)

3) Performance measures : standard costing (표준원가 차이분석)

⇨ 표준원가에 의한 차이분석은 14장에서 자세히 논의한다.

(2) Revenue center (수익중심점)

1) Manager is responsible for revenue only

2) Example: sales department (판매부문)

3) Performance measures : sales variance analysis (매출차이분석)

(3) Profit center (이익중심점)

1) Manager is responsible for revenue and costs

2) Example : 판매지역, 각 점포단위, 사업부 등

3) Performance measures : 매출에서 통제할 수 있는 원가를 차감한 이익

⇨ 주로 공헌이익으로 성과측정

(4) Investment center (투자중심점)

1) Manager is responsible for investments, revenue and costs

2) Example : 개별회사, 분권화된 사업부 등

3) Performance measures : ROI, RI, EVA

⇨ 투자중심점의 성과지표는 16장에서 자세히 논의한다.

※ Hilton Worldwide Holdings, Marriott International

- The maintenance department: cost center

- The sales department: revenue center

- The hotel manager: profit center

- The regional manager: investment center

3 Controllable costs

(1) Controllable costs

책임중심점 관리자(responsibility center manager)가 자신의 권한으로 통제할 수 있는 원가로서 직위가 높을수록, 장기간이 될수록 통제가능원가의 범위는 증가한다.

(2) Uncontrollable costs

책임중심점 관리자(responsibility center manager)가 자신의 권한으로 통제할 수 없는 원가로서 성과평가에 포함하지 않는다.

4 Performance report

성과보고서는 책임중심점의 성과평가를 위하여 필수적으로 작성되는 보고서로 예산과 실제성과 및 차이가 표시된다. 성과보고서를 통하여 경영자는 예외에 의한 관리(management by exception)를 할 수 있다. 책임중심점별로 성과평가를 하기 위한 성과보고서는 다음과 같다.

	Actual Results	Flexible Budget	Static Budget
Sales revenues	$AP \times AQ$	$BP \times AQ$	$BP \times BQ$
Variable costs	$AVC \times AQ$	$BVC \times AQ$	$BVC \times BQ$
Contribution margin	$ACM \times AQ$	$BCM \times AQ$	$BCM \times BQ$
Fixed costs	AFC	BFC	BFC
Operating income	xxx (1)	xxx (2)	xxx (3)

AQ : actual sales quantity   BQ : budgeted sales quantity

AP : actual sales price   BP : budgeted sales price

AVC : actual unit variable costs   BVC : budgeted unit variable costs

ACM : actual unit contribution margin   BCM : budgeted unit contribution margin

AFC : actual total fixed costs   BFC : budgeted total fixed costs

(1) Static budget variance (고정예산차이)

The static budget is based on the level of output planned at the start of the budget period. The static-budget variance is the difference between the actual result and the corresponding budgeted amount in the static budget.

$$\text{Static budget variance} = \text{Actual} - \text{Static budget} = (1) - (3)$$

static budget variance $> 0 \Rightarrow$ favorable variance (F)

static budget variance $< 0 \Rightarrow$ unfavorable variance (U)

(2) Flexible budget variance (변동예산차이)

A flexible budget calculates budgeted revenues and budgeted costs based on the actual output in the budget period. The flexible-budget variance is the difference between an actual result and the corresponding flexible-budget amount.

Flexible budget variance = Actual − Flexible budget = (1) − (2)

(3) Sales volume variance (매출조업도차이)

The difference between the static-budget and the flexible-budget amounts is called the sales-volume variance.

Sales volume variance = (2) − (3)
= Static budget variance − Flexible budget variance
= BCM × AQ − BCM × BQ

⇨ 매출조업도차이는 변동예산과 고정예산의 차이를 의미하지만, 변동예산상의 공헌이익과 고정예산상의 공헌이익의 차이를 의미하기도 한다.

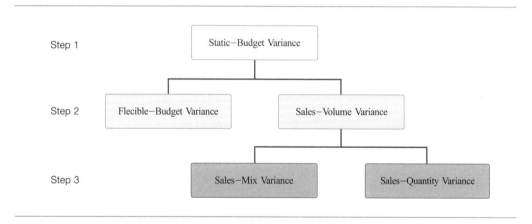

[그림 13−1] Overview of variances

Example – 1

Michelin manufactures tires for the Formula I motor racing circuit.

For 20X1, it budgeted to manufacture and sell 3,000 tires at a variable cost of $74 per tire and total fixed costs of $54,000. The budgeted selling price was $110 per tire. Actual results in 20X1 were 2,800 tires manufactured and sold at a selling price of $112 per tire. The actual total variable costs were $229,600, and the actual total fixed costs were $50,000.

Prepare a performance report that uses a flexible budget and a static budget.

(1) Actual result

AQ = 2,800, AP=$112, AVC= $229,600 ÷ 2,800 = $82,

ACM = 112 − 82 = $30, AFC = $50,000

Operating income = 2,800 × $30 − $50,000 = $34,000

(2) Flexible budget

BQ = 3,000, BP = $110, BVC = 74,

BCM = 110 − 74 = $36, BFC = $54,000

Operating income = 2,800 × $36 − $54,000 = $46,800

(3) Static budget

Operating income = 3,000 × $36 − $54,000 = $54,000

(4) Static budget variance = $34,000 − $54,000 = (−)$20,000 U

(5) Flexible budget variance = $34,000 − $46,800 = (−)$12,800 U

(6) Sales volume variance = $46,800 − $54,000 = (−)$7,200 U or

$$= -20,000 - (-12,800) = (-)\$7,200 \text{ U or}$$

$$= (2,800 - 3,000) \times \$36 = (-)\$7,200 \text{ U}$$

5 Sales variance

수익중심점(revenue center)의 성과평가를 위한 차이분석을 매출차이분석(sales variance)라고 한다.

(1) Sales price variance (매출가격차이)

매출가격차이는 실제매출액과 변동예산상의 매출액의 차이를 말한다.

$$\text{Sales price variance} = AP \times AQ - BP \times AQ$$

(2) Sales volume variance (매출조업도차이)

매출조업도차이는 변동예산상의 공헌이익과 고정예산상의 공헌이익의 차이를 의미하며, 매출배합차이(sales mix variance)와 매출수량차이(sales quantity variance)로 세분화 된다.

$$\text{Sales volume variance} = BCM \times AQ - BCM \times BQ$$
$$= \text{Sales mix variance} + \text{Sales quantity variance}$$

(3) Sales mix variance (매출배합차이)

The sales-mix variance is the difference between (1) budgeted contribution margin for the actual sales mix and (2) budgeted contribution margin for the budgeted sales mix.

$$\text{Sales max variance} = AQ \times BCM - EAQ \times BCM$$

EAQ: Expected Actual Quantity (실제 판매수량 중 예상 배합비율에 해당되는 판매수량)
EAQ = Total actual quantity × Budgeted sales mix percentage

(4) Sales quantity variance (매출수량차이)

The sales-quantity variance is the difference between (1) budgeted contribution margin based on actual units sold of all products at the budgeted mix and (2) contribution margin in the static budget.

The two components of the sales-quantity variance are (a) the difference between the actual market share and the budgeted market share (the market-share variance) and (b) the difference between the actual market size in units and the budgeted market size in units (the market-size variance).

$$\text{Sales quantity variance} = \text{EAQ} \times \text{BCM} - \text{BQ} \times \text{BCM}$$

매출조업도 분석을 정리하면 다음과 같다.

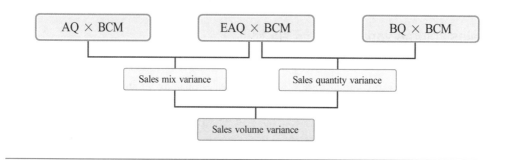

Example-2

Coca-Cola manufactures and sells two soft drinks: Cola and Sprite.

⟨Budgeted data⟩

Products	Cola	Sprite
Selling price	$100	$60
Variable cost per unit	60	40
Cartons sold	400	600

⟨Actual data⟩

Products	Cola	Sprite
Selling price	$120	$70
Variable cost per unit	82	46
Cartons sold	540	660

Compute the sales price variance, the total sales-volume variance, the total sales-mix variance, and the total sales-quantity variance.

(1) UCM

Budgeted UCM of Cola = 100 − 60 = $40

Budgeted UCM of Sprite = 60 − 40 = $20

Actual UCM of Cola = 120 − 82 = $38

Actual UCM of Sprite = 70 − 46 = $24

(2) EAQ

Budgeted total quantity = 400 + 600 = 1,000

Actual total quantity = 540 + 660 = 1,200

Budgeted sales mix percentage of Cola = 400 / 1,000 = 40%

Budgeted sales mix percentage of Sprite = 600 / 1,000 = 60%

EAQ of Cola = 1,200 × 0.4 = 480

EAQ of Sprite = 1,200 × 0.6 = 720

(3) Sales price variance

Cola : $(120 - 100) \times 540 = 10,800$ F

Sprite : $(70 - 60) \times 660 = 6,600$ F

Total $= 10,800 + 6,600 = 17,400$ F

(4) Sales volume variance

Cola : $(540 - 400) \times 40 = 5,600$ F

Sprite : $(660 - 600) \times 20 = 1,200$ F

Total $= 5,600 + 1,200 = 6,800$ F

(5) Sales mix variance

Cola : $(540 - 480) \times 40 = 2,400$ F

Sprite : $(660 - 720) \times 20 = 1,200$ U

Total $= 2,400 - 1,200 = 1,200$ F

(6) Sales quantity variance

Cola : $(480 - 400) \times 40 = 3,200$ F

Sprite : $(720 - 600) \times 20 = 2,400$ F

Total $= 3,200 + 2,400 = 5,600$ F

※ Flexible budget variance

Cola : $(38 - 40) \times 540 = 1,080$ U

Sprite : $(24 - 20) \times 660 = 2,640$ F

Total $= -1,080 + 2,640 = 1,560$ F

03   MCQ (Multiple Choice Questions)

01. Which one of the following best identifies a profit center? (CMA)

    a. The Information Technology Department of a large consumer products company.

    b. A large toy company.

    c. The Production Operations Department of a small job-order machine shop company.

    d. A new car sales division for a large local auto agency.

02. Characteristics of a responsibility accounting system include all of the following except that (CMA)

    a. responsibility for performance according to budget must be linked to the appropriate authority.

    b. the system should encourage employee involvement and participation.

    c. cost centers are responsible for revenues as well as common costs.

    d. each level of management is responsible for their department's operations and employees.

03. Sara Bellows, manager of the telecommunication sales team, has the following department budget.

Billings - long distance	$350,000
Billings - phone card	75,000
Billings - toll free	265,000

Her responsibility center is best described as a (CMA)

    a. cost center.   b. revenue center.

    c. profit center.   d. investment center.

04. Teaneck Inc. sells two products, Product E and Product F, and had the following data for last month.

	Product E		Product F	
	Budget	Actual	Budget	Actual
Unit sales	5,500	6,000	4,500	6,000
Unit contribution margin	$4.50	$4.80	$10.00	$10.50

The company's sales mix variance is (CMA)

a. $3,300 favorable.   b. $3,420 favorable.

c. $17,250 favorable.   d. $18,150 favorable.

05. The following performance report was prepared for Dale Manufacturing for the month of April.

	Actual Results	Static Budget	Variance
Sales units	100,000	80,000	20,000F
Sales dollars	$190,000	$160,000	$30,000F
Variable costs	125,000	96,000	29,000U
Fixed costs	45,000	40,000	5,000U
Operating income	$ 20,000	$ 24,000	$ 4,000U

Using a flexible budget, Dale's total sales-volume variance is (CMA)

a. $4,000 unfavorable.   b. $6,000 favorable.

c. $16,000 favorable.   d. $20,000 unfavorable.

· 정답 및 해설

1. ⟨a⟩와 ⟨c⟩는 cost center

⟨b⟩는 investment center

⟨d⟩는 자동차 제조회사가 아닌 자동차 판매회사이기 때문에 profit center이다.

정답 : d

2. Cost center는 수익에 대해서는 통제 불가능이다.

정답 : c

3. 통신판매부서는 revenue center이다.

정답 : b

4. Budget sales mix ratio: E + F = 5,500 + 4,500 = 10,000 이므로 E = 0.55, F = 0.45

SMV(E) = (AP − EAP) × BCM = (6,000 − 12,000 × 0.55) × 4.50 = −2,700

SMV(F) = (AP − EAP) × BCM = (6,000 − 12,000 × 0.45) × 10 = +6,000

Total = −2,700 + 6,000 = +3,300 (F)

정답 : a

5. BCM = (160,000 − 96,000) ÷ 80,000 units = \$0.80

SVV = (AP − BP) × BCM = (100,000 − 80,000) × 0.80 = +16,000

정답 : c

04 / TBS (Task-Based Simulation)

Problem-1

Libbey Corporation sells two brands of wine glasses: Plain and Chic.

Libbey provides the following information for sales in the month of June 20X1:
- Static-budget total contribution margin : $15,525
- Budgeted units to be sold of all glasses : 2,300 units
- Budgeted contribution margin per unit of Plain : $5 per unit
- Budgeted contribution margin per unit of Chic : $12 per unit
- Total sales-quantity variance : $2,700 U
- Actual sales-mix percentage of Plain : 60%

All variances are to be computed in contribution-margin terms.

• Instruction •

1. Calculate the sales—quantity variances for each product for June 20X1.

2. Calculate the individual—product and total sales—mix variances for June 20X1.

3. Calculate the individual product and total sales—volume variances for June 20X1.

Problem-2

KIM Printers, Inc., produces luxury checkbooks with three checks and stubs per page. Each checkbook is designed for an individual customer and is ordered through the customer' bank. The company' operating budget for 20X1 included these data:
- Number of checkbooks : 15,000
- Selling price per book : $20
- Variable cost per book : $8
- Fixed costs for the month : $145,000

The actual results for 20X1 were as follows:
- Number of checkbooks produced and sold : 12,000
- Average selling price per book : $21
- Variable cost per book : $7
- Fixed costs for the month : $150,000

The executive vice president of the company observed that the operating income for 20X1 was much lower than anticipated, despite a higher-than-budgeted selling price and a lower-than-budgeted variable cost per unit. As the company' management accountant, you have been asked to provide explanations for the disappointing 20X1 results. KIM Printers develops its flexible budget on the basis of budgeted per-output-unit revenue and per-output-unit variable costs without detailed analysis of budgeted inputs.

· Instruction ·

1. Prepare a static—budget—based variance analysis of the 20X1 performance.

2. Prepare a flexible—budget—based variance analysis of the 20X1 performance.

Problem-3

Ben & Jerry's Company produces the basic fillings used in many popular frozen desserts and treats—vanilla and chocolate ice creams, puddings, meringues, and fudge. Ben & Jerry's uses standard costing and carries over no inventory from one month to the next. The ice-cream product group's results for June 20X1 were as follows:

	Actual results	Static Budget
Units (pounds)	350,000	335,000
Revenues	$2,012,500	$1,976,500
Variable manufacturing costs	1,137,500	1,038,500
Contribution margin	$875,00	$938,000

KIM, the business manager for ice-cream products, is pleased that more pounds of ice cream were sold than budgeted and that revenues were up. Unfortunately, variable manufacturing costs went up, too. The bottom line is that contribution margin declined by $63,000, which is less than 3% of the budgeted revenues of $1,976,500. Overall, KIM feels that the business is running fine.

• Instruction •

1. Calculate the static—budget variance in units, revenues, variable manufacturing costs, and contribution margin. What percentage is each static—budget variance relative to its static—budget amount?

2. Break down each static—budget variance into a flexible—budget variance and a sales— volume variance.

3. Calculate the selling—price variance.

Control & Performance Measures

Chapter

14

Standard Costing

1 Standard cost

(1) Predetermined target costs under efficient conditions

표준원가란 효율적인 상황에서의 원가를 말하며 단순히 예측되는 원가만을 의미하는 예산 (budget)과는 다른 개념이다. 즉, 효율적 상태의 예산이 곧 표준인 것이다.

(2) Functions

1) The standard is a planning tool

Flexible budgeting에서는 표준을 원가의 예측도구로 사용한다.

2) The standard is a control tool

실제원가와 표준원가를 비교하는 차이분석을 사용하여 원가를 통제한다.

3) The standard is a cost measurement tool

표준은 재고자산의 원가계산과정을 단순화 및 신속화 할 수 있다.

(3) Industry

표준원가는 산업의 형태화 관계없이 적용할 수 있다. 즉, 제조업뿐만 아니라 서비스업에서 도 적용이 가능하며, 개별원가계산 또는 종합원가계산 모두 적용이 가능하다.

(4) GAAP

표준원가에 의한 재고자산의 기록 방식은 현재 미국 회계기준(GAAP)에서 허용되고 있다. 따라서 표준원가에 의한 회계처리는 고정제조간접원가(FOH)를 재고자산으로 기록하는 전부 원가계산으로 하여야 한다.

2 Standard types

(1) Ideal standards

1) Standard costs which could be achieved under perfect condition.

2) With no allowance for spoilage or breakdown.

(2) Currently attainable standards

1) Standard costs which could be achieved under efficient condition.

2) With allowance for spoilage or breakdown.

⇨ currently attainable standards으로 원가를 통제하는 것이 ideal standards으로 원가를 통제하는 것 보다 더 목적적합하다

3 Variance analysis

표준원가제도에서 중요한 핵심은 차이분석이며 이때 차이는 다음과 같이 정의 된다.

$$\text{Variance} = \text{Actual cost} - \text{Standard cost}$$

Variance > 0 ⇨ Actual cost $>$ Standard cost ⇨ Unfavorable variance(U)
Variance < 0 ⇨ Actual cost $<$ Standard cost ⇨ Favorable variance(F)

Variances facilitate management by exception. Management by exception is a practice whereby managers focus more closely on areas that are not operating as expected and less closely on areas that are.

Example-1

ZARA Corporation designs and manufactures T-shirts. It sells its T-shirts to brand-name clothes retailers. ZARA's 20X1 budget and actual results are as follows:

〈Budget〉

Standard cost per unit = $5

〈Actual〉

Actual finished goods = 20 units

Total actual manufacturing cost = $120

Total standard cost = 20 units × $5 = $100

Variance = $120 − $100 = +20 (U)

경영자는 재고자산 20개의 원가를 $100로 계산하여 의사결정을 하며 불리한 차이 $20에 대해서는 책임부서를 찾아 통제한다. 회계처리는 다음과 같다.

Dr) Inventory   100   Cr) Cash   120
    Variance   20

Variance > 0 ⇨ Unfavorable variance(U) ⇨ Debit account

Variance < 0 ⇨ Favorable variance(F) ⇨ Credit account

variance account balance는 마감 전에 다음과 같이 제거한다.

If not significant, close out them to CGS.

If significant, allocated them to CGS and appropriate ending inventories.

차이분석은 원가의 형태에 따라 다음과 같이 구분한다.

− Direct material variance

− Direct labor variance

− Variable overhead variance

− Fixed overhead variance

02 Variance analysis

1 Direct material variance

(1) Price and quantity variance

A price variance is the difference between actual price and standard price, multiplied by the actual input quantity, such as direct materials purchased.

A quantity variance is the difference between the actual input quantity used (such as square yards of cloth) and the standard input quantity allowed for actual output, multiplied by standard price. A quantity variance is sometimes called a usage variance or an efficiency variance.

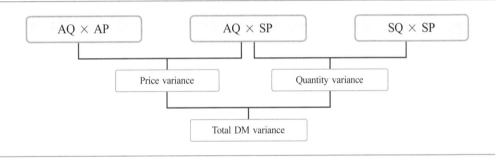

AQ: 직접재료의 실제투입량　　　　AP: 직접재료단위당 실제가격
SQ: 실제 산출량에 허용된 표준투입량　　SP: 직접재료단위당 표준가격

$$Price\ variance = AQ \times (AP-SP)$$
$$Quantity\ variance = SP \times (AQ-SQ)$$

※ 직접재료의 구입수량과 투입수량이 다른 경우

　직접재료의 구입수량과 투입수량이 다르다면 가격차이는 실제 구입수량 기준으로 계산하고, 수량차이는 실제 투입수량을 기준으로 계산한다.

$$Price\ variance = AQ^* \times (AP-SP)$$
$$Quantity\ variance = SP \times (AQ-SQ)$$

AQ*: 직접재료의 실제구입량

Example-2

ZARA Corporation designs and manufactures T-shirts. It sells its T-shirts to brand-name clothes retailers. ZARA's 20X1 budget and actual results are as follows:

⟨Budget⟩

DM standard per unit : 2 pounds per unit

Standard price per pound : $5

⟨Actual⟩

Actual output produced : 100 units

Actual DM purchased were 250 pounds at $6 per pound

Actual DM used were 210 pounds.

(1) Price variance

= AQ* × (AP−SP) = 250 pounds × ($6−$5) = +$250 (U)

(2) Quantity variance

= SP × (AQ−SQ) = $5 × (210 pounds − 200 pounds) = +$50 (U)

(3) Total direct material variance

= 250 + 50 = +$300 (U)

가격차이는 구입시점에서 인식하며, 수량차이는 투입시점에서 인식하는데 이를 회계처리하면 다음과 같다.

When purchased		When used	
Material inventory	1,250	WIP	1,000
Price variance	250	Quantity variance	50
Various accounts	1,500	Material inventory	1,050

(2) Variance analysis

직접재료 가격차이는 가격결정 권한이 있는 구매부서의 성과로 평가하며, 직접재료 수량차이는 제조부서의 성과로 평가한다.

Variance	Responsibility department
Price variance	Purchase department
Quantity variance	Production department

Causes for price variance

- Purchasing manager negotiated the direct materials prices more skillfully.
- Purchasing manager switched to a lower—price supplier.
- Purchasing manager ordered larger quantities and obtains quantity discounts.
- Unexpected materials prices changes.
- Purchasing manager negotiated favorable prices because of he was willing to accept unfavorable terms on factors other than prices (lower—quality material).

Causes for quantity variance

- Poor design of products or processes
- Poor work on the production line because of under—skilled workers
- Inappropriate assignment of labor or machines to specific jobs
- Suppliers not manufacturing materials of uniformly high quality

(3) Graph analysis

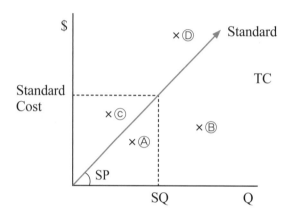

	Price	Quantity
A	F	F
B	F	U
C	U	F
D	U	U

[그림 14-1]

2 Direct labor variance

(1) Rate and efficiency variance

A rate variance is the difference between actual price and standard price, multiplied by the actual input quantity.

An efficiency variance is the difference between the actual input quantity used and the standard input quantity allowed for actual output, multiplied by standard price.

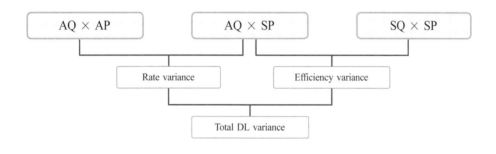

AQ: 실제 직접노동시간   AP: 직접노동시간당 실제임률

SQ: 실제 산출량에 허용된 표준직접노동시간   SP: 직접노동시간당 표준임률

$$\text{Rate variance} = AQ \times (AP - SP)$$
$$\text{Efficiency variance} = SP \times (AQ - SQ)$$

Example-3

ZARA Corporation designs and manufactures T-shirts. It sells its T-shirts to brand-name clothes retailers. ZARA's 20X1 budget and actual results are as follows:

⟨Budget⟩

DL standard per unit : 3 hours per unit
Standard price per hour : $2

⟨Actual⟩

Actual output produced : 100 units
Actual DL used were 290 hours at $2.10 per hour

(1) Rate variance

= AQ × (AP−SP) = 290 hours × ($2.1 − $2.0) = +$29 (U)

(2) Efficiency variance

= SP × (AQ−SQ) = $2 × (290 hours − 300 hours) = −$20 (F)

(3) Total direct labor variance

= 29 − 20 = +$9 (U)

직접노무원가의 표준원가 회계처리는 다음과 같다.

WIP	600	
Rate variance	29	
	Various accounts	609
	Efficiency variance	20

(2) Variance analysis

직접노무원가 가격차이(rate variance)는 인사채용 권한이 있는 인사부서의 성과로 평가하며, 직접노무원가 능률차이(efficiency variance)는 제조부서의 성과로 평가한다.

Variance	Responsibility department
Rate variance	Personnel department
Efficiency variance	Production department

Causes for rate variance

- Personnel manager changes hourly wages
- Personnel manager hired under-skilled workers.
- Increase overtime work

Causes for efficiency variance

- Workers worked more slowly or made poor-quality products that required reworking.
- Personnel manager hired under-skilled workers.
- Production scheduler inefficiently scheduled work.
- Maintenance department did not properly maintain machines.
- Budgeted time standards were too tight.

3 Variable overhead variance

(1) Spending and efficiency variance

The variable overhead spending variance is the difference between the actual variable overhead cost per unit of the cost-allocation base and the budgeted variable overhead cost per unit of the cost-allocation base, multiplied by the actual quantity of variable overhead cost-allocation base used.

The variable overhead efficiency variance is the difference between actual quantity of the cost-allocation base used and budgeted quantity of the cost-allocation base that should have been used to produce the actual output, multiplied by the budgeted variable overhead cost per unit of the cost-allocation base.

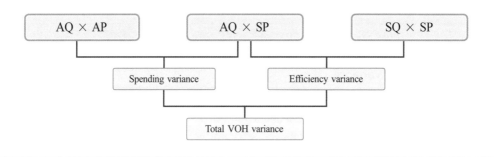

AQ: 실제 배부기준수   AP: 배부기준단위당 VOH 실제배부율
SQ: 실제 산출량에 허용된 표준배부기준수   SP: 배부기준단위당 VOH 예정배부율

$$\text{VOH Spending variance} = AQ \times (AP - SP)$$
$$\text{VOH Efficiency variance} = SP \times (AQ - SQ)$$

직접재료원가(DM)는 재료 수량, 직접노무원가(DL)는 노동시간과 같은 직접 추적이 가능한 조업도가 존재하지만 제조간접원가(MOH)는 직접 추적이 되는 조업도가 존재하지 않으므로 노동시간이나 기계시간과 같은 배부기준을 미리 설정하여 시간당 배부율을 결정하여야 한다. 따라서 제조 간접원가의 표준가격인 SP는 정상원가계산(normal costing)의 예정 배부율을 의미한다.

> **Example-4**

ZARA Corporation designs and manufactures T-shirts. It sells its T-shirts to brand-name clothes retailers. Factory overhead is allocated to units produced on the basis of standard direct labor hours. ZARA's 20X1 budget and actual results are as follows:

〈Budget〉

Direct labor standard per unit : 3 hours per unit

ZARA estimated variable factory overhead of $1,000 based on normal capacity of 400 hours

〈Actual〉

Actual output produced : 100 units

Actual direct labor used were 290 hours.

Actual variable factory overhead was $740.

(1) SP = $1,000 ÷ 400 hours = $2.50 per hour

(2) VOH Spending variance

$= AQ \times (AP - SP) = \$740 - 290$ hours $\times \$2.5 = +\$15$ (U)

(3) VOH Efficiency variance

$= SP \times (AQ - SQ) = \$2.50 \times (290$ hours $- 300$ hours$) = -\$25$ (F)

(4) Total VOH variance = 15 − 25 = −$10 (F)

변동제조간접원가의 표준원가 회계처리는 다음과 같다.

WIP	750	
Spending variance	15	
Various accounts		740
Efficiency variance		25

(2) Variance analysis

변동제조간접원가의 불리한 소비차이는 전기료, 소모품등의 지출을 낭비한 경우에 발생하며, 불리한 능률차이는 배부기준으로 선정한 노동시간이나 기계시간을 표준보다 더 사용하는 경우에 발생한다. 따라서 변동제조간접원가 소비차이(spending variance)과 능률차이(efficiency variance)는 모두 제조부서의 성과로 평가한다.

Variance	Responsibility department
Spending variance	Production department
Efficiency variance	Production department

Causes for spending variance

- Unexpected energy or indirect material prices change.
- Budget error
- Waste of energy or indirect material

Causes for efficiency variance

- Workers worked more slowly.
- Production scheduler inefficiently scheduled work.
- Maintenance department did not properly maintain machines.
- Budgeted time standards were too tight.

4 Fixed overhead variance

(1) Spending and volume variance

The fixed overhead spending variance is the difference between actual fixed overhead costs and fixed overhead costs in the flexible budget.

There is no efficiency variance for fixed overhead costs. That' because a given lump sum of fixed overhead costs will be unaffected by how efficiently machine-hours are used to produce output in a given budget period.

The production-volume variance, also referred to as the denominator-level variance, is the difference between the budgeted and allocated fixed overhead amounts on the basis of actual output produced. The production-volume variance arises only for fixed costs.

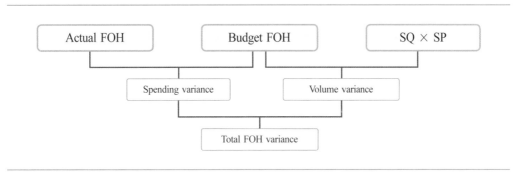

SQ: 실제 산출량에 허용된 표준배부기준수   SP: 배부기준단위당 FOH 예정배부율

FOH Spending variance = Actual FOH − Budget FOH
(Production) Volume variance = Budget FOH − SP × SQ

원가통제목적의 고정제조간접원가는 budget FOH를 사용하지만, 제품원가계산목적의 고정제조간접원가는 SP × SQ를 사용한다. 이때 발생하는 차이를 조업도차이(volume variance)라고 한다.

Example-5

ZARA Corporation designs and manufactures T-shirts. It sells its T-shirts to brand-name clothes retailers. Factory overhead is allocated to units produced on the basis of standard direct labor hours. ZARA's 20X1 budget and actual results are as follows:

⟨Budget⟩

Direct labor standard per unit : 3 hours per unit

ZARA estimated fixed factory overhead of $2,000 based on normal capacity of 400 hours

⟨Actual⟩

Actual output produced : 100 units

Actual fixed factory overhead was $2,100

(1) SP = $2,000 ÷ 400 hours = $5 per hour

(2) FOH Spending variance

= Actual FOH − Budget FOH = $2,100 − $2,000 = +$100 (U)

(3) Volume variance

= Budget FOH − SP × SQ = $2,000 − $5 × 300 hours = +$500 (U)

(4) Total FOH variance = 100 + 500 = +$600 (U)

고정제조간접원가의 표준원가 회계처리는 다음과 같다.

WIP	1,500	
Spending variance	100	
Volume variance	500	
Various accounts		2,100

(2) Variance analysis

고정제조간접원가의 불리한 소비차이는 유형자산에 대한 자본적 지출을 낭비하거나 관리가 잘못되어 감가상각비가 더 발생한 경우로서 이에 권한이 있는 부서가 책임져야 한다. 하지만 조업도차이(volume variance)는 표준원가를 원가계산목적으로 전부원가계산방법에 따라 제품에 배부한 하기 위하여 예산으로 정한 기준조업도와 실제조업도가 차이가 나서 발생하는 것으로 어느 부서에도 책임을 물을 수 없는 통제 불가능한 차이이다. 표준원가에서 발생하는 차이(variance) 중에서 유일하게 통제 불가능한 차이는 조업도차이이다.

Variance	Responsibility department
Spending variance	Maintenance department etc.
Volume variance	Uncontrollable

Causes for spending variance

- Higher plant−leasing costs
- Higher depreciation on plant and equipment
- Higher salary paid to the plant manager.
- Budget error

Causes for volume variance

- 전부원가계산에서는 고정제조간접원가(FOH)도 제품원가로 계산하여야 하기 때문에 제품 수량에 비례하여 표준원가를 배부하여야 한다. 따라서 사전에 예측한 정상조업도와 실제 조업도가 일치하지 않은 경우에 발생한다. 위의 예제에서는 사전에 예측한 조업도는 400시간이었지만 실제 제조된 제품 100개에 허용되는 표준시간은 300시간으로 100시간의 차이가 발생하며 이 차이가 조업도 차이를 발생시킨다. 이러한 차이를 제거하기 위해서는 사전에 제품 100개를 정확히 예측하여 300시간을 사전에 예측한 조업도로 선정하여야 하지만 이는 현실적으로 불가능하므로 통제 불가능한 차이이다.

5 Integrated analysis of overhead variances

제조간접원가는 다음과 같이 4분법, 3분법, 2분법에 의하여 차이분석을 한다.

	4-ways	3-ways	2-ways
VOH Spending	VOH-Spending	Spending	Budget (Controllable)
FOH Spending	FOH-Spending		
VOH Efficiency	Efficiency	Efficiency	
FOH Volume	Volume	Volume	Volume

앞의 예제를 3분법으로 분석하면 다음과 같다.

1) Spending variance = VOH-Spending variance + FOH-Spending variance

   $$= \$15 \text{ (U)} + \$100 \text{ (U)} = \$115 \text{ (U)}$$

2) Efficiency variance = $25(F)

3) Volume variance = $500 (U)

앞의 예제를 2분법으로 분석하면 다음과 같다.

1) Budget variance = Spending variance + Efficiency variance

   $$= \$115 \text{ (U)} + \$25 \text{ (F)} = \$90 \text{ (U)}$$

2) Volume variance = $500 (U)

제조 간접원가 총 차이는 $590의 불리한 차이가 발생하였지만 이 중 $90의 불리한 차이는 통제가 가능하고 $500의 불리한 조업도 차이는 통제가 불가능하다.

03 MCQ (Multiple Choice Questions)

01. Under a standard cost, the materials usage variances are the responsibility of

    a. production and industrial engineering.

    b. purchasing and industrial engineering.

    c. purchasing and sales.

    d. sales and industrial engineering.

02. A favorable materials price variance coupled with an unfavorable materials usage variance would most likely result from

    a. machine efficiency problems.

    b. product mix production changes.

    c. the purchase and use of higher than standard quality materials.

    d. the purchase of lower than standard quality materials.

03. An unfavorable materials price variance coupled with a favorable materials usage variance would most likely result from

    a. machine efficiency problems.

    b. product mix production changes.

    c. the purchase and use of higher than standard quality materials.

    d. the purchase of lower than standard quality materials.

04. A difference between standard costs used for cost control and budgeted costs

    a. can exist because standard costs must be determined after the budget is completed.

    b. can exist because standard costs represent what costs should be, whereas budgeted costs represent expected actual costs.

    c. can exist because budgeted costs are historical costs, whereas standard costs are based on engineering studies.

    d. cannot exist because they should be the same amounts.

05. Franklin Products has an estimated practical capacity of 90,000 machine hours, and each unit requires two machine hours. The following data apply to a recent accounting period.

Actual variable overhead	$240,000
Actual fixed overhead	$442,000
Actual machine hours worked	88,000
Actual finished units produced	42,000
Budgeted variable overhead at 90,000 machine hours	$200,000
Budgeted fixed overhead	450,000

Of the following factors, Baltimore's production volume variance is most likely to have been caused by (CMA)

    a. a wage hike granted to a production supervisor.

    b. a newly imposed initiative to reduce finished goods inventory levels.

    c. acceptance of an unexpected sales order.

    d. temporary employment of workers with lower skill levels than originally anticipated.

06. Frisco Company recently purchased 108,000 units of raw material for $583,200. Three units of raw materials are budgeted for use in each finished good manufactured, with the raw material standard set at $16.50 for each completed product. Frisco manufactured 32,700 finished units during the period just ended and used 99,200 units of raw material. If management is concerned about the timely reporting of variances in an effort to improve cost control and bottom-line performance, the materials purchase price variance should be reported as (CMA)

a. $6,050 unfavorable.

b. $9,920 favorable.

c. $10,800 unfavorable.

d. $10,800 favorable.

07. A company isolates its raw material price variance in order to provide the earliest possible information to the manager responsible for the variance. The budgeted amount of material usage for the year was computed as follows.

• 150,000 units of finished goods × 3 pounds/unit × $2.00/pound = $900,000

Actual results for the year were the following.

Finished goods produced	160,000 units
Raw materials purchased	500,000 pounds
Raw materials used	490,000 pounds
Cost per pound	$2.02

The raw material price variance for the year was (CMA)

a. $9,600 unfavorable.

b. $9,800 unfavorable.

c. $10,000 unfavorable.

d. $20,000 unfavorable.

08. Randall Company uses standard costing and flexible budgeting and is evaluating its direct labor. The total budget variance can usually be broken down into two other variances identified as the (CMA)

    a. direct labor rate variance and direct labor efficiency variance.

    b. direct labor cost variance and the direct labor volume variance.

    c. direct labor rate variance and direct labor volume variance.

    d. direct labor cost variance and direct labor efficiency variance.

09. Richter Company has an unfavorable materials efficiency (usage) variance for a particular month. Which one of the following is least likely to be the cause of this variance? (CMA)

    a. Inadequate training of the direct labor employees.

    b. Poor performance of the shipping employees.

    c. Poor design of the production process or product.

    d. Poor quality of the raw materials.

10. The JoyT Company manufactures Maxi Dolls for sale in toy stores. In planning for this year, JoyT estimated variable factory overhead of $600,000 and fixed factory overhead of $400,000. JoyT uses a standard costing system, and factory overhead is allocated to units produced on the basis of standard direct labor hours. The denominator level of activity budgeted for this year was 10,000 direct labor hours, and JoyT used 10,300 actual direct labor hours. Based on the output accomplished during this year, 9,900 standard direct labor hours should have been used. Actual variable factory overhead was $596,000, and actual fixed factory overhead was $410,000 for the year. Based on this information, the variable overhead spending variance for JoyT for this year was (CMA)

    a. $24,000 unfavorable.   b. $2,000 unfavorable.

    c. $4,000 favorable.   d. $22,000 favorable.

11. When using a flexible budgeting system, the computation for the variable overhead spending variance is the difference between (CMA)

    a. actual variable overhead and the previously budgeted amount.

    b. the previously budgeted amount and actual inputs times the budgeted rate.

    c. the amount applied to work-in-process and actual variable overhead.

    d. actual variable overhead and actual inputs times the budgeted rate.

12. The best basis upon which cost standards should be set to measure controllable production inefficiencies is

    a. engineering standards based on ideal performance.

    b. normal capacity.

    c. recent average historical performance.

    d. engineering standards based on attainable performance.

13. Which of the following management practices involves concentrating on area that deserves attention and placing less attention on area operating as expected?

    a. Management by objectives.   b. Responsibility accounting.

    c. Benchmarking.   d. Management by exception.

14. The standard direct material cost to produce a unit of FG is four pounds of material at $2.50 per pound. During 20X1, 420 pounds of material costing $1,190 were purchased and 390 pounds of material were used to produce 100 units of FG. What was the material price variance for 20X1?

    a. $140 unfavorable.   b. $140 favorable.

    c. $25 unfavorable.   d. $25 favorable.

15. The standard direct material cost to produce a unit of FG is four pounds of material at $2.50 per pound. During 20X1, 420 pounds of material costing $1,190 were purchased and 390 pounds of material were used to produce 100 units of FG. What was the material usage variance for 20X1?

a. $140 unfavorable.

b. $140 favorable.

c. $25 unfavorable.

d. $25 favorable.

16. (주)경성기계는 내부관리목적으로 표준원가회계제도를 도입하고 있다. 당기 변동제조간접원가 예산은 ₩6,000,000, 고정제조간접원가 예산은 ₩8,000,000이며, 기준조업도는 1,000 직접노동시간이다. 당기 실제 직접노동시간은 800시간이었다. 변동제조간접원가 능률차이가 ₩300,000(불리)이라면 고정제조간접원가 조업도차이는 얼마인가? (K–CPA)

a. 2,000,000 unfavorable.

b. 2,000,000 favorable.

c. 200,000 unfavorable.

d. 200,000 favorable.

17. 다음은 ㈜한강의 표준원가 및 생산활동 자료이다.
㈜한강의 직접재료가격차이는 얼마인가? 단, 직접재료와 재공품, 제품의 기초 및 기말재고는 없는 것으로 가정한다. (K–CPA)

완제품 실제생산량	1,000개
직접재료 표준구매가격	₩64/kg
직접재료 표준사용량	21kg/완성품 1개
직접재료 실제발생원가	₩1,400,000
직접재료수량차이	₩64,000 유리

a. 110,000 unfavorable.

b. 110,000 favorable.

c. 120,000 unfavorable.

d. 120,000 favorable.

18. ㈜한강의 당기 초 생산활동과 관련된 예산자료는 다음과 같다.
당기의 실제생산량은 1,100단위이었고 실제제조간접원가 총액은 ₩355,000이었다.
제조간접원가 총차이를 통제가능차이와 조업도차이는 각각 얼마인가? (K-CPA)

구분	예산
생산량(기준조업도)	1,000단위
고정제조간접원가 총액	₩200,000
단위당 변동제조간접원가	₩125

a. 17,500 unfavorable / 20,000 unfavorable

b. 17,500 unfavorable / 20,000 favorable

c. 17,500 favorable / 20,000 unfavorable

d. 17,500 favorable / 20,000 favorable

· 정답 및 해설

1. 재료비 수량차이는 제조부서 또는 공정설계부서의 책임이다. <정답> : a

2. 가격차이가 유리하면 싼 가격에 구입한 것이고, 수량차이가 불리하면 수량이 많이 투입되었다는 의미이므로 표준보다 재료의 품질이 낮은 상황이다.

<정답> : d

3. 가격차이가 불리하면 비싼 가격에 구입한 것이고, 수량차이가 유리하면 수량이 적게 투입되었다는 의미이므로 표준보다 재료의 품질이 높은 상황이다.

<정답> : c

4. 예산은 효율성이 반영되지 않은 예측자료이며, 표준은 효율성이 반영된 목표자료이다. <정답> : b

5. Estimated capacity = 90,000 hours
   Standard capacity = 42,000 units × 2 = 84,000 hours
   예상 생산수량보다 실제 생산수량이 적기 때문에 불리한 조업도 차이가 발생하였다.
   제품 재고량을 줄이게 되면 생산수량이 적어지므로 b가 정답

<정답> : b

6. Price variance = $583,200 − 108,000 × 16.50 ÷ 3 = −10,800 <정답> : d

7. Price variance = 500,000 × (2.02 − 2.00) = +10,000 $ <정답> : c

8. DL variance = Rate variance + Efficiency variance <정답> : a

9. 불리한 직접재료 수량차이는 제조부서의 비효율성 또는 구매부서에서 품질이 낮은 재료의 구입이 원인이다.

<정답> : b

10. SP((VOH))= $600,000 ÷ 10,000H = $60
    Spending variance (VOH) = $596,000 − 10,300 H × $60 = −22,000 <정답> : d

11. Spending variance (VOH) = Actual VOH − AQ × SP   정답 : d

12. 비효율성을 제거하기 위해서는 과거 경험보다는 공학적인 분석이 적절하며 a는 이
    상적이지만 달성 가능성이 없기 때문에 달성 가능성을 반영한 d가 정답
                                                              정답 : d

13. 차이분석을 초점으로 분석하는 경영기법을 management by exception이라고 한다.
                                                              정답 : d

14. Price variance = $1,190 − (420 pounds × $2.50) = +$140 (U)
                                                              정답 : a

15. Quantity variance = (390 pounds − 400 pounds) × $2.50 = −$25(F)
                                                              정답 : d

16. FOH rate = 8,000,000 ÷ 1,000시간 = @8,000
    VOH rate = 6,000,000 ÷ 1,000시간 = @6,000
    Efficiency variance = 300,000(U) = (800시간−SQ) × 6,000 → SQ = 750시간
    Volume variance = 8,000,000 − 750시간 × 8,000 = 2,000,000 (U)
                                                              정답 : a

17. SP × SQ = 64 × 1,000개 × 21kg = 1,344,000
    Quantity variance = −64,000(F) = SP × AQ − 1,344,000 → SP × AQ = 1,280,000
    Price variance = 1,400,000 − 1,280,000 = 120,000 (U)
                                                              정답 : c

18. FOH rate = 200,000 ÷ 1,000개 = @200
    Volume variance = 200,000 − 1,100개 × 200 = −20,000(F)
    Controllable variance = 355,000 − (1,100개 × 125 + 200,000) = +17,500(U)
                                                              정답 : b

04 / TBS (Task-Based Simulation)

Problem-1

IKEA Inc., is a privately held furniture manufacturer. For 2014, IKEA had the following standards for one of its products, a wicker chair:

⟨Standards per Chair⟩
- Direct materials : square yards of input at $5 per square yard
- Direct manufacturing labor : 0.5 hour of input at $10 per hour

The following data were compiled regarding actual performance: actual output units (chairs) produced, 2,000; square yards of input purchased and used, 3,700; price per square yard, $5.10; direct manufacturing labor costs, $8,820; actual hours of input, 900; labor price per hour, $9.80.

• Instruction •

1. Show computations of price and efficiency variances for direct materials and direct manufacturing labor. Give a plausible explanation of why each variance occurred.

2. Suppose 6,000 square yards of materials were purchased (at $5.10 per square yard), even though only 3,700 square yards were used. Compute the price and efficiency variances under this approach.

Problem-2

Wilo Company manufactures water pumps and uses a standard cost system.
The standard factory overhead costs per water pump are based on direct labor hours and are as follows:

Variable overhead (4 hours at $8/hour) : $32
Fixed overhead (4 hours at $5*/hour) : $20
Total overhead cost per unit : $52
* Based on a capacity of 100,000 direct labor hours per month.

The following additional information is available the month of November:
- 22,000 pumps were produced although 25,000 had been scheduled for production.
- 94,000 direct labor hours were worked at a total cost of $940,000
- The standard direct labor rate is $9 per hour.
- The standard direct labor time per unit is 4 hours.
- Variable overhead costs were $740,000
- Fixed overhead costs were $540,000

• Instruction •

Determine direct labor, variable overhead and fixed overhead variances. (CMA)

The French Bread Company bakes baguettes for distribution to upscale grocery stores. The company has two direct-cost categories: direct materials and direct manufacturing labor. Manufacturing overhead is allocated to products on the basis of standard direct manufacturing labor-hours.

Following is some budget data for the French Bread Company:
- Direct manufacturing labor use : 0.02 hours per baguette
- Variable manufacturing overhead : $10.00 per direct manufacturing labor-hour
- Fixed manufacturing overhead : $4.00 per direct manufacturing labor-hour
- Planned (budgeted) output : 3,200,000 baguettes

The French Bread Company provides the following additional data for the year ended December 31, 20X1:
- Actual production : 2,800,000 baguettes
- Direct manufacturing labor : 50,400 hours
- Actual variable manufacturing overhead : $680,400
- Actual fixed manufacturing overhead : $272,000

• Instruction •

1. Compute the flexible-budget variance, the spending variance, and the efficiency variance for variable manufacturing overhead.

2. Prepare a variance analysis of fixed manufacturing overhead cost.

Problem-4

The Singapore division of a Canadian telecommunications company uses standard costing for its machine-paced production of telephone equipment. Data regarding production during June are as follows:

- Variable manufacturing overhead costs incurred : $618,840
- Variable manufacturing overhead cost rate : $8 per standard machine-hour
- Fixed manufacturing overhead costs incurred : $145,790
- Fixed manufacturing overhead costs budgeted : $144,000
- Denominator level in machine-hours : 72,000
- Standard machine-hour allowed per unit of output : 1.2
- Units of output : 65,500
- Actual machine-hours used : 76,400
- Ending work-in-process inventory : 0

• Instruction •

Prepare an analysis of all manufacturing overhead variances. Use the 4-variance analysis framework.

KIMCPA Manufacturing Company's costing system has two direct-cost categories: direct materials and direct manufacturing labor. Manufacturing overhead (both variable and fixed) is allocated to products on the basis of standard direct manufacturing labor-hours (DLH). At the beginning of 20X1, KIMCPA adopted the following standards for its manufacturing costs:

	Input	Cost per output unit
Direct materials	5 lb. at $4 per lb.	$ 20.00
Direct manufacturing labor	4 hrs. at $16 per hr.	64.00
Variable manufacturing overhead	$8 per DLH	32.00
Fixed manufacturing overhead	$9 per DLH	36.00

Standard manufacturing cost per output unit = $152.00

The denominator level for total manufacturing overhead per month in 20X1 is 37,000 direct manufacturing labor-hours. KIMCPA's flexible budget for January 20X1 was based on this denominator level. The records for January indicated the following:

Direct materials purchased   40,300 lb. at $3.80 per lb.
Direct materials used   37,300 lb.
Direct manufacturing labor   31,400 hrs. at $16.25 per hr.
Total actual manufacturing overhead (variable and fixed) $650,000
Actual production   7,600 output units

· Instruction ·

For the month of January 20X1, compute the following variances, indicating whether each is favorable (F) or unfavorable (U):

1. Direct materials price variance, based on purchases
2. Direct materials efficiency variance
3. Direct manufacturing labor price variance
4. Direct manufacturing labor efficiency variance
5. Total manufacturing overhead spending variance
6. Variable manufacturing overhead efficiency variance
7. Production—volume variance

PART **III**

Control &
Performance Measures

Chapter

Performance Measure

Performance Measure

01 Performance measures for investment center

투자중심점(investment center)은 원가와 수익에 대한 통제 권한뿐만 아니라 투자에 대한 권한을 부여받은 책임중심점이므로 투자중심점 관리자를 성과평가할 때에는 이익과 투자를 동시에 고려하여야 한다.

투자중심점 성과측정치로 이용되는 지표는 다음과 같다.

- 투자수익률(ROI)
- 잔여이익(RI)
- 경제적 부가가치(EVA)

1 ROI (Return on investment)

(1) ROI 의의

투자수익률(ROI : return on investment)은 미국의 화학기업 듀퐁(Dupont)사가 사업부를 평가하기 위하여 최초로 사용한 것으로 영업이익을 투자액으로 나누어 계산한 수익성 지표이며, 투자된 자본 한 단위가 획득한 영업이익의 비율을 나타낸다.

$$ROI = Income \div Investment$$

* Income = operating income
* Investment = average total assets
(투자액은 일반적으로 평균가액을 사용하지만 기업에 따라서 기초금액 또는 기말금액을 사용하기도 한다.)

(2) DuPont method of profitability analysis

듀퐁 분석은 화학업체인 듀퐁에서 근무하던 브라운(Donaldson Brown)이 1920년대 고안한 재무 분석 기법으로 다음과 같다.

$$
\begin{aligned}
\text{ROI} &= \text{Income} \div \text{Investment} \\
&= (\text{Income} \div \text{Revenues}) \times (\text{Revenues} \div \text{Investment}) \\
&= \text{Return in sales} \times \text{Investment turnover}
\end{aligned}
$$

* Return in sales = operating profit margin (매출액이익률)
* Investment turnover = asset turnover (자산회전율)

(3) 투자수익률(ROI)을 증가시키는 방법

① Increase in income

② Decrease in investment

③ Increase in return on sales

④ Increase in investment turnover

Example-1

Sales revenues : $20,000

Beginning operating assets : $4,000

Ending operating assets : $6,000

Operating income : $1,250

Required rate of return = cost of capital = 10%

Calculate return on investment (ROI) using operating income as a measure of income and average total assets as a measure of investment.

(1) ROI = $1,250 ÷ $5,000 = 25%

⇨ ROI가 최저필수수익률(자본비용)보다 더 크기 때문에 투자성과는 양호하다.

(2) DuPont method of profitability analysis

Return in sales = $1,250 ÷ $20,000 = 6.25%

Investment turnover = $20,000 ÷ $5,000 = 4

ROI = 6.25% × 4 = 25%

(4) Decision making

1) Division manager's decision making

투자중심점 관리자는 다음과 같이 의사결정을 한다.

① 신규투자안의 ROI > 투자 전 사업부의 ROI ⇨ Accept the project

② 신규투자안의 ROI < 투자 전 사업부의 ROI ⇨ Reject the project

2) Corporation's decision making

기업전체관점에서는 다음과 같이 의사결정을 한다.

① 신규투자안의 ROI > Required rate of return ⇨ Accept the project

② 신규투자안의 ROI < Required rate of return ⇨ Reject the project

3) 준 최적화 현상(sub-optimization)

ROI로 성과평가를 하게되면 사업부 관리자의 의사결정과 기업전체관점에서의 의사결정이 일치하지 않는 준최적화 현상이 발생할 수 있다.

(5) ROI의 장점

- 계산이 간편하고, 투자액을 고려하므로 투자중심점 성과평가에 유용하다.
- 비율로 표현되기 때문에 투자규모가 다른 사업부 성과비교에 유용하다.

(6) ROI의 단점

- 준 최적화 현상(sub-optimization)이 발생할 수 있다.
  ⇨ 잔여이익(RI)과 경제적 부가가치(EVA)는 준최적화 현상이 발생하지 않는다.
- 고객만족도와 같은 비재무적 성과도 중요한데 재무적 성과만을 고려한다.
- 회계적 이익은 현금흐름과 일치하지 않으며, 화폐의 시간가치를 고려하지 않는다.

Example-2

Google Corporation's capital cost is 10%. One of division managers considers a project that will generate $100 million operating income per year on initial investment of $500 million. The division's current operating income is $250 million and its average operating asset is $1,000 million. The manager receives a bonus based on the division's ROI. Should the division manage accept the project? Why or why not?

(1) Division manager's decision making

   1) Current ROI = $250 ÷ $1,000 = 25%

   2) Project ROI = $100 ÷ $500 = 20%

   3) ROI after accepting the project = $350 ÷ $1,500 = 23.3%

     Division manager는 이 투자안을 채택하면 사업부의 ROI가 25%에서 23.3%로 감소하기 때문에 이 투자안을 기각할 것이다.

(2) Corporation's decision making

     기업전체의 관점에서 보면 투자안의 ROI(20%)가 기업의 자본비용(10%)보다 크기 때문에 이 투자안을 채택하여야 한다. 이처럼 ROI로 투자중심점을 성과평가하게 되면 기업전체의 목표와 사업부의 목표가 불일치하는 준 최적화 현상이 발생한다.

2 RI (Residual income)

(1) RI의 의의

투자수익률(ROI)로 투자중심점의 성과평가를 할 경우에는 준최적화 현상이 발생하는데 이를 극복하기 위하여 고안된 것이 잔여이익이다. 잔여이익(RI : residual income)은 미국의 GE사에서 주로 사용하였던 평가기법으로 영업자산으로부터 획득해야 할 최소한의 이익을 초과하는 영업이익을 말한다.

$$RI = Income - (Investment \times Required\ rate\ of\ return)$$

* Required rate of return = cost of capital

(2) 잔여이익(RI)을 증가시키는 방법

① Increase in income

② Decrease in investment

③ Decrease in required rate of return

(3) ROI와 RI의 관계

ROI = Income ÷ Investment ⇨ Income = ROI × Investment

RI = Income − (Investment × Required rate of return)

   = ROI × Investment − (Investment × Required rate of return)

   = Investment × (ROI − Required rate of return)

위의 식을 바탕으로 ROI와 RI의 관계는 다음과 같다.

$$ROI > Required\ rate\ of\ return \Rightarrow RI > 0$$
$$ROI = Required\ rate\ of\ return \Rightarrow RI = 0$$
$$ROI < Required\ rate\ of\ return \Rightarrow RI < 0$$

(4) Decision making

투자중심점 관리자는 다음과 같이 의사결정을 한다.

① 신규투자안의 RI > 0 ⇨ Accept the project

② 신규투자안의 RI < 0 ⇨ Reject the project

이러한 의사결정은 기업전체의 의사결정과도 일치하기 때문에 잔여이익으로 성과평가를 하면 준최적화현상을 막을 수 있다.

(5) RI의 장점

- 투자액을 고려하므로 투자중심점 성과평가에 유용하다.
- 준 최적화 현상(sub-optimization)을 방지할 수 있다.
- 투자안의 위험을 최저필수수익률에 반영할 수 있다.

(6) RI의 단점

- 투자규모가 다른 사업부의 성과평 비교가 어렵다.
- 고객만족도와 같은 비재무적 성과도 중요한데 재무적 성과만을 고려한다.
- 회계적 이익은 현금흐름과 일치하지 않으며, 화폐의 시간가치를 고려하지 않는다.

Example-3

Sales revenues : $20,000

Beginning operating assets : $4,000

Ending operating assets : $6,000

Operating income : $1,250

Required rate of return = cost of capital = 10%

Calculate residual income (RI) using operating income as a measure of income and average total assets as a measure of investment.

(1) RI = $1,250 − ($5,000 × 10%) = $750

　　⇨ 잔여이익 $750는 영업이익에서 투자에 대한 자본비용(기회비용)을 차감하고도
　　　 $750의 이익이 남았다는 의미이다.

(2) ROI 〉 Required rate of return ⇨ RI 〉 0

　　ROI = $1,250 ÷ $5,000 = 25%

　　RI = $5,000 × (0.25 − 0.10) = $750

Example-4

Google Corporation's capital cost is 10%. One of division managers considers a project that will generate $100 million operating income per year on initial investment of $500 million. The division's current operating income is $250 million and its average operating asset is $1,000 million. The manager receives a bonus based on the division's RI. Should the division manage accept the project? Why or why not?

(1) Division manager's decision making

　　1) Current RI = $250 − ($1,000 × 10%) = $150

　　2) Project RI = $100 − ($500 × 10%) = $50

　　3) RI after accepting the project

　　　= $350 − ($1,500 × 10%) = $200 or

　　　= $150 + $50 = $200

Division manager는 이 투자안을 채택하면 사업부의 RI가 $150에서 $200로 증가하기 때문에 이 투자안을 채택할 것이다.

(2) Corporation's decision making

기업전체의 관점에서 보면 투자안의 ROI(20%)가 기업의 자본비용(10%)보다 크기 때문에 이 투자안을 채택하여야 한다. 이처럼 RI로 투자중심점을 성과평가하게 되면 기업전체의 목표와 사업부의 목표가 일치하여 준 최적화 현상이 발생하지 않는다.

3 EVA (Economic Value Added)

(1) EVA의 의의

경제적 부가가치(EVA : economic value added)는 미국의 경영컨설팅 회사 Stern & Steward사가 사용한 기업가치 평가방법이다. 경제적 부가가치는 잔여이익(RI)을 투자자 관점에서 보다 정교하게 만든 경제적 이익(economic profit)으로 다음과 같이 계산한다.

$$
\text{EVA} = \text{After-tax operating income} - (\text{WACC} \times \text{Investment})
$$

* After-tax operating income = operating income $\times$ (1- tax rate)
* WACC : Weighted-average cost of capital
* Investment = Total assets - Current liabilities
          = Long-term assets + Working capital

가중평균자본비용(WACC)은 외부차입의 타인자본비용(cost of debt)과 주주에 대한 자기자본비용(cost of equity)용을 가중평균한 자본비용을 말하며 다음과 같이 계산한다.

$$
\text{WACC} = \text{cost of debt} \times (1-\text{tax rate}) \times w_d + \text{cost of equity} \times w_e
$$

* w_d = Market value of debt $\div$ (Market value of debt + Market value of equity)
* w_e = Market value of equity $\div$ (Market value of debt + Market value of equity)

(2) EVA와 RI의 차이

경제적 부가가치(EVA)와 잔여이익(RI)은 경제적 이윤을 측정한 것이지만 다음과 같은 점에서는 다르다.

	RI	EVA
Income	세전이익	세후이익
Investment	총자산	총자산-유동부채
Opportunity cost	required rate of return	WACC

(3) MVA (Market-Value Added)

　시장부가가치(MVA)는 금융시장에서 형성된 기업가치에서 주주와 채권자가 실제 투자한 금액을 차감한 금액으로 미래 예상되는 경제적 부가가치(EVA)의 현재가치를 합한 것이다.

(4) EVA의 장점

- 투자액을 고려하므로 투자중심점 성과평가에 유용하다.
- 준 최적화 현상(sub-optimization)을 방지할 수 있다.
- 투자안의 위험을 가중평균자본비용에 반영할 수 있다.
- EVA가 증가하면 기업가치가 증가하므로 주주와 경영자의 이해관계가 일치하여 대리인비용을 줄일 수 있다.

(5) EVA의 단점

- 계산이 어렵다.
- 고객만족도와 같은 비재무적 성과도 중요한데 재무적 성과만을 고려한다.

Example-5

Operating income : $15,000

Tax rate : 20%

Total assets : $100,000

Current liabilities : $10,000

WACC : 10%

Calculate EVA(economic value added) and RI.

(1) EVA

    1) Income $= 15,000 \times (1 - 0.2) = \$12,000$

    2) Investment $= 100,000 - 10,000 = \$90,000$

    3) EVA $= 12,000 - (90,000 \times 0.1) = \$3,000$

(2) RI

    1) Income $= \$15,000$

    2) Investment $= \$100,000$

    3) RI $= 15,000 - (100,000 \times 0.1) = \$5,000$

02 / Balanced Scorecard(BSC)

1 Balanced Scorecard

균형성과표(BSC : Balanced Scorecard)는 1992년 Kaplan & Norton이 개발한 성과평가방법으로 기존의 ROI나 RI와 같은 전통적인 성과측정치인 재무적 지표 (financial measure)의 한계점을 지적하고 재무적 지표이외에 비재무적 지표로도 성과를 측정하자는 이론이다.

	Traditional	BSC
Financial measure	Include	Include
Non-financial measure	Exclude	Include

2 BSC의 특징

(1) Strategy-focused

BSC는 기업의 목표를 달성하기 위한 경영자의 전략과 그 수행에 따른 성과평가를 통합적으로 하기 위한 도구이다. 따라서 전략적 목표에 따라 성과평가 기준이 변경된다.

(2) Balanced performance measure

전통적인 재무적 측정치 외에 비재무적 측정치도 성과평가에 포함하는 방법으로 단기적인 성과평가에 그치지 않고 장기적 성과를 균형 있게 평가하고자 한다.

(3) Cause-and-effect linkages

BSC에서 강조하는 4가지 측면의 지표사이에는 서로 인과관계를 갖고 있고 이를 보여주는 체계를 전략지도(Strategy map)이라고 한다. 인과관계에서 원인이 되는 지표를 선행지표 (leading indicators)라고 하고 그 결과로 나타나는 자료를 후행지표(lagging indicators)라고 한다.

3 Key performance Indicators (KPI)

BSC는 성과지표를 아래 그림에서 제시하는 것처럼 4가지 관점으로 구분한다.

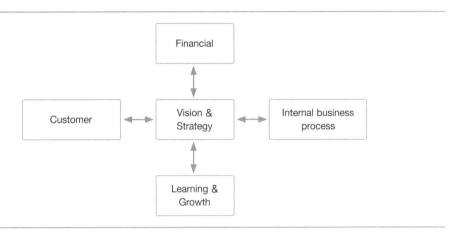

[그림 15-1]

(1) Financial perspective

재무적 관점은 주주를 위한 이익과 기업 가치를 얼마나 향상시켰는가를 평가하는 것으로 다음과 같은 성과측정치들이 있다.

- Stock price
- Operating income
- Return on sales
- Revenue growth
- ROI(return on investment)
- RI (residual income)
- EVA(economic value added)

(2) Customer perspective

고객 관점은 목표시장에서 기업이 얼마나 성공하였는지를 평가하는 것으로 다음과 같은 성과측정치들이 있다.

- Market share (시장점유율)

- Customer satisfaction (고객만족도)

- Customer relation (고객 유지율)

- Customer acquisition (고객 확보율)

- Number of customer complaints

(3) Internal business process perspective

내부 프로세스 관점은 고객에게 가치를 창출하기 위하여 내부 운영이 얼마나 향상되었는지를 평가하는 것으로 다음과 같이 3가지로 구분된다.

1) Innovation process

고객의 욕구를 충족시키기 위한 신제품의 개발과 관련된 평가지표이다.

- Operating capabilities

- Number of new products or services

- New-product development times

- Number of new patents

- Break-even time

2) Operating process

기존 제품의 운영과정의 성과지표로 품질, 원가 및 시간관 관련된 성과측정치가 이용된다.

① Process time: cycle time, lead time, on-time delivery

② Process quality: number of defects, number of returns

③ Process cost: cost per unit, rework cost

3) Post-sales service process

제품을 고객에게 인도한 후의 프로세스에 대한 성과지표이다.

- Time taken to replace or repair defective products

- Hours of customer training for using the product

(4) Learning-and-Growth perspective

학습과 성장관점은 핵심 내부프로세스를 향상하기 위하여 종업원, 정보시스템 및 조직기반의 성과가 얼마나 향상되었는지를 평가하는 것이다.

1) Employee measures

- Employee education and skill levels
- Employee-satisfaction ratings
- Employee turnover rates
- Percentage of employee suggestions implemented
- Percentage of compensation based on individual and team incentives

2) Technology measures

- Information system availability
- Percentage of processes with advanced controls

4 Components of BSC

BSC의 구성내용은 다음과 같다.

(1) Objectives : 전략적 목표

(2) Measures : 성과측정치

(3) Initiatives : 실행수단

(4) Targets performance : 목표성과

(5) Baseline performance : 현재성과

다음은 고객관점(customer perspective)의 균형성과표 사례이다.

Objectives	Measures	Initiatives	Target performance	Baseline performance
시장점유율 증가	시장점유율	고객의 미래욕구 파악	7%	6%
고객만족도 증가	고객만족도 조사	고객에 초점을 맞춘 판매조직 강화	상위점수 고객비율 95%	상위점수 고객비율 90%

5 Strategy maps

균형성과표의 4가지 관점의 성과지표의 인과관계를 이를 보여주는 체계를 전략지도 (Strategy map)이라고 한다.

[그림 15-2]

위의 그림에서 적시배송이 달성되면 고객만족도가 증가하고 따라서 기업의 ROI가 증가하는 체계를 나타낸 것이다. 이때 Customer satisfaction 지표는 On-time delivery에 대해서는 후행지표 (lagging indicator)이지만, ROI에 대해서는 선행지표(leading indicator)이다.

03   MCQ (Multiple Choice Questions)

01. After investing in a new project, Lee Company discovered that its residual income remained unchanged. Which one of the following must be true about the new project? (CMA)

    a. The net present value of the new project must have been negative.

    b. The return on investment of the new project must have been less than the firm's cost of capital.

    c. The return on investment of the new project must have been equal to the firm's cost of capital.

    d. The net present value of the new project must have been positive.

02. Which of the following perspectives under BSC measures a company's customer relation?

    a. Financial.   b. Customer.

    c. Internal business process.   d. Learning and growth

03. Which of the following perspectives under BSC measures a company's on-time delivery?

    a. Financial.   b. Customer.

    c. Internal business process.   d. Learning and growth

04. Which of the following perspectives under BSC measures a company's EVA?

    a. Financial.   b. Customer.

    c. Internal business process.   d. Learning and growth

05. Which of the following perspectives under BSC measures a company's IT expenditure per employee?

    a. Financial.   b. Customer.

    c. Internal business process.   d. Learning and growth

1. 잔여이익의 변화가 없다는 것은 투자안의 RI = 0이며 ROI = k를 의미한다.

정답 : c

2. 고객만족도는 customer의 성과지표이다.

정답 : b

3. 적시에 납품하는 것은 process의 성과지표이다.

정답 : c

4. EVA는 재무적 성과지표이다.

정답 : a

5. 종업원과 관련된 성과는 주로 learning & growth의 성과지표이다.

정답 : d

04 / TBS (Task-Based Simulation)

Problem-1

NIKE Company produces a wide variety of outdoor sports equipment. Its newest division, Golf Technology, manufactures and sells a single product—AccuDriver, a golf club that uses global positioning satellite technology to improve the accuracy of golfers' shots. The demand for AccuDriver is relatively insensitive to price changes. The following data are available for Golf Technology, which is an investment center for Outdoor Sports:

Total annual fixed costs : $30,000,000
Variable cost per AccuDriver : $ 500
Number of AccuDrivers sold each year : 150,000
Average operating assets invested in the division : $48,000,000

· Instruction ·

1. Compute Golf Technology' ROI if the selling price of AccuDrivers is $720 per club.

2. If management requires an ROI of at least 25% from the division, what is the minimum selling price that the Golf Technology Division should charge per AccuDriver club?

Problem-2

Fill in the following blanks:

	Company A	Company B	Company C
Revenues	$ 500,000	$200,000	?
Operating income	$ 150,000	$ 60,000	?
Investment	$ 250,000	?	$1,000,000
Income as a percentage of revenues	?	?	3.0%
Investment turnover	?	?	2
ROI	?	6%	?

Problem-3

다음은 ㈜누리의 남부사업부와 중부사업부의 대차대조표와 손익계산서 자료 일부이다.

	남부 사업부	중부 사업부
총자산	₩2,000,000	₩10,000,000
유동부채	500,000	3,000,000
세전영업이익	250,000	2,000,000

㈜누리의 가중평균자본비용 계산에 관련된 자료는 다음과 같다.

장기부채	시장가치 ₩7,000,000	이자율 10%
자기자본	시장가치 7,000,000	자본비용 14%

법인세율은 40%이다. 남부사업부와 중부사업부의 경제적 부가가치(EVA)는 얼마인가? (단, 각 사업부에는 동일한 가중평균자본비용을 적용한다.) (K-CPA)

Tesla Auto Company operates a new car division (that sells high-performance sports cars) and a performance parts division (that sells performance-improvement parts for family cars). Some division financial measures for 20X1 are as follows:

	New Car Division	Performance Part Division
Total assets	$33,000,000	$28,500,000
Current liabilities	6,600,000	8,400,000
Operating income	2,475,000	2,565,000
Required rate of return	12%	12%

• Instruction •

1. Calculate return on investment (ROI) for each division using operating income as a measure of income and total assets as a measure of investment.

2. Calculate residual income (RI) for each division using operating income as a measure of income and total assets minus current liabilities as a measure of investment.

3. Tesla Auto Company, whose tax rate is 40%, has two sources of funds: long–term debt with a market value of $18,000,000 at an interest rate of 10% and equity capital with a market value of $12,000,000 and a cost of equity of 15%. Applying the same weighted–average cost of capital (WACC) to each division, calculate EVA for each division.

Problem-5

Munich Reinsurance is a reinsurance and financial services company. Munich Reinsurance strongly believes in evaluating the performance of its standalone divisions using financial metrics such as ROI and residual income. For the year ended December 31, 20X1, Munich Reinsurance's CFO received the following information about the performance of the property/casualty division:

Sales revenues	$1,200,000
Operating income	200,000
Total assets	1,250,000
Current liabilities	250,000
Debt (interest rate: 6.25%)	600,000
Common equity	400,000

For the purposes of divisional performance evaluation, Munich Reinsurance defines investment as total assets and income as operating income (that is, income before interest and taxes). The firm pays a flat rate of 20% in taxes on its income.

• Instruction •

1. What was the net income after taxes of the property/casualty division?

2. What was the division's ROI for the year?

3. Based on Munich Reinsurance's required rate of return of 10%, what was the property/casualty division's residual income for 20X1?

4. Munich Reinsurance's CFO has heard about EVA and is curious about whether it might be a better measure to use for evaluating division managers. Munich Reinsurance's four divisions have similar risk characteristics. Munich Reinsurance's debt trades at book value while its equity has a market value approximately twice that of its book value. The company's cost of equity capital is 12%. Calculate EVA for the property/casualty division.

Control & Performance Measures

Chapter

Quality Control

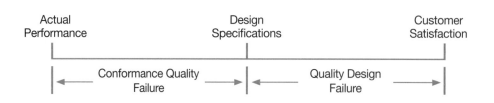

Chapter 16 Quality Control

01 Quality control

1 Quality

품질이란 다음과 같이 두 가지의 개념으로 구분할 수 있다.

(1) Quality of design

설계품질은 제품의 사양이 고객의 요구를 얼마나 잘 반영하고 있는지에 대한 품질이다.

(2) Quality of conformance

적합품질은 제품의 성능이 제품의 설계명세서에 얼마나 합치되고 있는지에 대한 품질이다.

이 두 가지 품질 개념을 비교하면 [그림 16−1]과 같다.

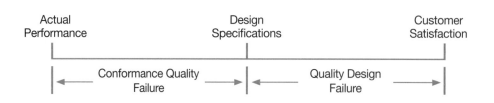

[그림 16−1]

2 Cost of Quality

품질원가는 일정 품질수준을 유지하기 위하여 투입되는 원가을 말하며 다음과 같이 분류한다.

Cost of quality	Prevention costs	Control costs (= cost of conformance)
	Appraisal costs	
	Internal failure costs	Failure costs (= cost of non-conformance)
	External failure costs	

통제원가(control costs)는 불량품의 발생을 방지하기 위하여 투입하는 원가이며, 실패원가(failure costs)는 실제로 불량품이 발생하여 지출하는 비용을 말한다. 전통적인 품질관리에서는 통제원가를 증가하면 불량률과 실패비용은 감소하고, 통제원가를 감소하면 불량률과 실패비용은 증가한다.

[그림 16-2]에서 보는 것처럼 전통적인 관점에서는 전체적인 품질원가를 최소화하기 위해서는 통제원가(control costs)와 실패원가(failure costs)사이의 적절한 균형이 필요하다고 본다. 그러나 [그림 16-3]에서 보는 것처럼 최근의 관점은 예방원가를 증가하는 것이 불량률의 감소 및 총 품질원가를 최소화에 가장 효과적이라고 본다. 즉, 무결점(zero-defect)의 상태가 총품질원가를 최소화하는 최적수준으로 보는 것이다.

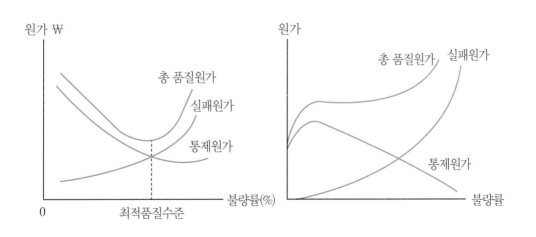

[그림 16-2] 전통적인 관점　　　　　[그림 16-3] 최근의 관점

(1) Prevention cost (예방원가)

Costs incurred in predicting the production of products that do not confirm to specifications.

- Design engineering
- Quality training
- Process engineering
- Suppliers evaluation
- Preventive equipment maintenance
- Testing of new materials

(2) Appraisal cost (평가원가)

Costs incurred in detecting which of the individual units of products do not confirm to specifications.

- Inspection
- Product testing T

(3) Internal failure cost (내부실패원가)

Costs incurred when non−confirming products are detected before it is shipped to customers.

- Spoilage
- Rework
- Scrap
- Machine repairs
- Downtime caused by quality problems

(4) External failure cost (외부실패원가)

Costs incurred when non−confirming products are detected after it is shipped to customers.

- Warranty repairs and replacements
- Product recalls
- Liability arising from defective products
- Returns and allowances arising from quality problems
- Lost sales arising from reputation for poor quality

3 Statistical quality control (SQC)

통계적 품질관리란 품질관리부에서 통계적 기법을 사용하여 제품이나 서비스의 품질을 관리하는 것으로 모집단(population)을 대표하는 표본(sample)을 통계적으로 추출하는 품질관리방법이다. 통계적 품질 관리 방법에는 Control chart, Pareto diagram, Cause-and-effect diagram 등이 있다.

(1) Control chart

관리도(control chart)는 생산 공정상태가 관리한계를 벗어나는 경우 그 원인을 규명하고 조정하여 다시 공정을 안정시키는 통계적 품질관리 방법 중의 하나이다. 관리한계는 공정의 변동이 일정 범위 내에 있는가의 여부를 판단하는 기준으로 중심선으로부터 관리상한 (upper control limit)과 관리하한 (lower control limit)을 설정한다.

[그림 16-4]는 복사기를 제조하는 기업의 관리도의 사례이다.

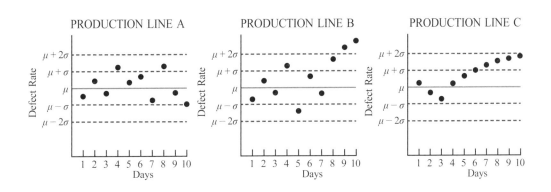

[그림 16-4]

(2) Pareto diagram

파레토 분석은 경제학의 80% : 20%의 법칙인 파레토 법칙을 품질관리 분야에 응용한 것으로 전체 중에서 중요한 것은 단지 소수이고 나머지 부분은 사소한 것이라는 철학에서 출발한다. 즉, 불량의 핵심원인을 찾기 위하여 발생빈도 (frequency)를 파악하고 이를 수정하는 기법이다.

[그림 16-5]는 복사기를 제조하는 기업의 파레토분석의 사례이다.

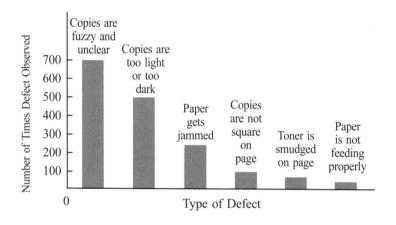

[그림 16-5]

(3) Cause-and-effect diagram (Fish-bone diagram)

품질의 문제를 발생시키는 잠재적인 핵심요인들(potential causes)을 파악하고, 그 원인들 간에 존재하는 상호관계를 분석하는 도표이다.

[그림 16-6]은 복사기를 제조하는 기업의 사례이다.

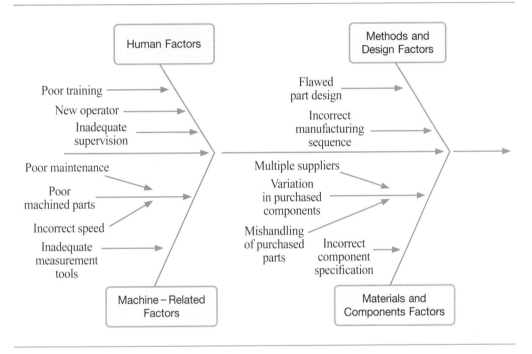

[그림 16-6]

4 Total quality control (TQC)

종합적 품질관리(TQC)는 품질 관리를 경영자가 하는 경영 관리의 중요한 부분으로 못 박고, 제조 부문 뿐만 아니라 판매, 서비스, 영업까지 기업의 모든 부문에 일관하여 행하는 종합적 관리 체제를 말한다. SQC가 품질 관리부라는 전문적인 부서를 통하여 품질을 통제하였다면 TQC는 품질 관리가 전 부서와 종업원들에게까지 확대되는 것을 말한다.

GE의 생산관리 및 품질관리의 책임자였던 파이겐바움(Feigenbaum) 박사는 품질에 대한 책임을 제조부문에 국한시키지 않는 전사적인 접근방법을 개발함으로써 전세계의 품질운동에 크게 기여하였다. 고객입장에서의 불만족스런 제품설계, 비능률적 유통, 부적절한 마케팅, 불충분한 지원활동 아래서는 제조에서의 품질이 달성될 수 없다고 주장하였다.

5 Total Quality Management (TQM)

종합적 품질경영(TQM)은 TQC에서 발전한 기법으로 제품 및 서비스의 품질만 개선하는 것이 아닌 조직의 전부문의 품질을 향상하는 품질경영 기법으로 품질은 최종적으로 고객이 결정하며 검사보다는 예방에 초점을 둔다. 즉, TQM은 고객만족을 최우선시하는 품질관리 기법이다. TQM은 일본의 토요타 자동차에서 JIT와 함께 도입한 품질관리 기법으로 다음과 같은 경영기법들을 동반한다.

(1) TQM의 구성요소

　　1) 고객 만족

　　2) 종업원 참여

　　3) 지속적 개선 (continuous improvement)

(2) Line-stop : 불량품이 발생하는 즉시 공정을 중단하는 제도

(3) Poke-yoke : 불량품이 검사대를 통과하는 것을 자동적으로 방지하는 시스템

(4) PDCA cycle

　　1) Plan : 개선할 대상을 파악하여 계획을 수립하고

　　2) Do : 계획을 실행에 옮기고

3) Check : 결과를 검토하고

4) Act : 문제점을 파악한 후 재실행하는 반복과정.

6 Six sigma

식스 시그마(six sigma)는 100만 개의 제품 중 3~4개의 불량만을 허용하는 3~4PPM(Parts Per Million) 경영을 말한다. 시그마(σ)는 보통 통계학에서 오차 범위를 나타내며, 경영학에서는 제품의 불량률을 나타내는 데 사용된다.

Six sigma는 1987년 미국 모토롤라에 의해 처음 고안되었으며, 제너럴 일렉트릭(GE)은 1996년 모든 사업 분야에 six sigma를 적용하기 시작했다.

Six sigma추진 조직은 다음과 같은 벨트제도로 대표된다.

① Champion

식스 시그마를 조직전체에 파급시키는 역할을 수행하는 경영층

② Master black belt

블랙벨트 취득자로서 통계적인 도구에 심도 있는 훈련을 받음

③ Black-belt

식스시그마 개선 프로젝트 리더 (추진 책임자)

④ Green belt

상대적으로 작은 규모의 프로젝트를 책임지고 수행

⑤ White belt

7 Quality Assurance (QA)

(1) Malcom Baldrige National Quality Awards (미국)

품질경영 분야에서 세계적으로 권위를 인정받는 상으로 1987년에 당시 상무 장관이었던 말콤 볼드리지의 제안으로 제정되었다.

(2) The Deming Prize (일본)

1951년 수학자 데밍의 공적을 기념하고 품질 붐을 조성하기 위해 개설된 상으로 TQM 운동의 효시가 되었고 일본자동차의 품질이 미국을 지배하게 된 계기가 된 상이다.

(3) ISO series

International Organization for Standardization(ISO)가 인증하는 국제품질 인증제도로서 다음과 같은 종류가 있다.

1) ISO 9000 series: 품질경영시스템의 인증
2) ISO 14000 series: 환경경영 보증제도

8 Time

(1) Operational measure of time

경쟁적 요소로서의 시간의 측정은 다음 2가지로 구분된다.

Customer–response time	Time from when a customer places an order for a product to when the product is delivered to the customer.
On–time performance	Which the product is actually delivered at the time it is scheduled to be delivered.

Customer–response time을 자세히 살펴보면 [그림 16–7]과 같다.

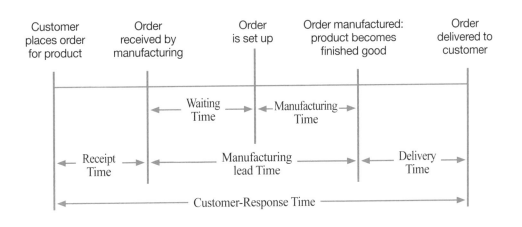

[그림 16–7]

(2) Break-even time(BET)

BET is the time from when the initial concept for a new product is approved by the management until when the cumulative present value of net cash inflows equals the cumulative present value of net cash outflows.

9 Theory of constraints (TOC)

(1) Theory of constraints (TOC)

The theory of constraints (TOC) describes methods to maximize operating income when faced with some bottleneck operations. The objective of the TOC is to increase throughput margin while decreasing investments and operating costs.

제한된 자원으로 인하여 일부공정에 병목현상이 나타나는 경우 이를 해결하는 이론을 제약 조건이론이라고 한다.

(2) Bottleneck

An operation or resource where the demand exceeds the available capacity

(3) Throughput margin

Throughput margin = revenues − direct material costs of the goods sold

(4) Investment

Investments = (a) + (b) + (c)

(a) material costs in direct materials, work−in−process, and finished goods

(b) R&D costs

(c) capital costs of equipment and buildings.

(5) Operating costs

Operating costs equal all costs of operations (other than direct materials) incurred to earn throughput margin. Operating costs include costs such as salaries and wages, rent, utilities, and depreciation.

10 Benchmarking

Benchmarking is the continuous process of comparing the levels of performance in producing products and services and executing activities against the best levels of performance in competing companies or in companies having similar processes.

There are four primary types of benchmarking: internal, competitive, functional, and generic.

(1) Internal benchmarking

Internal benchmarking is a comparison of a business process to a similar process inside the organization.

(2) Competitive benchmarking

Competitive benchmarking is a direct competitor-to-competitor comparison of a product, service, process, or method.

(3) Functional benchmarking

Functional benchmarking is a comparison to similar or identical practices within the same or similar functions outside the immediate industry.

(4) Generic benchmarking

Generic benchmarking broadly conceptualizes unrelated business processes or functions that can be practiced in the same or similar ways regardless of the industry.

02 / MCQ (Multiple Choice Questions)

01. Three of the basic measurements used by the Theory of Constraints (TOC) are (CMA)

    a. gross margin (or gross profit), return on assets, and total sales.

    b. number of constraints (or subordinates), number of non-constraints, and operating leverage

    c. throughput (or throughput contribution), inventory (or investments), and operational expense.

    d. fixed manufacturing overhead per unit, fixed general overhead per unit, and unit gross margin (or gross profit).

02. Quality programs normally include a number of techniques to find and analyze problems. The technique commonly used to analyze the source of potential problems and their locations within a process is called a

    a. Control Chart.   b. Pareto Diagram.

    c. Fishbone Diagram.   d. Value Chain Analysis.

03. The primary reason for adopting TQM was to achieve

    a. greater customer satisfaction.   b. reduced delivery time.

    c. reduced delivery charges.   d. greater employee participation.

04. Quality is achieved more economically if the company focuses on

    a. appraisal costs.   b. prevention costs.

    c. Internal failure costs.   d. external failure costs.

05. The cost of scrap, rework, and tooling changes in a product quality cost system is categorized as a(n)

a. training cost.

b. external failure cost.

c. Internal failure cost.

d. prevention cost.

• 정답 및 해설

1. TOC의 3가지 성과지표는
   throughput contribution, investments and operational expense이다.

   정답 : c

2. 잠재적 문제점을 진단하는 것은 Fishbone Diagram이다.

   정답 : c

3. TQM의 목표는 고객만족도의 극대화 및 품질관리이다.

   정답 : a

4. 가장 효율성이 높은 품질비용은 예방 비용이다.

   정답 : b

5. Rework는 대표적인 내부 실패 비용이다.

   정답 : c

03   TBS (Task-Based Simulation)

Problem-1

Safe Travel produces car seats for children from newborn to 2 years old. The company is worried because one of its competitors has recently come under public scrutiny because of product failure. Historically, Safe Travel's only problem with its car seats was stitching in the straps. The problem can usually be detected and repaired during an internal inspection. The cost of the inspection is $5.00 per car seat, and the repair cost is $1.00 per car seat. All 200,000 car seats were inspected last year, and 5% were found to have problems with the stitching in the straps during the internal inspection. Another 1% of the 200,000 car seats had problems with the stitching, but the internal inspection did not discover them. Defective units that were sold and shipped to customers needed to be shipped back to Safe Travel and repaired. Shipping costs are $8.00 per car seat, and repair costs are $1.00 per car seat. However, the inspection. Negative publicity will result in a loss of future contribution margin of $100 for each external failure.

• Instruction •

1. Calculate appraisal cost and internal failure cost.
2. Calculate out-of-pocket external failure cost.
3. Determine the opportunity cost associated with the external failures.
4. What are the total costs of quality?
5. Safe Travel is concerned with the high up-front cost of inspecting all 200,000 units. It is considering an alternative internal inspection plan that will cost only $3.00 per car seat inspected. During the internal inspection, the alternative technique will detect only 3.5% of the 200,000 car seats that have stitching problems. The other 2.5% will be detected after the car seats are sold and shipped. What are the total costs of quality for the alternative technique?

Problem-2

Cell Design produces cell phone covers for all makes and models of cell phones. Cell Design sells 1,050,000 units each year at a price of $10 per unit and a contribution margin of 40%. A survey of Cell Design customers over the past 12 months indicates that a disturbing number of customers were disappointed because the products they purchased did not fit their phones. Cell Design's managers want to modify their production processes to develop products that more closely match Cell Design's specifications.
The current costs of quality are as follows:

Prevention costs	$210,000
Appraisal costs	$100,000
Internal failure costs	
Rework	$420,000
Scrap	$ 21,000
External failure costs	
Product replacements	$315,000
Lost sales from customer returns	$787,500

The QC manager and controller have forecast the following additional costs to modify the production process.

CAD design improvement	$150,000
Improve machine calibration to specifications	$137,500

• Instruction •

1. If the improvements result in a 60% decrease in customer replacement cost and a 70% decrease in customer returns, what is the impact on the company's operating income?

2. Calculate prevention, appraisal, internal failure, and external failure costs as a percentage of total quality costs and as a percentage of sales before and after the change in the production process.

Problem-3

(주)시그마는 품질원가의 측정을 위해 품질관련 활동원가를 계산하고 있다. 다음 나열된 품질관련 활동원가 중 예방원가(prevention cost of quality)에 포함되어야 할 금액은? (K-CPA)

활 동	활동원가(또는 비용)
품질방침기획 및 선포활동	₩ 10
선적 전에 발견된 부적합품 재작업활동	20
반품 재작업활동	30
예방적 설비보수 및 유지활동	40
미래 판매기회상실에 따른 기회비용	50
제품품질검사 및 시험활동	60
원부자재 공급사 평가활동	70
반품 재검사활동	80
품질교육 및 훈련활동	90

· Instruction ·

위에서 나열된 품질관련 활동원가 중 예방원가(prevention costs), 평가원가(appraisal costs), 내부실패원가(internal failure costs) 및 외부실패원가(external failure costs)에 포함되어야 할 금액은 각각 얼마인가?

8th
Managerial Accounting

2023년 11월 01일 8판 1쇄 발행

저 자 | 김용석
편집·디자인 | 유진강(아르케 디자인)
인쇄·제본 | 천광 인쇄

펴낸이 | 김용석
펴낸곳 | (주) 이러닝코리아
출판등록 | 제 2016-000021
주 소 | 서울시 금천구 가산동 60-5번지 갑을그레이트밸리 A동 503호
전 화 | 02)2106-8992
팩 스 | 02)2106-8990

ISBN 979-11-89168-31-5   93320